Principles of Data Management and Presentation

Principles of Data Management and Presentation

JOHN P. HOFFMANN

UNIVERSITY OF CALIFORNIA PRESS

University of California Press, one of the most distinguished university presses in the United States, enriches lives around the world by advancing scholarship in the humanities, social sciences, and natural sciences. Its activities are supported by the UC Press Foundation and by philanthropic contributions from individuals and institutions. For more information, visit www.ucpress.edu.

University of California Press
Oakland, California

Library of Congress Cataloging-in-Publication Data

Names: Hoffmann, John P. (John Patrick), 1962—author.
Title: Principles of data management and presentation / John P. Hoffmann.
Description: Oakland, California: University of California Press, [2017] |
    Includes bibliographical references and index. | Description based on print version record and CIP data
    provided by publisher; resource not viewed.
Identifiers: LCCN 2017005895 (print) | LCCN 2017012555 (ebook) | ISBN 9780520964327 (epub and ePDF) |
    ISBN 9780520289956 (cloth : alk. paper) | ISBN 9780520289949 (pbk. : alk. paper)
Subjects: LCSH: Research—Methodology. | Research—Data processing—Management.
Classification: LCC Q180.55 (ebook) | LCC Q180.55 .H64 2017 (print) | DDC 001.4/2—dc23
LC record available at https://lccn.loc.gov/2017005895

Stata® is a registered trademark of StataCorp LP, 4905 Lakeway Drive, College Station, TX 77845 USA. SAS® and all other SAS Institute Inc. products or service names are registered trademarks in the USA and other countries.® indicates USA registration. SAS Institute, Inc., 100 SAS Campus Drive, Cary, NC 27513 USA. SPSS® is a registered trademark of SPSS, Inc., 233 S. Wacker Drive, 11th Floor, Chicago, IL 60606 USA. SPSS, Inc. is an IBM company. Their use herein is for informational and instructional purposes only.

Manufactured in United States of America

25 24 23 22 21 20 19 18 17 10 9 8 7 6 5 4 3 2 1

To Curtis

CONTENTS

PREFACE

The world is saturated with data. Readers of newspapers, magazines, blogs, and other media are exposed on a regular basis to data presented in words, tables, pictures, diagrams, and graphics. Customers of large retail establishments, patients who visit medical centers, students attending public and private schools, and many other people provide data—often unwittingly—that are used to predict their behaviors, medical conditions, and scores on various types of tests. You may not know what data you have provided in your life, but there is a high likelihood that information about you is part of a few large databases.

I have been teaching courses on data analysis and research methods to university students for many years. These types of courses can be challenging for students in the social and behavioral sciences, especially in disciplines that tend to attract those who are not comfortable with quantitative methods. Although I have found that most students can handle the coursework—at least in my home disciplines of sociology and criminology—I've come to recognize a tangible gap in the way students are taught to do research. This involves the bridge between statistics courses and research methods courses.

The typical approach for undergraduate students in the social and behavioral sciences (although this is also common in graduate programs) is to first complete an introductory course in statistics. This type of course typically teaches students about exploratory analyses, basic statistics (e.g., means, standard deviations), elementary statistical inference, and graphical representations of data (e.g., box plots, histograms). Introductory courses often conclude with units on correlations, analysis of variance (ANOVA), and simple linear regression models. In most of these courses, students are taught to use statistical software to conduct various types of analyses. Second, students take a course in research methods. This usually involves learning a little philosophy of science (epistemology, ontology), followed by a review of various research approaches, such as experiments, quantitative methods, and qualitative studies. In my department, students in this course are usually involved in a survey that requires them to become familiar with sampling, questionnaire design, interviewing techniques, and data entry. They are also exposed to theoretical issues in the field.

Finally, in some programs, students build on this material by taking more advanced courses, such as regression analysis or qualitative methods, or by applying what they've learned in a capstone course.

This sequence has existed for decades and may work relatively well, but I see the need to reconsider how students are taught to conduct research. I came to this conclusion after seeing the results of alumni surveys in which many of our students reported that they wished they had had more training in how to understand, manipulate, and use data to answer questions for their employers. This corresponds with a concern of some in the statistics education community that most students are not provided with *"data habits of mind"* that evolve mainly from working with data; these habits develop as students are taught to begin thinking about data at the very beginning of a research project, even before they examine a dataset (Baumer 2015; Finzer 2013, 5). I also noticed that many students who entered our graduate program could remember what means and correlations are used for and why one might choose a survey or an ethnographic approach to study some phenomenon, but they had a difficult time bridging the divide from understanding this material to conducting their own research. There seemed to be something missing, some gaps in their knowledge, skills, and experience.

After speaking with some colleagues and mulling this over, I worked with one of my fellow faculty members to design a new course that concerns the research process, with a special emphasis on understanding and using data. The course is called "Data analysis, management, and presentation" and has been a required course in my department for a little more than 10 years. However, the title does not include an important component: how to develop research questions. Although becoming familiar with data management and presentation is important and motivates this course, as well as this book, it should be clear that developing a good research project must begin with a good research question or problem to tackle. Thus, the first part emphasizes the general research process and how to develop good ideas and questions that guide subsequent data needs. In general, my goals for the course—and, derivatively, for this book—are to help students develop the skills learned in introductory statistics and research methods and complement them with a broader perspective on how to understand data and use them to conduct research projects. Given the strictures of a single semester and my own expertise, I've limited the course to working with quantitative data. This is not to say that other methods are not equally valuable, but given that most of my students will not go on to research careers, but often do take jobs that require familiarity with quantitative data and their uses, I thought it prudent to focus in one area.

The reading material for such a course is not available in a single location. Thus, I have used many books and articles to address particular aspects of the curriculum. Yet my concern that many students graduate from a social or behavioral science program without some useful research skills has convinced me that a single source would be valuable, hence the book you are now reading. But what are its general purposes? First, I hope to provide readers with a general understanding of some important aspects of social and behavioral science research. This is motivated not only by my experiences conducting research and teaching undergraduate and graduate students but also with a recent emphasis on *workflow*. This term has been borrowed from organizational studies to address the steps that a researcher should take to initiate and complete a research project (Kirchkamp 2013; Long 2009). Workflow is typically concerned with the part of a research project that involves the data, including the following steps: (a) collecting, compiling, and organizing a dataset; (b) planning the method of analysis; (c) analyzing the data; and (d) writing a report that describes and interprets the results of the analysis. One of the emphases that sets workflow apart from research steps as generally understood is that, for efficient workflow, each step should be carefully and fully documented so that a researcher can repeat each of them (if needed), share what was done with colleagues, and allow other researchers to reproduce or replicate the work. Although this book does not repeat in detail what others have recommended regarding workflow, this way of understanding a key part of the research process does influence what follows.

Second, although I find an emphasis on project workflow to be valuable because it reminds us to be well organized and carefully document each stage of the data and analysis work, a key feature of research studies is often omitted from discussions of workflow. That is, for a project to be timely and important, it is not enough to gather data and analyze them. There are key steps that must come first, especially identifying a research question or problem to guide the project. Thus, the first two chapters of this book discuss what research is in a general context and how to narrow down the scope of one's interest to a research question, problem, or hypothesis that may be investigated within the structure of a social science study.

Third, whereas many elementary statistics and research methods courses require students to use statistical software, they don't typically teach much about data management, including labeling and coding practices, missing data, and data cleaning. Exploratory analysis, a typical part of elementary statistics courses, is rarely linked to data management and cleaning, yet it can play a crucial role in helping students understand data better. Hence, data management is an area emphasized in this book.

Fourth, even though research methods courses do a fine job of teaching students how to collect data, I fear that many of them fail to provide some critical skills in understanding and handling data. In addition, students are rarely exposed to administrative data and how they may be combined from different sources into a dataset designed for a particular research objective. A substantial number of studies in the social sciences also use *secondary data*: those that have been collected by other researchers and made available to the research community. Secondary datasets offer a cost-effective way to conduct research, yet it is the rare course that teaches students about them in any detail. Thus, this book discusses several ways to acquire data.

Fifth, social science statistics and methods courses spend a substantial amount of time teaching students how to estimate models, but spend too little time, in my judgment, on how to present data. Many students are simply expected to learn about data presentation by preparing research posters and papers for courses, or, for some, to present at conferences. Much of their education about data presentation comes informally from mentors or from reading research articles in their field. This is an inefficient way to learn, though. Thus, one of my objectives is to provide some principles of data presentation, along with specific examples of good presentation practices. In other words, once we have a research question, gained access to and organized some data, and conducted an analysis, how can we effectively present the results so that various audiences can understand what we've done?

Now that I've described a few things this book is designed to accomplish, it may be helpful to discuss what it is not. First, this is not a book, at least not as usually presented, on research methods. There are plenty of excellent books on how to conduct research in general, with an abundance of information on different methods, such as experiments, surveys, and ethnographies. Many of these books also discuss issues such as research ethics, developing good questions, validity and reliability, sampling, and measurement techniques.

Second, the purpose of this book is not to teach readers about elementary or advanced statistics. Again, there are plenty of books that provide specific guidance on how to use statistical models to analyze data. Elementary statistics books present information on data collection, various exploratory techniques, graphical methods, hypothesis testing, Bayes's theorem, probability distributions, estimation and inference, nonparametric statistics, ANOVA, and comparing population parameters. More advanced books cover topics such as linear regression analysis, generalized linear models, survival models, simultaneous equations, and multivariate statistics. I assume that readers are familiar only with the statistical tools taught in an elementary statistics course. Along these lines, I try not to take a position that favors frequentist or Bayesian statistics. Although most of my own work has been within the frequentist framework, there is little in this book that could not apply to either analytic approach.

Third, this is not a book on statistical software. Software is used as a tool to illustrate the various concepts and principles used throughout, but the choice of software is secondary. Thus, readers will likely need to consult resources that fall outside this presentation for more information on using statistical and data management software. Nevertheless, Appendix A provides a brief introduction to three statistical software packages that are used in the examples sprinkled throughout the book: Stata®, SPSS®, and SAS®. It also points to resources for learning how to use each of these packages. Although the programming language and data analysis software R is not used for the examples, Appendix A provides a brief introduction to its capabilities as well.

Finally, this book is not designed to teach readers how to write research reports or articles, nor how to present conference posters or papers. Although the principles and tools presented herein include some important aspects of preparing reports of research, there are other, more comprehensive resources that describe how to write about numbers (Miller 2004; Morgan et al. 2002), how to prepare research articles (Baglione 2016; Becker 2007; White 2005), and how to put together research presentations (Cohen et al. 2012; Miller 2007b).

As suggested earlier, this book is designed to "fill in some gaps" that I see as especially stark in the way research is taught to undergraduate and graduate students in the social and behavioral sciences. I've found that their skill set in basic research methods and statistics tends to be sound, but there is more to the research process than the knowledge that is typically imparted in these courses. There are also some specific skills that are all too often missing from their education. I hope to fill in some of these gaps by offering this book.

A BRIEF DESCRIPTION OF THE CHAPTERS

The chapters are designed to be read in the order presented, although readers with research experience may wish to skip around to find topics that interest them.

Chapter 1 addresses why we conduct research and some of the benefits of research to the individual, community, and society in general. It describes generally what research is and reviews various types of research, such as exploratory, descriptive, and analytical/explanatory research. There is also a discussion of impediments to sound research, some characteristics of research that make it interesting and persuasive, and the general research process. The goal of the chapter is to get readers thinking about research, why it is important, and how we can make it sound and useful.

Chapter 2 focuses on how to develop research questions. It begins with an emphasis on narrowing in on interesting topics that others will also find stimulating and significant. This is followed by a discussion of the role of using various techniques to move from a topic to a reasonable research question. The next section addresses theories, concepts, and arguments. The idea of a conceptual model is utilized to outline this issue, along with concepts and statements that can be used to construct these models.

Chapter 3 addresses some fundamental issues regarding data, such as what they are and how they are characterized in the social sciences. The next topic addressed in this chapter is measurement, in particular, some ways that researchers move from concepts to variables. The next chapter describes some principles of data documentation, as well as different coding strategies that are common in the social and behavioral sciences. This is followed by an overview of some principles of data management, which include data cleaning and screening practices, and naming conventions. Finally, some principles of file management are presented.

Because many research projects in the social and behavioral sciences use secondary data (typically quantitative data that have been collected by another researcher and made available through a data repository or in some other way), Chapter 5 emphasizes some positive and negative aspects of this type of data. Examples of large data repositories that share data freely with researchers are listed. The next section describes some common ways to download data and import them into software useful for data management and analysis. The software examples include Stata, SPSS, and SAS, but also discuss how text files are particularly useful for conducting research with different software platforms.

Since learning how to gather primary data is one of the principal goals of research methods courses, which may be a prerequisite for courses that use this type of book, some more general principles regarding the creation of datasets from primary data collection are provided in Chapter 6. The chief emphasis is on understanding some principles of creating quantitative datasets, including how to combine administrative data to good effect.

The last few years have seen growing interest in missing data and their implications for social and behavioral science research. There are now many tools for handling missing data. Chapter 7 begins with a discussion of different types of missing data and their implications for research and data analysis. It then outlines several techniques for handling missing values, with an emphasis on providing a straightforward description of how to use state-of-the-art methods, maximum likelihood and multiple imputation, for attenuating missing data problems. This chapter presents material that is at a slightly more advanced level than the material in other chapters, so readers may wish to focus on its first three sections to gain a general understanding of missing data.

Chapter 8 provides an overview of the principles used in effective data presentation, including those based on research on cognitive processing and recognition to illuminate how people tend to see and interpret data when it is presented to them in tables or graphics. This includes an emphasis on comparisons, pattern recognition/perception, the use of color, dimensionality, and data ordering and labeling that help tables and graphics meet the goals of clarity, precision, and efficiency. A key objective of this chapter is to get readers to think about how their research questions and the audience should guide the most effective ways that the data are presented.

Chapter 9 addresses principles of designing tables to present research findings. It discusses various principles of organization, data ordering, and using labels, titles, legends, and notes. The aim is to help the reader design tables that convey the main message of the data and analysis.

The final chapter is an overview of common types of graphics, their respective strengths and weaknesses (relative to the design principles discussed in Chapter 8), and how the choice of a particular graphic depends on the type of data or analysis that one wishes to present. Additional principles of creating effective graphics are discussed. The overarching goal of Chapters 9 and 10 is to provide principles and examples so that one's audience or readers are most likely to reach an efficient level of understanding. The last section of the chapter mentions some innovative ways of presenting data, such as with dynamic and interactive graphics. It also provides readers with suggestions of where to go next to find good tools for data presentation through visualization.

A BIT MORE ON SOFTWARE

I have used many statistical and data management software platforms over the last 30 years. I began many years ago with SPSS, moved to SAS, shifted to SPlus and Stata, and have recently relied on R for many analytical tasks. I've also used MS Access and various spreadsheet software for data management tasks, and have dabbled with data visualization and presentation software (e.g., FlowVella, Visual.ly, Tableau, Prezi). However, I teach classes mainly with Stata because it is particularly efficient as a teaching tool. Given that the types of courses and readers who might benefit from the material in this book likely use a variety of software, though, I have tried to provide diversity by presenting some of the information that follows in Stata, SPSS, and SAS. The program R, which is growing rapidly in popularity because of its breadth of capabilities and its cost (free), is also discussed in Appendix A. I also show some data in spreadsheets, mainly imported from comma-separated values (csv) text files, which provide a good cross-platform for downloading data and moving them into statistical software. Almost any spreadsheet software may be used to import and examine data, such as Numbers for Mac, Google Sheets, Apache OpenOffice, MS Excel, or LibreOffice Calc. In the discussion of program documentation and the preparation of program files, I rely mainly on Notepad++ since it is a widely used and easily accessible text editing software. However, there are many other options available, such as Vim, Emacs, TextPad, TextEdit, or Sublime Text. Finally, although I use OS X, Linux, and MS Windows operating systems (depending on the computer), the following material was created on MS Windows and OS X based computers. With a few exceptions, most of the application software used herein may be run with a variety of operating systems.

LEARNING RESOURCES

This book is accompanied by a publisher's website that includes material to enhance the learning experience of the reader. The website includes the statistical software code and the datasets used in the examples. Although Chapters 4 and 5 emphasize that original datasets should be in text format, the datasets on the website are also available in Stata, SPSS, and SAS formats (www.ucpress.edu/go/datamanagement).

ACKNOWLEDGMENTS

I owe so much to the many students I've taught over the years, especially those who have been in my data management, statistics, and research methods courses. They have taught me how to teach (although I have only myself to blame for the remaining limitations), and I've shared in their struggles to understand data and analysis. At the risk of forgetting some, I am especially indebted to Liz Warnick, Dallin Everett, Mandy Workman, Daehyeon Kim, Colter Mitchell, Bryan Johnson, and Scott Baldwin. Some of my colleagues who have taught similar courses have been especially gracious in sharing their experiences and material with me, including Brayden King, Lance Erickson, Carter Rees, and Eric Dahlin. I owe much to those at the University of California Press and IDS Infotech Ltd. who shepherded this work to print. This includes Seth Dobrin, Kate Hoffman, Chris Sosa Loomis, Renee Donovan, Jack Young, Mansi Gupta, S. Bhuvneshwari, and many others who work for these remarkable organizations. Finally, I thank Lynn, Brian, Christopher, Brandon, and Curtis for making family life the center of my existence. This book is dedicated, in particular, to Curtis, whose music and science will one day change the world.

ONE

Why Research?

It seems that every day brings another report of some research finding. A quick Internet search of news articles that appeared on an otherwise ordinary day in June revealed, among other stories, that California just approved a publicly funded gun research center, the Netherlands began a campaign to identify and reduce research misconduct, a geological study discovered that some parts of the San Andreas Fault are sinking and others are rising, a nutrition study suggested that broccoli is healthier than previously thought because its phenolic compounds have notable antioxidant properties, and a survey revealed that about 31% of people admit to snooping on a friend or loved one by looking at their cell phones. As suggested by just a single day's news coverage, research is a huge enterprise, employing millions of people worldwide and resulting in thousands of reports, articles, and books every year. The American Association for the Advancement of Science (2016) estimates that the US government spends about $70 billion per year on various forms of research.

But many people have questioned the value of some of this funded research. We regularly see debates about the value of research on global warming, firearms, health-care systems, and many other topics. In addition, conservative politicians such as US Senator Tom Coburn of Oklahoma publish annual reports of federal government waste, taking particular glee in pointing out what are considered dubious scientific studies. For example, the 2014 *Wastebook* highlights studies of gambling monkeys, mountain lions on treadmills, and synchronized swimming by brine shrimp. Yet, there is clearly much to be gained from good research. Without it, there is little doubt that death, illness, and injury rates would be much higher. Food production would be substantially lower. The field of forensic science would be much more primitive, thus impeding efforts to solve crimes and catch criminals. Producing

enough power to light homes, operate cars, and run businesses would be much more difficult. The list goes on and on.

Social science often gets a particularly bad rap because some do not consider it a true "science." But it has also contributed not only to making the world a better place, but also to
increasing our understanding of the way people, social groups, communities, and institutions function and interact. Let's examine a few examples of social science research to see
what it has taught us. As you read the following illustrations, think of what broader implications each has for understanding the social world and perhaps even improving people's lives.

In the mid-1960s, the social psychologist Stanley Milgram wanted to determine how
close or far apart people were socially. He devised a project in which he mailed a letter to random people who lived in several Midwestern US cities. The letter asked them if they person-
ally knew an individual—again selected randomly—who lived in Boston, Massachusetts. If
they did, they were to send the letter to this person. If not, they were to send the letter to a
friend or relative who was more likely to know the person in Boston. He then examined how
many times, on average, the letters that reached the person had been sent. This led to the
famous phrase about "six degrees of separation," which was based on the average number of
times the letter was forwarded (Milgram 1967). Even though the project and its findings
have been criticized in the ensuing years (Watts 2004), it has motivated hundreds of subsequent studies on social networks and led to the proliferation of social network analysis as a
valuable research tool for the social sciences. In what other ways might social networks be
important for understanding the way people interact and how this affects their lives?

In the early 1990s, political scientist Bruce Keith and his colleagues wished to understand better what it means to be a political independent. Whereas many people in the United
States identify as a Democrat or a Republican, a plurality claim they are independent and
don't identify with either political party. Understanding what this signifies has important
implications for voting behavior and the public's support of political figures and their policies. Keith et al. (1992) determined that a large number of independents are actually fairly
consistent in voting for Democratic or Republican candidates. Thus, regardless of how they
label themselves, only a relatively small percentage of voters are truly "independent." What
might this finding suggest for other questions about how people identify with groups and
engage in civic life?

Finally, most residents of a town or city can distinguish the "good" neighborhoods from
the "bad" neighborhoods. Good neighborhoods tend to be safe, whereas bad neighborhoods
tend to be dangerous, places where the risk of falling victim to crime is high. Often, we perceive of bad neighborhoods as those with vacant lots, graffiti, and boarded-up buildings.
Sociologists Robert Sampson and Stephen Raudenbush (2004) sought to understand
whether these signs of "disorder" were valid markers of dangerous areas. By carefully studying dozens of Chicago neighborhoods, they found that it was less the explicit "dangerous-
ness" of a neighborhood—as measured by criminal activity or physical decay—that predicted whether people judged a neighborhood as qualitatively bad or good, but instead
whether there was more poverty and minorities who lived in a neighborhood. In other

words, neighborhoods can get labeled as bad or good based on the types of people who live in them, regardless of how objectively safe they are. What consequences does this finding have for understanding social and ethnic relationships, the health and development of communities, and how the criminal justice system operates?

I hope it is clear that each of these studies, while important in its own right, illustrates the value of social science research. We know that scientific research has led to many improvements in the world, from longer lives due to medical advances to rapid transit from one part of the globe to another. Although perhaps not considered as beneficial, research in the social and behavioral sciences has also led to a better understanding of society, with the potential to improve lives, relationships, and communities. For example, social network studies, many of which are motivated by Stanley Milgram's research, have led to more effective health education and intervention programs (e.g., Kim et al. 2015), thus serving to improve health among underserved groups of people. Sampson and Raudenbush's study might lead to more just policing strategies and help prevent police shootings in minority neighborhoods (a problem that has plagued several US communities over the past few years).

WHY RESEARCH?

Although most of us will never conduct research that is as influential as these notable examples, we may nevertheless find satisfaction in the design and execution of a good research project. Perhaps some of you will also be involved in research that will improve the human condition. This book discusses some of the principles and tools that are at the foundation of social scientific research. Before embarking on this discussion, though, it may be helpful to think a bit more about why we conduct research. Here are four broad reasons (Booth et al. 2008).

- *Research helps us develop a deeper understanding of questions and answers.* This assumes we wish to know the answer to some important questions that research can provide, such as those that involve patterns of behavior, factors that influence social problems, or why some forms of government or social policies seem to work better than others. It is also a good way—some argue a critical way—to identify *facts*: those bits of information for which there is evidence to indicate they genuinely exist. This is often contrasted with *opinions*: beliefs about some issue that depend largely on the holder's point of view. We'll return to the issue of evidence later. Research can be especially important when it comes to studies of health, safety, and economic well-being—research can improve and save lives.

- *Research helps explain the world around us.* Research can help us understand and explain how things operate and why events occur. I may not want to be able to explain something because I wish to change it, but rather simply because I'm curious about why it operates the way it does. Although this reason is often considered the domain of "pure research" in fields such as physics, many social scientists are also interested in explaining why people or social groups behave or believe the way they do. This is not because they want to change behaviors or beliefs, but rather because they are curious about them. This can be especially satisfying when other people or groups seem different or peculiar from the researcher's perspective. It can help us unmask our own preconceptions about others.

- *Some people find pleasure in solving puzzles.* In the social sciences, researchers often gain satisfaction by answering questions that others have not thought of or have not been able to answer in the past. For example, what, if any, influence do neighborhood factors have above and beyond the influence of families or schools on the way young people behave? If a young person moves from an impoverished neighborhood to a wealthy neighborhood, should we expect her chances of attending college to improve? Or does her likelihood of going to college depend mainly on her family's station and influence? This might be considered a puzzle that has not been solved yet.

- *Research provides a learning environment.* By conducting research, we may learn new and more advanced skills. This furnishes training to conduct more sophisticated forms of research. One way to think about this is that early involvement in research is a type of apprenticeship that might lead to a vocation at which you can excel (or at least support yourself!).

These four reasons need not be independent of one another, though. Someone's pleasure in solving research puzzles may certainly be related to her interest in answering a question or to comprehending how the world and its inhabitants operate.

WHAT IS RESEARCH?

But what do we mean by the term *research*? Most dictionary definitions of this word use terms such a systematic exploration, discovery, or investigation. For example, the *Oxford English Dictionary* (2016) defines the noun form of research as "the systematic investigation into and study of materials and sources in order to establish facts and reach new conclusions." In a guide to research practices in the social sciences, DePoy and Gitlin (2016, 3) offer the following definition:

> Research is . . . multiple, systematic strategies to generate knowledge about human behavior, human experience, and human environments in which the thinking and action processes of the researcher are clearly specified so that they are logical, understandable, confirmable, and useful.

In this context, research is a systematic set of transparent procedures designed to produce knowledge. Systematic refers to a fixed plan that can be repeated. Transparent means that the procedures used are clear and understandable. Thus, research is a process of fixed and clear steps that is aimed at revealing something that is unknown, poorly understand, or even to assess a statement of fact ("Watching violent films makes teenagers more aggressive"). Moreover, some suggest that it is fundamentally about identifying a problem and finding a solution (Booth et al. 2008). Research includes many kinds of information or data gathering exercises. In general, we wish to collect information—in a systematic and documentable way—to solve a problem, answer a question, or perhaps even generate more questions.

Research Involves Telling a Story

A useful way of thinking about research is to relate it to telling a story. Simply put, research involves the following: *Something happened, it's important, and I want to tell you about it.* Good stories include *themes*—key things the story tries to tell or teach the reader—and *plots*—information and events that are organized in a logical and recognizable order. Good stories are *narratives*: they connect events, sometimes in clever and unexpected ways. One of the tasks of research is to describe and explain how events are connected. Yet there is often an aspect of research that sets it apart from a story about Uncle Joe and how he lost a family heirloom when he went surfing. Although the heirloom may be valuable to some family members, researchers usually wish to tell stories that are important in a more general sense. As related earlier, Professors Sampson and Raudenbush told a story about how people identify and label Chicago neighborhoods based on the types of people living in them. A theme of this story is that what we perceive with our eyes and interpret with our minds do not necessarily reflect reality. Our general perception of the physical environment is influenced largely by who we see in that environment. In general, research tells stories—like many good stories—about things that apply broadly.

Research Is about Making Comparisons

Research also involves comparisons. When researchers wish to answer a question, such as whether a drug abuse prevention program is effective, they are concerned with comparing those who were exposed to the prevention program to those who were not. Even when they observe only one group, it is important to think about what would have happened to members of that group—or a similar group—if they had had a different experience. Similarly, how does the group under investigation compare to other groups who may behave similarly or who live under similar conditions but behave differently? For example, suppose an ethnographer is studying a group of methamphetamine users in rural Missouri. It is usually helpful—even if only implicitly—to consider how those in this setting compare to those in other settings, such as in inner-city St. Louis or rural South Dakota. How might their use of methamphetamine serve a similar or different purpose than use among other users? Does their motivation to use or eventually abstain differ from the experiences of others? What implications does the broader social or cultural milieu have for their use vis-à-vis others' use?

A term that is frequently used when thinking about research as a comparison is *counterfactual*. This refers to attempting to infer what would have happened if some other experience than that observed had occurred. For instance, when an experiment is conducted and only one group—the experimental group—is given the stimulus (such as when only one group of people watches a violent encounter), the counterfactual asks what would have happened to those in the comparison group if they had been given the same stimulus. An assumption is that they would have reacted in a similar way—thus demonstrating the same outcome. This assumption is made more realistic by randomization, a process designed to make the groups comparable in most conceivable ways. If they are comparable, then the only difference between them is the stimulus that they experienced. However, we may never observe the true counterfactual (Mumford and Anjum 2013). Yet, imagining it by thinking explicitly about comparisons among research participants is a useful mental exercise that helps answer questions.

Research Is a Type of Argumentation

Another useful way to think about research is that it is a type of argumentation (Booth et al. 2008). Argumentation refers to the process of developing and assessing arguments. However, the type of argument referred to here is not an angry or hostile verbal exchange between two opponents. Rather, we are interested in two relevant types of arguments. The first type, *rhetorical*, provides information—or a set of supporting statements—to persuade someone that some claim is accurate ("ocean waters appear blue because of the way water absorbs light waves"). A *claim* is simply an assertion that something is true. Rhetorical arguments are used in many spheres, from a teacher who tells her students which ethnic groups vote most often in local elections to the radio personality who claims that a politician is wrong on some issue and provides reasons, such as by discussing the politician's voting record and public statements. The second type, *dialogical*, examines different, perhaps opposing, claims and tries to reach agreement on which one is most accurate (Driver et al. 2000). Research is appropriate for evaluating dialogical arguments since it is important to consider alternative explanations for phenomena. Explanatory research is especially well suited for examining *scientific arguments*: the process of using scientific methods to demonstrate that some process or claim is the most reasonable or valid, usually when compared to some alternative process or claim (Khine 2012).

Discussions of argumentation typically identify and distinguish three components: *claims*, *warrants*, and *data*. The following two sentences provide an illustration of an argument:

> Michael Jordan was a better basketball player than Kobe Bryant (claim). He won more NBA championships and most valuable player awards (data) because he was more talented physically, a better team player, and had a stronger drive to succeed (warrants).

Thus, a warrant is a principle or statement that provides a way to connect the claim to the data. It may describe a general source of reasoning that covers a broad area within which the specific claim occurs. For example, to be successful at team sports requires not just physical skills, but also the ability to work well with teammates and to be mentally focused. This general perspective might offer the following warrant that could then be used to support a claim:

> Basketball players, even if they are matched against others who are equal in innate physical ability, are better if they play team ball and have a stronger motivation to succeed. Basketball is not just a physical game, but also a team sport that requires mental discipline and drive.

The data in this context are the facts—the valid pieces of information—that are used to support the claim. The combination of data and warrants provides the *evidence* to bolster the claim. Arguments may also include qualifiers that state the conditions when the argument holds (Jordan was a better NBA player, but he may not have been better than Kobe Bryant in high school or in international play). There might even be situations in which the claim is not accurate (Newton's laws of motion do not operate at the subatomic level; Toulmin 1958).

Research is useful for both developing and testing arguments. Since good research generates good information in the form of data, we may strengthen our arguments by relying on research that supports one view over another. Furthermore, as already mentioned, research is an integral part of examining scientific arguments. When someone proposes an explanation for a physical or social phenomenon—which takes the form of an argument—it may be tested using the methods of research. In particular, research is used to determine whether the evidence—the data and warrants—is valid, and thus whether the claims are accurate. We may check whether Michael Jordan really did win more championships than Kobe Bryant and perhaps even study their actual play to determine who was more physically talented (although subjectivity is likely to creep in). In order to determine if the evidence is valid, it is important to ask some questions: Did it come from a trustworthy source? When was the evidence gathered? From where was it collected? Was it developed based on sound principles of logic and research? What biases or political manipulations may have affected it? Klass (2012, chapter 3) provides a good overview of problems—such as logical fallacies and other issues—that can undercut even the most reasonable arguments and evidence. Several of these that affect the quality of research are discussed in the next section.

Claims and warrants are also used to develop theories. However, there are other components needed as well. How theories and claims are linked to research and the questions that drive it are discussed in chapter 2.

CLASSIFYING RESEARCH

There are various ways of understanding the general purposes of research. This typically involves, though, the type of research undertaken. In most social scientific disciplines, research is classified into one of three types: exploratory research, descriptive research, and explanatory or analytical research.

Exploratory research involves conducting a background review to gather information about a question or problem and some preliminary steps to try to understand it better. For example, suppose a scholar is interested in the effects of criminal forfeiture laws but has no prior experience conducting research on this topic. She might begin by reading books and research articles, and interviewing a few legislators, judges, attorneys, US Marshals, and those whose property has been seized under these laws. She might also examine one or two court cases that involved the application of these laws. Not only does this lead to a better understanding of the topic, but also suggests the best research method for studying particular questions regarding criminal forfeiture laws. Perhaps our inquisitive scholar decides that a survey is the best way to gather data that can then be used to answer a specific research question. Or an ethnographic study may offer a better approach. Exploratory work is often needed to make informed decisions about how a research project should be conducted (McNabb 2010).

Descriptive research includes gathering information to find out what is happening. It may involve information about a single variable. For example, what percentage of mothers in Canada breastfeed their babies? How long, on average, do they breastfeed? What percentage of young people, ages 12–17, in the state of Colorado have ever drunk an alcoholic beverage? Descriptive research may also include identifying an association between two variables, such as with a correlation coefficient: What is the correlation or statistical association between frequency of alcohol use and grades in school among teenagers? Is teen alcohol use more common in the United States or Canada?

Explanatory or analytical research involves gathering information to determine the causes of or explanations for some phenomenon. Thus, some scholars distinguish descriptive and *causal* research (Remler and Van Ryzin 2015). An explanation provides reasons or interpretations for some observed pattern or phenomenon; it answers questions regarding why or how something occurred ("The Iraqi invasion of Kuwait in 1990 occurred because . . ."). In the social and behavioral sciences, as well as the physical/natural sciences, hypotheses are often used as a way to test a predetermined explanation. A *hypothesis* is a statement about the presumed relationship between two or more variables. It is usually tested by gathering data and determining whether the relationship between the variables matches the predictions of the hypothesis. Nevertheless, most types of studies, even if they use good data, are not, by themselves, sufficient for establishing a causal relationship. This is particularly true in *observational studies*: those projects in which the researcher has little to no control over what conditions participants are exposed to. Since so much social scientific research relies on observational data, this third type is identified best as explanatory research.

There are situations, however, when researchers do have some control over what happens to participants; thus, quasi-experimental and experimental designs are not unknown in the social scientific community. For example, suppose a researcher hypothesizes that moving children from poor neighborhoods to wealthy neighborhoods will make them more likely to graduate from high school or less likely to engage in violent behavior. This hypothesis might be driven by the researcher's descriptive research; it showed that these children are at risk of dropping out of school or of becoming involved in violent activities. How might this hypothesis be tested? The researcher first takes a randomly selected group of children and moves them (as well as, hopefully, their families) from poor neighborhoods (this must be defined carefully) to wealthier neighborhoods. Then, by comparing these children to those who remained in the poor neighborhoods, the researcher determines whether the evidence supports or refutes the hypothesis. Nevertheless, even if the hypothesis is supported, this type of research should also—if one wishes to move from description to explanation—have a good reason for what it is that underlies the differences among the children, if there are any. In other words, researchers should have a logical set of reasons why or how these changes occurred. This is where theory and conceptualization come into play.

These three categories do not exhaust the possible types of research, however. Some people, for example, are interested primarily in prediction. This may be reasonable in, say, the medical research community. I don't particularly care why ibuprofen cures my headaches; just being able to predict that it will and will not, on the other hand, make me sick or unhealthy in other ways is enough for me. Thus, the fact that some team of medical researchers found out that this medication predicts a cessation of headaches is sufficient. Yet, prediction has also become a common goal in the growing field of *data mining* (also called *data analytics* or by the euphemism "big data"). Data mining is a general method for uncovering patterns in large datasets (Han et al. 2012). In practice, this usually involves developing statistical models that predict some outcome with a relatively high degree of accuracy. Although it is a technique that is beginning to make headway in the social sciences (Attewell and Monaghan 2015), data mining is used most often to help companies to predict the characteristics of their customers, such as what products they are most likely to purchase. There are certainly analogous situations faced by social scientists, but most of these researchers are concerned with developing reasonable explanations of phenomena.

Another type of research involves advocacy. Perhaps the best-known example of advocacy research is practiced in the legal profession (Firebaugh 2008). A defense attorney, for example, conducts research in order to help her client stay out of jail; this type of research typically involves searching for evidence that shows that the client did not commit the crime (or that contradicts the opposing attorney's evidence). This is not to say that the legal profession engages only in advocacy research (reading of a few law review articles quickly dispels this impression), only that it is a common method in an adversarial system. Yet members of the social science community would not be satisfied with such a one-sided effort. Instead, social scientists are supposed to consider all reasonable evidence, including that which might cast doubt on a hypothesis or favored answer to a research question. To do otherwise is a violation of the tenets and ethical guidelines of most social and behavioral science disciplines.

There are several other ways of classifying research, with a common approach concerned with distinguishing various research methods. Since an assumption is that readers have already had some experience with a research methods course, they are not covered in any detail here. Many books on research methods offer a good overview of the different approaches used in the social and behavioral sciences, such as experiments, observational studies, case studies, and qualitative or ethnographic methods (see Ragin and Amoroso 2011; Remler and Van Ryzin 2015).

This book, although it contains strategies and principles that can help with several of these types of research, is concerned mainly with descriptive and explanatory research. In other words, one of its initial purposes is developing and examining research questions that presuppose that some level of exploratory research has already been completed, but that does not have mere prediction or advocacy as its end goal. Furthermore, as mentioned in the preface, the techniques discussed in the following chapters are designed chiefly for data that are quantitative or include only a relatively small number of qualitative categories.

IMPEDIMENTS TO CONDUCTING SOUND RESEARCH

Now that we've defined research, discussed a few of its characteristics, and classified its different types, it is important to consider some common obstacles to conducting quality research. In this age of electronic communication, quick access to information (which can be overwhelming), and publication glut, it is easy to fall into a trap of emphasizing research quantity over quality. The tools available for conducting some modicum of research have become relatively simple to use, and we are awash in data that appear to be easy to analyze and mine for seemingly important findings. I had a colleague who once, as a practical joke, claimed that there was a new statistical program called "hypothesis test." It was advertised in a flyer that my friend posted near a university computer lab as a method for generating hypotheses and using readily available datasets to prove their validity. He told me that people flocked to his office to get their hands on this program so they could use it as the basis for writing research reports (publishing articles and achieving tenure is of utmost importance!). This illustrates an unfortunate situation: many researchers wish to find a simple path to achieving research results. Yet, as some smart people have reminded us, "research is hard" and it is even harder to conduct cutting-edge research (Gelman and Loken 2014, 464; Schwartz 2008). With this in mind, the following describes some common impediments to sound research.

Heuristics, Assumptions, and Cognition Traps

Heuristics are simple rules that are usually the result of socialization and evolutionary processes. They help explain how people make decisions, arrive at judgments, and solve problems, especially when they are faced with complex challenges or incomplete information. For example, when confronted with some statement of fact, a person might judge it based on examples that come easily to mind (the *availability heuristic*). Someone is told that a school shooting has occurred and this triggers her to think that the perpetrator is a young male with mental health problems. Heuristics often work well to simplify decision-making but may also lead to biases. Assumptions play a similar role: they are conditions or associations that are taken for granted irrespective of the evidence. For example, people often assume that individuals' gender or ethnicity allow a quick judgment of their involvement in legitimate or deviant behaviors. This might lead to a disproportionate research emphasis on deviant behavior among people of color or on females as caregivers. In general, humans seem to be hardwired to create stories about events from incomplete or even faulty evidence (Kahneman 2011). As an example of the risk of assumptions, for many years medical research focused mainly on men, with the notion that the findings could be generalized to women. We have since learned that this is normally not the case (Torpy et al. 2003).

Heuristics and assumptions, when they are based on flawed logic or evidence, can lead to *cognition traps* (Shore 2008). These are approaches to problems that are inflexible or grounded in rigid views of how the world operates. For instance, some people see the world in binary terms: good or evil, nice people versus ill-mannered people. Yet the world tends to be much more nuanced and complex than this. As the social sciences teach us, people or social groups may be magnanimous or selfish depending on the circumstances they find themselves in. One way to avoid these traps is to realize that what makes people and groups do the things they do is complicated and can rarely be narrowed down to a single cause or personal trait. In addition, we need to avoid the tendency that what we would have done in a particular situation is somehow rational or unbiased, so that what others do, if they take another path, is irrational. Yet this is a common outcome of *ethnocentrism*: viewing others based on one's own cultural or social standards.

A similar problem can occur when we hold strong ideological views. It is often difficult for people to let go or modify their assumptions about some outcome or piece of information—such as whether a social policy is worth implementing—when they adhere strongly to, say, a traditional or progressive view of the way the world (should) work. In fact, there is a psychological phenomenon known as the *backfire effect* that can be a key problem for both generating research and convincing others of the accuracy of research. The backfire effect occurs as people reject valid evidence that does not support their beliefs and actually develop even stronger beliefs that favor their position (Nyhan and Reifler 2010). For instance, someone who is already convinced that American Pit Bull Terriers are the most vicious dogs, but is presented with evidence that they are actually no more aggressive than several other breeds (Duffy et al. 2008), may actually end up with a stronger belief about their viciousness. Good social researchers try to avoid the cognition traps and be on the lookout for backfire effects by considering various points of view. As mentioned later, researchers should also consider whether their audience might also be affected by these issues.

Not Understanding What Has Already Been Done

This is why reading the research literature on a topic is so important. We need to know what others have done before us in order to identify the unanswered questions. Suppose a researcher wishes to conduct a study of why people join a particular group, such as a religious organization. Before embarking on this study, he should determine whether others have conducted similar research so that his work is original and not redundant, or whether more research is needed on this issue. As suggested earlier, this mandates that some exploratory research is carried out prior to developing one's own research project. Of course, it is easy to get overwhelmed by the research literature, especially when considering commonly studied phenomena. A strategy that often takes substantial practice to develop is learning how to read the literature in one's field (Shore 2016). This is discussed a bit later with an eye toward using previous studies to develop interesting and important research questions.

Poor Data

We may have a fantastic research question that is original and timely, but unless we have good data that effectively measure the phenomena we're interested in, we cannot adequately answer questions, test hypotheses, or solve problems. A key challenge for the social sciences is whether we can accurately measure phenomena we're interested in. Some things are simply so vague as to make measurement extremely difficult; others are hard to pin down since they may shift quickly. We also often rely on individuals to tell us how they feel, what opinion or belief they hold, or what they did during a certain period of time. This is affected, however, by many things, such as their understanding of the words that make up the question, their memories, their mood, and their motivation to provide valid answers. As the noted anthropologist Margaret Mead purportedly said, "What people say, what people do, and what they say they do are entirely different things." In general, a vital concern is whether we are measuring what we think we are measuring (e.g., happiness, depression, juvenile delinquency). Moreover, researchers often rely on data from samples. This leads to questions regarding what the sample represents, how it was selected, whether it is biased in some way, and several other conditions. Thus, a good understanding of questionnaire design, measurement strategies, and sampling is needed in order to conduct sound research. There are many excellent books available that instruct researchers about how to choose samples and collect good data (e.g., Bradburn et al. 2004; Groves et al. 2009).

Poor or Ill-Suited Methods

We may have a good research question and sound data, but if the methods used to conduct the research are of poor quality or not suited to the task, we may be misled by the results of the research. In general, it is important to use a method that is best designed to answer the research question or solve the research problem (Leek and Peng 2015). If one wishes to document the number of violent crimes in a city over a certain time period, an ethnographic study is unlikely to be useful. However, if one wishes to understand how people in a particular neighborhood tolerate or ignore the violence that occurs around them, then an ethnographic study is likely a good choice. Similarly, in the study described earlier, Sampson and Raudenbush (2004) used surveys and systematic observations of neighborhood conditions to study people's perceptions. This was appropriate given the researchers' goals. However, it would have been impractical to rely only on an ethnographic study or an experimental method to gauge people's perceptions in the numerous Chicago neighborhoods. Once again, a solid understanding of the strengths and weaknesses of various research methods is a crucial part of executing and completing good research.

A Boring, Irrelevant, or Unanswerable Question or Problem

We might avoid cognition traps, have wonderful data, and utilize suitable methods, but sound research also requires an interesting or important question. Some research is simply not that interesting; the story it tells is boring. Or the research addresses an overly narrow phenomenon. Do people really care if travelers prefer seeing cows or goats when driving along rural roads in Nebraska? Some answers are also obvious or are so well known that more research is not needed. We know that practicing Mormons are less likely to drink alcohol than practicing Catholics; we don't need a research project to demonstrate this. The following section and the next chapter discuss a few ways to develop research questions that are at least somewhat exciting (to some people) and relevant. However, this should not be taken to imply that all research must be innovative. As discussed later, replication of research studies is a crucial endeavor that is not emphasized enough in the social sciences, yet is fundamental to the advancement of scientific understanding.

In addition, it is not uncommon to have an interesting question that simply cannot be answered with the tools available to social scientists. Although the social and behavioral sciences have made great strides in developing innovative research tools—often by borrowing techniques from other disciplines—there are still some things that are very difficult to do.

Impatience

As mentioned earlier, doing good research is hard. It takes skill, motivation, and patience. Yet, the demands on one's time are often onerous. Students usually have many tasks to complete by the end of a semester or before their graduate school funding runs out. Academic researchers are under pressure to publish regularly in order to get tenure, be promoted, and receive salary increases. Researchers who work in the private sector or for think tanks are often expected to win grants and contracts, get patents, and produce reports. Thus, there is constant pressure to complete research projects and write reports or articles. Unfortunately, this concern with haste may lead to shortcuts, errors, and misleading results. In one notable example, two Harvard economists published a research paper in which they showed that nations with high levels of debt had slower economic growth. It was subsequently discovered that an error in an MS Excel spreadsheet affected this finding; when it was corrected, there was little effect of debt on growth; in fact, it may have been the other way around, with growth affecting debt (Bell et al. 2015). Although it's not clear whether this error was the result of impatience, it demonstrates the importance of being careful with the data used in research projects. As carpenters have taught for years, measure twice, cut once. Or more to the point: check the data several times before beginning the analysis and be careful and systematic with the analysis.

HOW CAN WE MAKE RESEARCH INTERESTING AND PERSUASIVE?

A key goal of this book is to provide some helpful guidance on how to match your research aims with data. At this point, though, it is useful to consider the audience for your research. What are some general steps that will show people that your research is interesting and that they should care about what you are doing? The late Wayne Booth and his colleagues (2008) note that when we conduct and present research we should imagine having a conversation with members of an audience (which might include other researchers, policymakers, funding agencies, or the public). Thus, in order to persuade them that the research is important, try to connect with them in some way. What information should you provide them with that is most persuasive and comprehensible? First, consider their expertise, interests, and background. Are they experts on the topic? Should they be concerned with the topic in general or with specific aspects of it? Could they have preconceived notions or biases about the topic, such as those that might lead to cognition traps or backfire effects?

As you consider these issues, think about how they might affect your ability to impart one of more or more of the following.

- *I've found something interesting.* It's crucial to think about how you can interest the audience in what you've found. It is not unlike being a salesperson, as unfortunate as this may sound. It also requires that you present the information clearly. This might include a well-written document or a carefully prepared presentation. Chapters 8–10 discuss some principles and tools for effective data presentation.

- *I've found a solution to a problem that is (or should be) important to you.* This is particularly vital in a business environment or when interacting with an audience interested in public policy. For example, in an earlier phase of my life, I worked for a nonprofit organization that conducted research for several government agencies. Most of their staff members were interested in practical issues, such as what policies are most effective and efficient for reducing adolescent tobacco use, alcohol use, or other risky behaviors. They wanted to know where they should target their limited resources to make a difference that is measurable and satisfactory. How could they make their constituents (e.g., the public, legislators) happy or at least convince them that they were doing something useful with tax dollars? Hence, they needed to be convinced that the research that my organization conducted aligned with these goals. To use one example, it was much more important to this audience that we studied whether a cost-efficient community prevention program led to reductions in teen tobacco use than to do research on identifying the strongest statistical predictors of teen smoking.

- *I've found an answer to an important question.* This is what academic researchers probably spend most of their time on. The goal is to solve a conceptual problem; one that requires additional knowledge because we don't have a complete understanding of it. This doesn't have to be "pie in the sky" work or fall under the designation "pure research" because a research project might, eventually, influence the development of practical solutions, effective policies, or answers to broader questions. For example, suppose someone conducts a descriptive study on homeless people living under bridges in San Francisco. This researcher may simply be interested in describing the types of people who live in these conditions. Do they tend to be males or females? Natives of San Francisco or from elsewhere? What is their range of ages and educational backgrounds? Although this research might have begun as a way to satisfy the researcher's intellectual curiosity, the study's findings may end up affecting subsequent research as well as policies regarding the homeless in general (e.g., what are their main health problems and treatment needs? How did they end up homeless in the first place?). Thus, just because a research project might seem to offer little to the practically minded person, it may make an important contribution at some future point (Booth et al. 2008, 19–20).

Hence, one of the keys to making our research interesting is to consider how to convince our audience that what we are doing is—at least potentially—important. Of course, some researchers find satisfaction when they've discovered something that simply seems interesting to them. But, more often than not, there is an audience that will share this interest; the trick is to find out who belongs to this audience and then find a way to reach them.

THE RESEARCH PROCESS

Books on research methods and on research, in general, describe the steps to conducting a study (O'Leary 2014). We shall refer to this as the *research process*, but it has also been called *research design* (Ragin and Amoroso 2011). It may be defined as the planning and execution of a project that is intended to answer a research question, solve a research problem, or test a hypothesis. A diagram of the research process is shown in figure 1.1. Note some of its important characteristics. The first two stages might be considered exploratory research, but should also include some of the suggestions outlined earlier to ensure that the research is interesting and persuasive, as well as not overly redundant. Moreover, before one acquires the data, it is important to have a clear data collection and analysis plan. Too often, researchers rely on a favored method or analysis technique without carefully considering if the methods match the type of data that should be collected or the research goals.

The sixth step in figure 1.1 is called *workflow*. As mentioned in the preface, this term has been borrowed from organizational studies to address some of the steps that researchers should take to during the course of a study (Kirchkamp 2013; Long 2009). However, it may be considered a subset of the research process since it is concerned mainly with how the data are treated as part of the overall project. In particular, this focuses on the flow once data have been acquired through project completion. Since project workflow plays such a central role

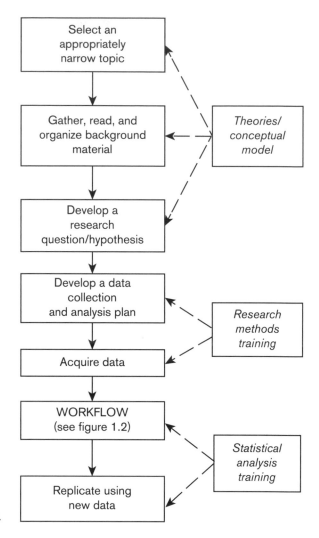

FIGURE 1.1 The research process.

in this book, figure 1.2 provides a diagram of some specific steps. Similar to the research process diagram, figure 1.2 is a bit misleading because, for most research projects, there is significant interplay among the steps. For instance, once one examines the data, it may be necessary to go back to the organization and cleaning stage. Similarly, a reviewer may point out at the presentation stage some problem with the analysis that necessitates going back to the methods or analyzing data stage. The sharing data stage is omitted by many researchers—perhaps for confidentiality or proprietary reasons—yet, when part of the workflow, it allows for *reproducibility* of the results. This refers to allowing other researchers access to the data and computer code so that they may validate the results and determine if they depend on peculiarities of the analysis (Kass et al., 2016; Peng et al. 2006). Note that it is not the same are replication since it does not involve new data.

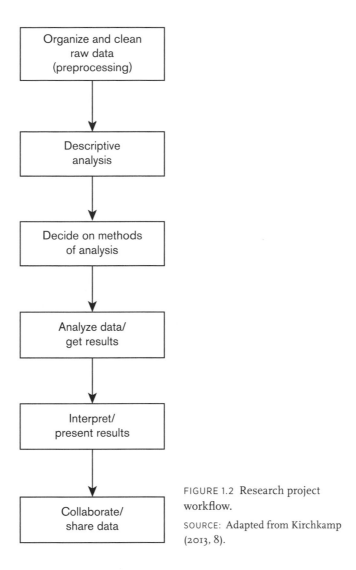

FIGURE 1.2 Research project workflow.

SOURCE: Adapted from Kirchkamp (2013, 8).

FINAL WORDS

Research is a valuable activity that involves identifying a question to be answered, a hypothesis to be tested, or a problem to be solved. It requires careful consideration of what is already known about a phenomenon, appropriate data in some form that may be used to get an answer to the question or help us understand the problem better, and tools to analyze the data in some manner and present the results of the analysis. This book focuses on questions and problems that may be examined using quantitative data. This chapter presents some ways to think about research, some impediments to quality research, and some methods to ensure that our research is timely and important. The next chapter explores how to develop and refine research questions by identifying topics, drawing on theory, building maps and conceptual models, and considering the role of arguments.

EXERCISES FOR CHAPTER 1

1. Select three or four articles from a recent issue of one of the prominent journals in your field. For example, if you are a sociologist, you might select the *American Journal of Sociology* or the *American Sociological Review*. Or, if you are a political scientist, you might choose the *American Political Science Review* or the *American Journal of Political Science*. Browse the articles and attempt to classify the research presented in them as exploratory, descriptive, or explanatory. Do you see any examples where more than one type occurs in the same article?

2. Look up a legal brief. A brief is a legal document that is presented to a court and argues why one side should win the case. Review the brief to get a flavor for how research may be used as advocacy. Contrast this with the way you might conduct research on the topic of the court case using a more balanced approach.

3. Using a favorite hobby, sport, or another area of interest, develop an argument that includes the three components discussed earlier: claims, warrants, and data. Discuss what additional evidence would be needed to evaluate your argument.

4. Locate and read an article from a media source that you think is biased in some way. For example, perhaps you think a certain online magazine is biased in a politically or socially conservative or liberal direction. Try to identify some assumptions and cognition traps the author tends to make or fall into. What is an example of a backfire effect that might result if someone was presented with information from this article?

5. Using one of the articles you selected in exercise 1, consider the steps described in it in terms of the research project workflow (figure 1.2). Which steps are described well? Which steps are unclear or not described at all? Do the authors provide instructions about how to access their data so that one may reproduce their results? If not, try to locate an article in one of your discipline's journals that does describe a way to access the data used in the analysis.

TWO

Developing Research Questions

The United States has the highest imprisonment rate in the western world, with more than 2 million inmates in state and federal prisons and county jails. This represents about 1 out of every 110 adults in the United States. Each year, more than 600,000 of these inmates are released back into the community. One of the problems many of them face is employment: some companies are hesitant to hire former prisoners and thus it is difficult to find a decent paying job. Though this is not a new or surprising piece of information, the sociologist Devah Pager was curious whether race also played a role in finding a job, for previous studies had suggested that African-Americans were less likely to be hired than Caucasians even when their experience and skill levels were similar. Therefore, she set up an experiment to test the question of whether a criminal record or race had a larger impact on finding a job. Pager conducted an experiment in which she sent four college students—two African-American and two Caucasian—to apply for a large number of job openings for entry level positions (no experience needed). The background of the students was virtually identical except for their race and their report of a prison record (which was randomly assigned—in other words, they had not actually been in prison, but reported that they had to a random set of employers). As anticipated, when they reported a prison record, they were less likely to be called back for an interview. There was a surprising finding, however: whereas 17% of the time the Caucasians with a "prison record" were called for an interview, only 14% of the time were the African-Americans with no "prison record" called for an interview. In other words, being an African-American seemed more detrimental to job prospects than having a criminal record (Pager 2008). Although one might have questions about this research, consider how asking a new question of an old research topic can lead to a surprising result.

Now let's see an example of what some might think of as a more dubious research question (you decide). In 2014, the Ig Nobel Prize in Psychology was given to a research team that used data mining of a huge dataset to find that depression and cat bites are associated, especially in women. In the abstract to their article, the researchers noted that 117,000 of 1.3 million patients in the database had depression (9%) and 750 patients had experienced cat bites (0.06%). Furthermore, "depression was found in 41.3% of patients with cat bites . . . [including 47% of women] compared to 24.2% of men presenting with a similar bite" (Hanauer et al. 2013). What do you think of their research question: "is being bitten by a cat associated with depression?" (Or is it the other way around: are cats more likely to bite depressed people?) By the way, Ig Nobel Prizes are given each year to "achievements that make people laugh and then think" (www.improbable.com/ig).

Recall that figure 1.1 in chapter 1 diagrammed the typical steps in the research process. The top part of the diagram involved selecting a topic and developing a research question. This is the part of the process discussed in this chapter. But what is a research question? As discussed in the last chapter, research is a set of transparent procedures that is designed to generate knowledge, such as answering a question, checking the veracity of a claim, or solving a problem. Thus, a research question is an inquiry designed to elicit information about a claim or a problem. It assumes that there are research methods available that may be used to gather this information. We'll discuss some important characteristics of research questions later. First, though, it's important to consider a broader issue: how are the topics that motivate particular research questions chosen by researchers?

SELECTING A TOPIC

How do researchers determine the specific topics they will study? This is the first step in determining which questions to ask and how to find answers to these questions. After all, if there is no way to answer a research question, then there is little point in asking it unless you simply like to imagine what the answers might be. For example, I might be interested in determining how many people died of the Black Death in Bath, England, during the year 1351, but it is unlikely I have tools to answer this question. So let's begin by considering how to find a topic for a research project. Where should one begin? The range of topics might be limited by disciplinary boundaries, so that's a good place to start. In the field I began in during my younger days—criminology—I was expected to conduct research on juvenile delinquency or criminal behavior. It would not have made much sense to study the effects of the Black Death in Bath, England, during the fourteenth century unless I could address its influence on criminal behavior or some closely related phenomena. Of course, if you have invested time in learning the range of topics examined by your discipline—perhaps by taking classes and reading books and articles in your field of study—then you've already narrowed the topics down to a certain degree. However, the social and behavioral sciences offer a substantial range of topics, from laboratory studies of rodents (psychology) to voting behaviors (political science) to national-level studies of human birth and death rates (demography/

sociology). Thus, let's consider how we might limit the scope of topics within an academic discipline (see Booth et al. 2008, for additional suggestions).

Try to Find a Topic That Interests You in Some Way

If you are a student taking a class that requires a research paper, this is not always possible (for instance, I found the study of corrections—which was a required part of the curriculum—terribly uninteresting when I was an undergraduate student). But let's assume you are taking a course that is at least somewhat interesting or that the course requirements are general enough to accommodate your interests. Or, are there particular courses that you've completed that were particularly fascinating? What did you find interesting about them: a specific subject, a theory, a required or recommended book or article? Sit down for a few minutes and think about the most fascinating topics you've come across in the field. Use your imagination, curiosity, and creative instincts. Consider what you've seen in the news media about this topic or issues that are meaningful to you (Foss and Waters 2007). What issues might be part of this topic? Take some notes or draw some pictures of the topic or issues that interest you. Sketch some relationships that seem intriguing:

Length of queue → *number of spontaneous social interactions per minute*

Personal income → *probability of voting*

Friendship networks → *happiness*

Perhaps the best, and most common, way to find topics is to read books and articles in the discipline (Alvesson and Sandberg 2013). The Internet makes it particularly easy to search for relevant books, articles, and reports; however, some care is needed since there is information overload for many topics. And it's not a good idea to spend too much time reading in depth before you have narrowed your topic to something manageable (White 2009). However, assume you are intrigued by studies of social deviance. Read a couple of chapters that look interesting from books with the term *social deviance* in the title (e.g., Rosoff and Pontell 2010; Weitzer 2002), or from topical journals such as *Deviant Behavior* and *Social Problems*. Pay particular attention to the conclusion section of journal articles; authors often describe what needs to be done now that they have completed their research. We'll return later to how journal articles are a good source of ideas. There might also be topics that seem well researched, but some of the key studies have never been replicated. A skeptical eye could point you toward potential flaws in the research that can be examined through replication. Or, you may think that replication is needed in order to ensure that a research finding that appears to have general support is valid. For example, Devah Pager's study discussed at the beginning of the chapter was conducted in Milwaukee, Wisconsin. Would the same results be found in other parts of the United States? Talk to colleagues, including instructors, about topics that are interesting. They can often point toward the most important material to read about a specific topic.

Consider a Problem That You Think Needs to Be Solved

It is helpful to think of research as a quest to solve a problem. Think about how common it is in the sciences to solve problems: mathematicians tackle algebra problems, physicists look for ways to produce cheap energy, and medical researchers try to find vaccines for human immunodeficiency virus (HIV). In the social sciences, problem-solving often means identifying some phenomenon that needs to be understood better in order to find solutions (e.g., homelessness in a city, methamphetamine use in a rural community). The key is that there is not sufficient knowledge or there is, at best, a poor understanding of the problem. Many of those in the research community actively seek out problems to work on; in fact, most consider the topics they work on as full of problems since they wish to gain information about them.

Similar to many types of problems, a research problem involves (1) a condition and (2) a cost or a consequence that someone doesn't like (Booth et al. 2008). The general condition of a research problem is, of course, not knowing something. I don't know what the association between experiencing a parental divorce and adolescent drug use is; I want to know more about it, though. My knowledge is incomplete. In addition, if I know more about this particular problem, I'll likely learn a little more about why some young people begin to use illegal drugs. This will not only increase my understanding of and curiosity about adolescent drug use, but it might also contribute to the research community's general understanding of this type of adolescent behavior. Furthermore, I can consider practical issues by thinking about how my research might be useful for preventing drug use or at least preventing the negative consequences of drug use by young people.

Make Sure the Topic Is Specific Enough (but Not Too Specific)

Choosing a specific topic that is neither too broad nor too narrow will allow you to complete the research in a reasonable amount of time. It is also important because, in the social and behavioral sciences, we generally tackle narrow topics. For example, why young people use illegal drugs is a huge area of inquiry that hundreds of researchers contribute to each year. I recently entered the term "adolescent drug use" in Google Scholar and limited the search to the previous two years. I stopped counting the number of articles listed after the 30th page. Thus, if you attempt to address this topic, you will likely have a lot of scattered information that is difficult to present concisely or in a report (this doesn't mean you shouldn't take on broad topics, especially if you're passionate about them, but just realize that you will need to invest a significant number of years). A more focused topic could be something like "Parents' mental health problems and adolescent drug use" or "Variations in the prevalence of adolescent drug use across different types of neighborhoods." Although both of these topics are still too broad to be examined in a single research project, the subject area is much more narrow and likely to yield interesting research questions.

Is There an Audience?

Recall that in chapter 1 we discussed the importance of considering your audience (Booth et al. 2008). As you are attempting to narrow the topic, don't forget to ask whether there is an

FIGURE 2.1 The steerage (photograph by Alfred Stieglitz).

audience interested in it. Suppose, for instance, that you are a psychologist who is intrigued by the way people use grammar when they write informally. The research in this area might be of interest to some of your fellow psychologists. However, you decide that you'd like to study whether religious people are more likely than others to confuse singular possessive cases and plural possessive cases when using surnames (e.g., James' dog is vicious vs. James's dog is vicious). Perhaps many religious people who read the Old Testament and derivative literature are used to seeing terms such as "Moses' writings" or "Moses' tablets." Before embarking on such an ambitious and time-consuming project, though, it's best to consider whether other psychologists are interested in this topic or whether they can be shown its importance.

Here's another example. Sociology has seen some growth in the area of visual studies: using photographs and other visual media as a research tool or as a way to understand how people and groups comprehend visual images, such as vacation photos and films. But will sociologists care if I wish to explore the social implications of a single photograph taken by Alfred Stieglitz, a famous early twentieth-century photographer? One of his photographs I find intriguing is called "The Steerage," taken in 1907 (figure 2.1). I read a story that Stieglitz's wife, Emmeline, loved to travel by ship. The story mentioned that, during a trip on the Kaiser Wilhelm II, Stieglitz grew tired of being around the wealthy people in first class, so he took a walk, camera in hand, to see the decks below where the lowest paying passengers had to stay, an area known as *the steerage*. The photograph he took during his walk is, I think, full of sociological implications concerning social class, early twentieth-century immigration, and even a wealthy person's discomfort with traveling in style while others were packed into much smaller spaces. However, it is unlikely—although not impossible—that I would generate much interest among sociologists if I wrote an assessment of only this photograph. Rather, a topic that would likely garner more interest is to consider how social class was represented by photographers in the early twentieth century, so a comparison of several photographs or photographers, perhaps accompanied by an analysis of commentary by photographers and art critics of the period, might make a good research project.

FROM TOPIC TO RESEARCH QUESTION

Once the topic is sufficiently narrow—although this issue should continue to be on your mind—it is next important to think about a how to use it to derive a research question. First, though, it is essential to recognize that research questions must be answerable (Andrews 2003). This means that they should be limited to those inquiries that they may be answered within the confines of a research project and using the methods available. A question such as "why does religion exist?" is far too broad an inquiry for present purposes, although it might be appropriate for one's life work (if done properly). A study of the dietary practices of Matsés people of Brazil might seem like a good idea, but if there is no way to get information on them, then there is little to gain by spending time developing a pertinent research question.

Moreover, research questions should be relevant, or you should be able to come up with a persuasive argument why they are relevant, to your discipline (Alvesson and Sandberg 2013). Some of the things that might seem interesting, though important, may not be relevant to your fellow sociologists, social workers, psychologists, or political scientists. With these qualifications in mind, what are some steps in deriving a research question?

Once You Have Identified a Topic, Ask Questions That Seem Interesting and Applicable

This will further help narrow the topic down to a manageable level. At this point, ask various questions about the topic; this may lead to some specific issues that are especially intriguing. Thinking about the topic, what are you curious about? Suppose, for example, that a researcher is interested in the topic of adolescent depression. She might then ask about differences among those who are depressed and those who are not. Is it just a genetic abnormality that leads to depression? Then, what effect might parents' mental health status or their parenting practices have on their children's risk of depression? Do early childhood experiences—such as neglect, punishment experiences, or being withdrawn or shy—affect this risk? Do the symptoms change over time? Does behavior affect the risk? What about relationships with siblings and friends?

Consider the previous example of early twentieth-century photographers. What was the background of Stieglitz and others who photographed people from different classes? What was the context of the photographs? Did the photographers intend them to be art, photojournalism, both, or neither? Did their photographs tend to involve urban or rural areas, or different ethnic or immigrant groups? Were these photographs commissioned by some organization or did the photographers work on their own? What were the reactions of art critics or others when the photographs were exhibited? How did these photographs compare to other media of the period?

Another set of questions directly involves imagining the audience: What is the value of these photographs for understanding social class in early twentieth-century America? Will an analysis of them provide any persuasive evidence to a social scientist interested in the general issue of social class or immigration? Can the researchers convince an audience that the questions have wider significance? Perhaps a skeptical critic would argue that photography is a marginal field for understanding social class or class differences since most photographers in the early twentieth century came from the middle or upper classes and they were opportunistic when taking photographs. Furthermore, they were idiosyncratic when it came to creating artistic representations, so there is little useful information to be obtained from their work for a social scientific or historical understanding of class or immigration. If this is a legitimate argument, then perhaps the researcher needs to find another angle or, unfortunately, another research topic.

Figuring out which questions to ask can be difficult. Fortunately, there are some useful guides. For example, psychologist and creativity expert Keith Sawyer (2013, 34–36) provides a set of questions derived from a CIA checklist that is useful for arriving at good research ideas. These include the following:

Why does this problem need to be solved? What can we gain by solving it?

What don't I understand yet?

What information is available? Is it sufficient? Are there sources of information available?

What is the scope of the problem? What is *not* the problem?

What are some parts of the issue or problem (break it down into components)?

What cannot be changed regarding this problem? What factors must remain constant?

Can you think of a similar problem or a different angle? Identifying analogous problems can be helpful.

You may be able to come up with other questions (see Foss and Waters 2007, Sak 2011). The point of this exercise is to narrow the topic down in such a way that a research question can emerge.

Identify a Gap

Earlier, we discussed a key way to find topics: reading books and articles in your discipline. As you narrow down the issues that interest you and read material about these issues, you will find that there are often well-settled questions that should normally be avoided (Campbell et al. 1982; unless replication is needed), but there are also almost always gaps in the literature (White 2009). Gaps exist for various reasons. Most often, they are present because a large majority of studies can offer only limited information about any research topic. Since research questions are, by their nature, rather narrow, there will almost always be more to know about a subject area.

It is not always easy to identify gaps, however. One efficient technique is to pay particular attention to the discussion and limitations sections of journal articles. These sections often provide a good way to find out what needs to be done regarding a particular topic. For example, suppose a researcher is interested in the association between stressful life conditions and illegal drug use. She reads an article in a recently published academic journal and notes the following sentence in the discussion section: "The next step is to determine whether adolescent males and females are affected differently by stress and whether this has any implications for initiating drug use." This suggests—although it is important to locate and read other articles to make sure—that the study of stress and illegal drug use has not evaluated differences between males and females. Perhaps this is worth considering.

Here is an example from an actual study. In the discussion section of a journal article on voting behavior and climate change skepticism, the authors wrote:

> Voting for a politically conservative party leads to higher levels of climate change skepticism, whereas voting for more liberal parties leads to lower levels of skepticism. . . . [But] in countries where there is more bipartisan political support for responses to climate change, we might expect to find lower and more stable levels of climate change skepticism. (McCrea et al. 2016, 1327, 1329).

In other words, the researchers studied this issue with data from one nation, yet if we examined this issue across nations, we might find that the answers are more nuanced than their results showed. This suggests a research project that uses data from different countries and asks whether the presumed connection between voting for a particular political party and climate change skepticism depends on how closely the parties agree about how governments should respond to climate change.

I've noticed that something that many students are worried about is disagreeing with or criticizing experts in their field about the choice or utility of a research question. ("He's a PhD level researcher so he must know so much more than me about research. Who am I to criticize?") However, this should not cause any anxiety because considering potential gaps, omissions, or even flaws in research is a common way that new ideas are generated or new research gets done. As mentioned earlier, most research questions are by design narrow and researchers can only tackle a thin slice of any topic in a single study. Thus, there is nothing wrong with thinking that there is another way to approach a research problem.

In addition, there may be healthy disagreement about the results of research projects because, from one's perspective, there are (1) flaws in the arguments, (2) flaws in the research methods and analysis, or (3) flaws in the interpretations. I once read an article in a prestigious criminology journal that claimed that school-level influences (e.g., student-teacher ratio; the proportion of poor children in a school) had no association with whether students misbehaved in school. However, individual characteristics, such as gender and school performance, did predict poor behavior. I looked at the way they did their study and realized that their data came from only seven schools. Knowing a bit about statistics, I suspected that this was not a large enough sample of schools to determine if there were school-level influences. I then used a dataset that had students from 1,000 schools and showed that when more schools were considered, school-level influences emerged as important. For example, schools where students, in general, were more involved in activities such as clubs and sports tended to have less misbehavior than in those schools with less student involvement.

As you read articles and look for gaps, consider some ways that research may be underdeveloped or even flawed. Moreover, think about alternative ways to tackle a particular research problem. Some issues to consider include the following:

- The researchers thought they were measuring some phenomenon, but you think there are other, perhaps even better ways, of measuring it. For instance, what did the researchers mean by "climate change skepticism" and how did this influence the way it was measured? Are there alternative questions that might be used to measure this form of skepticism?

- The researchers used a particular method, such as a quantitative approach, to examine a research question. It might also be useful to try a different method, such as a qualitative approach. Perhaps a study relied on survey data to examine the association between stress and alcohol use among young people, but you think qualitative interviewing might yield additional insight.

- There are alternative statistical methods one might use to study a problem. For example, a researcher may have used a linear technique when there was—in all likelihood—a nonlinear association. Suppose you come across a study of stressful life events and drug use that used a statistical model showing a linear relationship. You may think that these events only affect drug use up to a certain level, but the probability of use then decreases because highly stressed kids become depressed or withdrawn. Thus, understanding this issue might be advanced by studying nonlinear associations.

- From where were the data collected? Suppose that the sample used to examine a research question consisted of middle-class people from a Midwestern US city. Perhaps a sample from a Southern or Western US city would result in a different conclusion. Here, it is important to think about potential differences between people who live in different geographic areas. Similar questions about the source of the data include those about gender, race/ethnicity, socioeconomic status, nationality, and so forth.

- The researchers claimed that X influences Y, but actually you think that Y influences X. For example, the researchers examined whether voting for a particular political party affected subsequent views of climate change, but perhaps those views were already in place and then affected which party was more attractive to the voter.

- They claimed that X influences Y, but you think that some other factor affects both X and Y. For example, stress may not affect drug use; rather, poor parenting causes kids to experience stress and leads to drug use. In statistical terms, we say that poor parenting *confounds* the presumed association between stress and drug use.

- X influences Y only under certain circumstances. Suppose that some researchers studying welfare policies examined one nation that has a parliamentary democratic form of government. You might think it interesting to study these policies in nations with different forms of government (e.g., constitutional monarchy).

Use Theory

There are many definitions of the term *theory* and many ways that theories are used across academic disciplines. For example, Jonathan Turner (2013, 843) defines theory as "a mental activity revolving around the process of developing ideas that explain how and why events occur." As suggested by this definition, it is common to view theories as explanations of some phenomena that may be tested in some way (although this often differs across disciplines also). Inquiring into *how* and *why* things occur also provides the basis for many theories. For example, why did the US Civil War occur? How did the earth's surface temperature rise during the last 50 years? If a theory is a good explanation for a phenomenon, it should be a clear and thorough account and it should offer a better explanation than some other theory (Hoffmann 2003). Research questions are often designed as a test of theory through a deductive process or as a way to build a theory via induction. Figure 2.2 provides an illustration of the role that theories and research questions play in an ideal view of the way science progresses. Although some ideas have been labeled as laws in the social sciences—the law of demand, the iron law of oligarchy—it is rare to actually confirm that these laws are invariable across different conditions. In any event, this section focuses on using a theory to generate a research question.

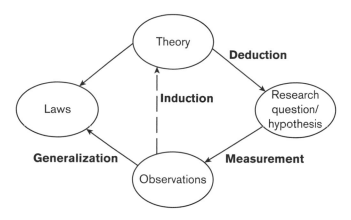

FIGURE 2.2 How science progresses.

A type of theory that is useful for generating research questions is identified by sociologist Robert K. Merton (1968) as "theories of the middle range." These are less abstract than broad explanations of human and societal actions and behaviors, such as rational choice theory, but more general than specific hypotheses or research questions. Middle range theories tend to focus on a particular set of variables that may be used to explain some outcome. For instance, Robert Agnew's (2006) general strain theory (GST) describes various types of subjective and objective stressors that are presumed to affect whether youth become involved in juvenile delinquency. Agnew also elaborates a set of intervening pathways that affect whether these stressors lead to illegal behaviors or some other outcome, such as depression. For example, if youth tend to respond to stressful situations with anger, they are likely to lash out violently and perhaps physically assault others when facing this type of condition. The theory may be used to develop specific research questions, such as one of those intimated earlier: do stressful life events, such as family fights or a death in the family, lead to a higher probability of initiation of marijuana use among adolescents?

Develop a Concept Map

A concept map is a way to depict the researcher's thought process as she attempts to move from a topic to a research question (Alvarez and Gowin 2010). It shows explicitly a set of terms that begin generally and then narrows the focus down until she reaches a research area that is appropriate for a single study. Concept maps are similar to *idea maps* that are designed to help people find solutions to problems (Sawyer 2013). Both types are intended to show a path from a broader topic to a narrow issue. A key part of this strategy involves using *concepts*. Although concepts are addressed in more detail later in the chapter, they may be defined for now as "generalized statements about [entire] classes of phenomena rather than specific statements of fact" (Becker 2008, 109). These statements are designed to say something about people, organizations, or other social units in general, without addressing only those that apply at some particular time or place. Some common concepts used in the social

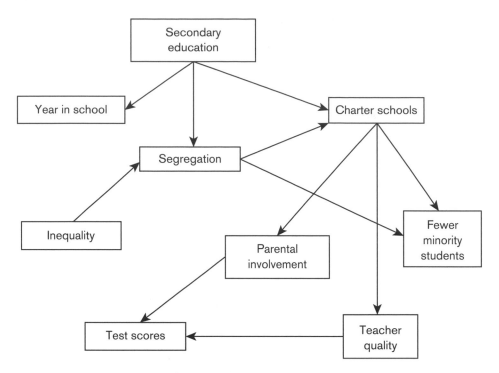

FIGURE 2.3 Concept map example. Research question: Do charter school students tend to have higher test scores because of greater parental involvement or because of higher quality teachers?

sciences are racial inequality, bureaucracy, juvenile delinquency, nationalism, prejudice, stereotype, and gender.

Although there are different ways to construct concept maps, the most useful is hierarchical in which the researcher

1. selects a topic and develops some concepts related to the topic;

2. ranks the concepts hierarchically from the most general to the most specific; and

3. arranges the concepts according to their hierarchical position and relationship to one another (Alvarez and Gown 2010, 5).

There are sometimes branches in the map that do not end up contributing to the research question, but are useful because they provide additional context for the topic. For instance, suppose a researcher is interested in the general topic of secondary education, such as what happens in high schools in the United States. What are some concepts related to the topic of education? From the literature in sociology and educational research, here are a few: test scores, grades, year in school, school choice, charter schools, curriculum, teacher quality, parental involvement, segregation, school attachment and commitment, inequality, and extracurricular activities. In reading the literature, the researcher also notices that several descriptive studies indicate that students in charter schools have higher scores on standardized tests than students in noncharter schools. How might this information be used in a concept map? Assuming the researcher is familiar with the literature, has some interest in particular aspects of education, and has carefully thought about the process that affects student performance, figure 2.3 provides an example.

This is a simple and unrefined example of a concept map, but it illustrates some key points. However, one area that likely needs improvement involves the enhancement of concepts, which can be ambiguous (what is meant by parental involvement? teacher quality?). So some revisions may be needed (O'Leary 2014). Nonetheless, carefully constructing and refining concept maps is a useful approach to developing research questions.

Identify a Hypothesis

Many social and behavioral scientists think that their studies should try to mimic, as close as possible, the natural and physical sciences. Recall from chapter 1 that a hypothesis is a statement about the presumed relationship between two or more variables. It is also sometimes described as an educated guess regarding an answer to a question. Most descriptions in the natural and physical sciences outline a specific set of five steps for the scientific method, one of which is to develop a hypothesis:

1. Observe a phenomenon.
2. Ask a question about the phenomenon.
3. *Develop a hypothesis.*
4. Conduct an experiment to test the hypothesis (which includes collecting and analyzing data).
5. Evaluate the evidence from the experiment to determine the veracity of the hypothesis (McClelland 2015).

The hypothesis must be testable and worded in such a way that it could be true or false (falsifiability). For some researchers, it is easier to think about research questions by identifying a specific hypothesis or set of hypotheses during the course of their study (Andrews 2003). This can be useful, especially if one thinks there is a clear or particularly important association between two concepts or variables. For example, a recent psychological study hypothesized that "job-based psychological ownership is positively related to job satisfaction" (Peng and Pearce 2015, 157). Job-based ownership means that the person thinks of her job and duties as her own rather than simply part of an organization. Hypotheses are normally derived directly from research questions, but specifying a hypothesis can also help refine a research question.

REFINING RESEARCH QUESTIONS

As mentioned earlier, research questions in the social sciences are often derived from theories. Since theories are fundamentally about explanation, it is important to recall that an explanation is a clear and thorough account of the issue that a researcher is studying. We wish to know why something occurred or how it happened. This is different than descriptive research questions that focus on when or where something occurred or who is involved in some phenomenon. Of course, research questions can apply to both descriptive and explanatory research.

Regardless of the type of research, questions may be modeled and refined by using concepts and propositions. As noted earlier, concepts are general statements about classes of a phenomenon rather than specific instances of a phenomenon. For example, a concept such as *stereotype* is designed to elicit an image of a general belief—often mistaken—about a group of people ("all hipsters wear skinny jeans"). Concepts are useful because they can provide a summary statement or term regarding a whole class of events or outcomes (Becker 1998). In a research project, they should be defined clearly: What does the concept mean? In some projects, the concepts used are understood well because they are so common in a particular research area. This lessens the need to define them. In addition, researchers must think about how to move from defining a concept to measuring it. Practically speaking, how will the data be used to identify a concept? This is a vital part of a process known as *operationalization* and is key to any research project. Concepts are measured using variables, which in quantitative social analyses are usually based on questions asked during surveys or interviews. We return to the issue of measurement and operationalization in chapters 4 and 5. For now, the focus is on the role of concepts in the formation and refinement of research questions.

A proposition is a statement that links two concepts together. The proposition "hipsters wear skinny jeans" connects the concept of hipster with the concept of skinny jeans. Similarly, the statement "job-based psychological ownership is positively related to job satisfaction" (Peng and Pearce 2015, 157) connects one concept, psychological ownership, with another, job satisfaction. Thus, a hypothesis is an example of a proposition.

Using Arguments

Chapter 1 includes a discussion of research as argumentation. It is helpful to revisit this section since thinking about arguments can help refine research questions. For example, consider that propositions are one type of claim ("crime rates are rising," "self-esteem is positively related to grades in high school"). When asking a research question, it is common to have a claim in mind, usually in the form of a proposition or hypothesis. For instance, the concept map shown in figure 2.3 includes the following research question: Do charter school students tend to have higher test scores because of greater parental involvement or because of higher quality teachers? This suggests two claims: (1) students in charter schools have higher test scores, than those in other public schools, because of greater parental involvement and (2) students in charter schools have higher test scores, than those in other public schools, because of higher-quality teachers. What arguments might support one of these two propositions? Are there reasons based on previous studies or a particular theoretical perspective? Note that the conjunction "because" is used in both propositions. However, it is useful, even if grammatically messy, to extend the claims by using "because" again: students in charter schools have higher test scores, than those in other public schools, *because* of higher-quality teachers *because* these teachers *do something better than other teachers* (Booth et al. 2008). This will help point toward (a) whether answering the research question is feasible, (b) what evidence is needed to evaluate it, and (c) whether it is relevant.

Another important aspect of using arguments is to be prepared to consider alternatives. Members of high school and college debate clubs know this principle well: they are taught that considering alternative explanations and arguments is essential to being a successful debater. Moreover, chapter 1 discussed cognition traps in which a person's views are rigid, such as when only one explanation is considered when evaluating some phenomenon. Given that the researcher is—or should be—in dialogue with the audience, it is essential that she be prepared to consider alternatives. For example, suppose that neither claim about charter schools is correct. An alternative explanation is that many charter schools are selective about which students they accept. They tend to reject applicants who have shown behavioral problems, low academic achievement, or don't have much motivation to do schoolwork. Therefore, charter schools self-select high achieving students who get high test scores regardless of what type of schools they attend or the quality of their teachers (Nichols-Barrer et al. 2016). Thinking about alternative explanations and attempting to consider them explicitly during the study will help improve the dialogical argument process that leads to supporting one proposition over the other and can, eventually, be used to suggest future directions for research on this issue.

Given the basic model of an argument (see chapter 1), some questions to ask that may help refine research questions and claims include the following:

- What are some alternative explanations to the claim or alternative answers – other than what I've presumed – to the question? (Direct a skeptical eye toward the claim and try to list some alternatives; see Klass [2012, chapter 3] for some reasons to be skeptical.)

- Has the question already been answered sufficiently that more research is not needed (e.g., we know that kids who use marijuana tend to associate with peers who use marijuana)?

- What evidence do I need to answer the question or determine if one claim is supported over another?

- Should this evidence be primarily qualitative, quantitative, experimental, historical, textual, based on a case study, or some combination of these? What type of data are needed? Should they come from surveys, experiments, administrative entities, or some other source?

It is best if you write down some notes about each of these issues. Keeping notes along the way will make it easier if you have to backtrack and change your specific question.

Think Like an Experiment

It is often helpful to think in terms of how might we answer the research question if we had extensive control over the groups we are interested in comparing. Suppose we could, for instance, randomly assign youth to charter schools or regular public schools. Given what we know from previous studies and from considering different possibilities, what might have happened if youth who attended regular public schools had attended charter schools? In other words, imagine the counterfactual situation. A variation of this is what the sociologist Howard Becker (2008, 20–21) calls the *null hypothesis trick*. This involves imagining if the phenomenon under consideration was the outcome of a purely random group of people. If interest is in test scores among charter school students, assume that charter schools are comprised of a completely random selection of students with various backgrounds. Would we expect to find the particular outcomes, such as higher test scores, if this was the case? Or would this be more likely if the students were not randomly selected? What would the selection process look like if it was not random? For example, good students and their parents—rather than students at random—may be more likely than bad or mediocre students to select charter schools.

Think Like a Historian (or a Detective)

Historians typically consider events that have already happened and then try to figure out why and how the event came about. Similarly, detectives and medical examiners usually don't begin their work until after a crime has been committed. Both types of researchers attempt to reconstruct events based on evidence that they acquire and then develop the most likely explanations given this evidence. Of course, they also need to consider the validity and strength of the evidence. Moreover, historians and detectives are interested in motives: what were the reasons that people or groups did the things they did that brought about the event (Shore 2008)? Once again, Howard Becker (2008, 39) has an analogous idea for conducting research: the *machine trick*. Imagine you are given a machine and wish to discover how it works. Perhaps the machine produces something, such as computer microchips (for fascinating examples, see the Science Channel show "How It's Made" [http://www .sciencechannel.com/tv-shows/how-its-made/videos]). What goes into its construction? How do the parts work together to make the machine operate? This is likened to *reverse engineering*: taking a machine apart in order to duplicate it. To think in this way, begin with the outcome that you wish to explain, such as higher test scores among students. Then, think backward, based on the background knowledge you've accumulated, to figure out what personal and social conditions would produce higher test scores. What evidence would be needed to understand these conditions better? Do the conditions include attendance at charter schools, certain types of teachers, or particular sorts of families? What else would such a machine

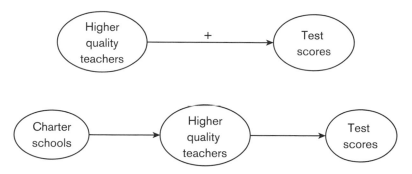

FIGURE 2.4 Example of two conceptual models.

need in order to operate? How does it produce higher test scores? What might be missing that would affect the success of the machine? This way of approaching a research question or issue is often useful for determining the quality and direction of the research.

Using Conceptual Models

In the social sciences, a conceptual model is a physical or diagrammatic representation of concepts and propositions. Some researchers prefer to call them "causal models," but this term implies more than most social science research projects can provide (see chapter 1), so it is avoided here. The diagrams are similar to flowcharts, yet the process shown relates to how one concept is thought to affect or be associated with another concept. They have also been used to depict theories, although some theories are too complex to be represented in this manner. Conceptual models are sometimes derived from concept maps, but they are more focused. For our purposes, we discuss just a couple of simple models by focusing on only two or three concepts linked by one or two propositions.

One of the values of conceptual models is that they strip research questions and claims down to their basic structure. Although there is a risk of oversimplification, it is a good idea to construct a conceptual model to determine if your research question and the claims you derive from it make sense (Whetten 2002). To construct one of these models in simple form, use oval shapes to represent concepts and arrows to represent propositions. Plus and minus signs are often placed on the arrows to indicate that the researcher thinks the association among the concepts is in a positive or a negative direction. For example, consider the earlier research question regarding test scores among students in charter schools. A couple of conceptual models are represented using the diagram in figure 2.4.

Although what these models represent is not entirely clear without additional context, they may be read as "the presence of higher quality teachers is positively related to higher test scores" and "charter schools tend to have higher quality teachers; thus, test scores tend to be higher." The second model assumes the first, which is much simpler, but the second model clarifies the claim better. Note that neither model explicitly shows the comparisons, though. What are charter schools being compared with? What constitutes the concept outside the boundary of high-quality teachers (low-quality teachers or all other teachers?). What types of test scores are the research questions concerned with? Thus, to understand conceptual models, a narrative that explains the research question or claim and the concepts should accompany them. As with the previous section, it is also important to ask additional questions regarding these conceptual models before moving along in the research process:

Are the concepts clear?

Is there a way to measure them?

Is evidence available with which to test whether the models are accurate?

What type of evidence is needed?

Are there alternative explanations that need to be considered?

AN EXAMPLE

We have touched upon a substantial number of ideas to guide the development of research questions. Let's now consider an example that uses a few of these ideas to narrow a research topic down to a research question. Suppose that we are given the task—perhaps by our employer or college teacher—to develop a research study on *recidivism*. The first thing to do is to figure out what this term means. According to the most common definitions, recidivism refers to a person's involvement in criminal behavior after he or she have been given sanctions or experienced some sort of formal state intervention for previous criminal activity. A literature review of research on recidivism further specifies this term as criminal behavior after serving a court-imposed sentence, such as time in jail or prison. Although there might be other ways to understand recidivism, this seems like a reasonable way to understand it.

Since this is such a broad topic, let's try to narrow it down a bit. Again, from the literature, it appears that most research on recidivism concerns those who have served time in state or federal prisons. Most of this research has also used large datasets collected by federal government agencies to track released prisoners and determine whether they are arrested for a crime from 1 to 3 years after release. Some questions we might ask at this stage include the following:

Who tends to recidivate (e.g., males or females, violent offenders or property offenders)?

When do they tend to recidivate (e.g., within the first three months)?

Why do they tend to recidivate (e.g., because they go back to hanging out with the same friends; they cannot find a job)?

Assuming the research is done in the United States, are those released in certain areas of the country more likely to recidivate?

FIGURE 2.5 Employment and recidivism conceptual model.

Imagine we decide that the most interesting issue involves the why question. It seems most important since if we understand why people recidivate, perhaps we can help inform programs to reduce it.

At this point, we review specific studies of recidivism and look for gaps, such as by carefully reading articles and paying close attention to hints at additional research that might be useful. One of the first things we notice is that most of the research over the past 10–15 years has been conducted on men rather than women. So it might be appropriate to limit our attention to women. There is also an article we find that provides an excellent summary of research on interventions that help reduce recidivism among women offenders (Gobeil et al. 2016). The authors of this article find that interventions such as drug treatment, employment training, and parenting programs while in prison led to a reduced likelihood of recidivism once female inmates were released. But, at this point, since the studies that were summarized in this article relied on general involvement in these intervention programs, we have little idea why or in what way they reduced recidivism. For example, did employment training improve their chances of getting a job once they were released?

At this point, let's consider a theory and how it might inform our attempt to hone in on a research question or hypothesis. In the field of criminology, one of the most popular explanations for criminal behavior is known as *social bond theory*. Briefly, this theory claims that people who are more attached and involved in conventional activities are less likely than others to commit criminal acts. For example, social bond theory has motivated studies that have found that when adults are gainfully employed in legitimate occupations, they are less likely to commit a crime, even if they are otherwise predisposed toward this sort of behavior (Uggen 1999). Thus, we reason that if employment training in prison does lead to employment after release, those women will be less likely to recidivate compared with women who did not receive this training. This leads to the conceptual model in figure 2.5.

It is now a good idea to consider the questions listed earlier: Are the concepts clear? Can they be measured? Is there evidence available to assess this conceptual model? Furthermore, what alternative explanations might also elucidate why employment programs lead to lower recidivism risk? For instance, perhaps especially violent prisoners cannot qualify for employment training and they are more likely than others to recidivate upon release. This example provides only one pathway to a potentially testable research question, but we could also have used other approaches, such as concept maps, to arrive at a research question.

1. Is the topic right for me?
   a. Is it interesting?
   b. Is the topic overly broad? Is it too narrow?
   c. Does it lend itself to a research question or set of questions?
   d. Can I manage my biases?
2. Is the research question right for the field?
   a. Has the question already been answered?
   b. Does a relevant audience, such as experts in the field, think it is relevant and important?
   c. Will the findings (potentially) be important?
   d. Will they make a contribution?
3. Is the research question well articulated?
   a. What theories, arguments, experimental thinking, and concept maps can be used to develop and refine the question?
   b. Can I articulate a hypothesis or a conceptual model based on the question?
   c. Are the concepts and propositions well defined?
   d. Are there unarticulated assumptions?
   e. What are some alternative explanations?

In addition to the issues outlined in this chapter, you should also ask yourself the following:

4. Can the research question be answered?
   a. Are data available?
   b. Are there datasets that already exist that might be used to answer the research question?
   c. If data sources do exist, can I gain access to them?
   d. Do I need to collect my own data? Is this feasible?
   e. Can I measure the concepts adequately to answer the research question?
   f. Do I have the right skills?
   g. Can I complete the research in time?
   h. Will it cost too much?
   i. Are there ethical problems?
5. Does the question meet the approval of my supervisor, advisor, or committee?
   a. Do they think I am on the right track?

FINAL WORDS

Research questions are an essential component of the research process. The proper identification of research questions ensures that the scope of the research is sufficiently narrow, valuable, interesting, answerable, and nonredundant. The research question is also central to the research process because it is related to each component of this process (White 2009). Research questions are typically developed by narrowing down a topic that the researcher finds interesting and important, and that remains at least partly unanswered. They often emerge through engagement with the research literature and by thinking creatively about puzzles or problems, but may also be derived from theories and concept maps, translated into hypotheses, and elaborated by considering relevant dialogical arguments, approaching them from different perspectives, and constructing conceptual models. Some combination of these methods will more often than not lead to a good research question, as well as testable claims.

As a final step, sidebar 2.1 provides a checklist of questions designed to determine whether a research question is generally appropriate (O'Leary 2014, 45). It follows most of the steps recommended in this chapter, and also includes additional considerations as you think about developing a research question and making it the centerpiece of a research project.

EXERCISES FOR CHAPTER 2

1. Select one of the following topics and use the research topic/question checklist, steps 1–3, to try to narrow it down to a research question, problem, or hypothesis. Make sure this is grounded in the research literature in some way.
   a. Binge alcohol use among young adults.
   b. Political activism among older adults.
   c. Access to mental health treatment in impoverished communities in the rural United States.
   d. Divorce and its effects on parent-child relationships.
   e. Trust in the police in urban areas of the United States and Canada.
   f. Eating disorders among minority female teenagers.
   g. Bullying and its consequences for elementary school students.
   h. Co-occurring mental health disorders among the homeless.
   i. The successes and failures of nonprofit environmental groups in Europe.
   j. China-Taiwan political relations in the twenty-first century.

2. If you didn't do this as part of exercise 1, draw a conceptual model of the research question or hypothesis.

3. Choose one of the concepts you would need to measure if you were to pursue a project on this research question or hypothesis. Conduct a literature review to determine how this concept has been measured in previous studies.

THREE

Data

What are data and how are they used? As we learn in this chapter, data represent information derived from a variety of sources. We use data in our everyday lives, often without even knowing it. In addition, you probably are regularly contributing data by tweeting and using Snapchat, Facebook, and other online media. Researchers rely on various forms of data to conduct studies and answer research questions. Thus, it is important to realize that the conclusions and recommendations from studies are only as good as the data that go into them. Consider, for instance, the following two examples.

In the late summer of 2015, a story in the national media reported that elementary school students were being given far too much homework. Whereas experts recommend about 10 minutes of homework per night per grade level, many students were assigned much more than this. Although not earth shattering, this caused some ripples about students being overwhelmed because of too much schoolwork and too little leisure time. However, as a researcher at the Brookings Institution pointed out, the data used in this study were collected from a sample of parents in only one northeastern city in the United States. Moreover, the parents filled out the survey with which the data were gathered in pediatricians' offices (Loveless 2015). The Brookings Institution researcher questioned whether the results of this study are particularly meaningful, given that they were based on a survey in one city and among parents who probably had quite a bit on their minds (is my child all right? Will the shot be painful?). In general, he criticized the data used to answer the research question and support the claim. What are your thoughts about the researcher's critique of the study? What might be some better ways to find data about this research topic?

The development of new pharmaceuticals to prevent and treat disease is a multibillion-dollar business. Even though getting a pharmaceutical to market takes years since there are strict safety requirements, adverse drug reactions are still a risk. In fact, the US Food and Drug Administration's (FDA) Adverse Events Reporting System (FAERS) indicated that there were about 123,927 deaths from legally prescribed pharmaceuticals in 2014, an increase of more than 300% since 2006 (FDA 2016). Much of this increase was attributable to the improper use of painkillers, but adverse reactions are still a major concern. One of the challenges is that the FDA has traditionally relied on prescribing physicians and emergency rooms to learn about these problems. However, some cases go unreported or might otherwise be lost in the bureaucratic system. Ahmed Abbasi, a professor of information technology at the University of Virginia, is leading a team of researchers who are attempting to learn about adverse drug reactions by analyzing social media data from websites, blogs, web forums, and social networking sites. Some of their early work has shown that this method of gathering data detects two-thirds of adverse events at least 15 months earlier than traditional reporting channels (Abbasi and Adjeroh 2014). What are some implications of this use of social media data? In what other ways might social media be used to study social and behavioral topics?

Data may be used for many positive purposes. As should be obvious, they are an essential part of the research process: data are needed so that researchers can explicitly examine research questions and test hypotheses. In this chapter, we consider data. What are they? What are some sources and types of data? What role do data play in the measurement process as concepts are translated into their empirical manifestations, variables? What are some types of variables used in the social and behavioral sciences? Finally, how do researchers organize data and variables so that they may use them in a project?

WHAT ARE DATA?

The word *data* has been used many times in the previous chapters. It is clearly an integral part of the research process. Yet, we hear this word so often that it is easy to overlook its definition. In brief, data are simply pieces of information (whereas a *datum* is one piece of information). Thus, data are around us at all times. Our minds are constantly collecting data through our sensory experiences: when driving a car, for example, we see and hear various stimuli that help us navigate. And our minds filter data constantly—we cannot process every bit of sensory input that we experience each moment. In fact, experiencing too much sensory data can lead to health disorders, such as sensory processing disorder and synesthesia. Stanley Milgram (1970), the social scientist introduced in chapter 1, even coined a term, *urban overload*, to refer to the often overwhelming sensory experiences among those living in large cities.

In the scientific community, data are a fundamental part of the research process—scientists need pieces of information to test conceptual models, solve problems, answer research questions, and evaluate hypotheses. Data provide the core of the evidence with which to examine the legitimacy of claims and arguments. But data are also used by companies to test and market their products, by schools to evaluate their students and teachers, by political campaigns to raise funds, and by governments to understand more about people, organizations, and economic and social conditions. An intriguing development is the emerging field of data science or data analytics. As mentioned in the introduction, data analytics uses large datasets—that can include terabytes of data (1 terabyte = 10^{12} bytes)—to develop predictive models that may then be used by organizations to understand people's tendencies better. The project to detect adverse drug reactions mentioned earlier is a good example of how data analytics may be used in a creative and useful way.

Although data are ubiquitous, social and behavioral scientists are concerned with specific types of data, especially those that are collected through a reliable, well-understood, and documented set of procedures. There is a special concern with *data quality* (Herzog et al. 2007). This includes the completeness, accuracy, and timeliness of the data; as well as whether they are appropriate for a specific task. It should be obvious that if pieces of information are incomplete, inaccurate, or out of date, then a research project will not be successful. You may recall that researchers are especially concerned with *validity* and *reliability*; each of these involves data quality. Validity refers generally to whether something is actually an indicator of what we think it is—is a datum an accurate indicator of, say, a person's age? Does a digital scale provide accurate data on a person's weight? Did the question about homework mentioned in the example that began this chapter yield correct data? Thus, there is the issue of whether the measurement strategies and data collection methods used in a study yield valid data.

Reliability concerns whether the data are consistent across different conditions. If we develop a question to gather data on a person's political ideology, will it yield the same response for a person from one day to the next? For instance, suppose we ask a group of people whether they consider themselves liberal, moderate, or conservative. For some, the response may be simple and so we might expect these people to give the same response a couple of days later. However, perhaps a subgroup of people are not native English speakers and are confused about what these labels mean. They may, therefore, give a different response a day or two later that might be influenced, for example, by something reported in the media. For this subgroup, the data would not be considered reliable. Consider once again the example that began this chapter. If we asked the parents during a relaxing time in their homes about their children's homework, would we expect the same answer as they gave in the physician's office?

Validity and reliability can become especially problematic when researchers use words that can be interpreted in different ways or that might not be familiar to some people. To give an unlikely example, suppose you were asked on a medical survey if you'd experienced epistaxis in the past six months. How would you respond? Perhaps you'd look it up on your smartphone, but it would be better if the survey asked simply if you'd had a nosebleed. Finally, another aspect of data involves their *integrity*: are the data unaltered from their source or have they been modified in some way (intentionally or unintentionally)? All of these aspects of data are concerned with whether the data are sound.

Most books on research methods discuss in detail numerous methods of data collection. For instance, books on my shelf discuss how to select samples, construct surveys and questionnaires, design qualitative studies, plan and perform experiments, and use mixed methods. There are also books that focus on each of these topics, as well as on case study techniques, textual analysis, historical methods, simulations, visual methods, social network data, meta-analysis, and several others. As mentioned at the outset, the goal of this book is not to cover the various methods that are utilized by the research community, but rather to consider specific parts of the research process in practical detail. We have already learned some valuable techniques for narrowing topics down to reasonable research questions and claims. And this section has introduced the topic of data. The next step is to consider some general sources and types of data.

SOURCES OF DATA

Suppose a researcher has defined an interesting research problem and perhaps even developed a conceptual model to explain some phenomenon. The next step in the research process (see figure 1.1) is to acquire data so that evidence may be brought to bear on whether the model is valid, invalid, or requires modification. The word *acquire* is used intentionally because, although descriptions of the research process typically use the term "collect data," there are actually various ways to obtain data for a project. It is often preferable—for reasons discussed later—to collect data specifically for a study, but some researchers do not have the resources to gather their own data and must rely on other sources.

There are various kinds of data used in the social and behavioral sciences, such as quantitative data, qualitative data, historical records, textual data, and so forth. However, at this point, it is helpful to distinguish three general sources of data: *primary sources*, *secondary sources*, and *tertiary sources*.

Primary sources are materials that researchers collect and use in their analysis. In history or literature, researchers look at original source material, such as letters and documents produced during a period under study. Social scientists typically think of *primary data:* data that the researcher collects and uses in some way. Thus, the data are considered new in some sense. This includes data from interviews conducted by the researcher and her team, focus groups, and ethnographic observations. A common type of primary data is collected through surveys that researchers design and administer. The answers to survey questions are then quantified and, usually, analyzed using statistical methods. Some researchers also collect primary data through experiments.

Secondary sources are materials that someone else has collected or produced but that another researcher might wish to use. This might be a book about a time period or an author's work that a researcher uses to support an argument ("Williams [2016], after conducting a thorough review of marriage records in York, claimed that Buttercup did marry Prince Humperdink, but that it took place in secret."). In the social sciences, this usually implies a *secondary dataset*, based on a survey or some other data collection technique, which someone else has compiled. A common source of secondary data is when a government agency sponsors a project designed to collect data that document some problem or phenomenon (e.g., illegal drug use in the United States; experiences of people living in poverty). A research team receives funding from the agency to collect and analyze the data. At some point, the dataset is placed in the public domain for other researchers to use. As discussed in the next chapter, there are several data repositories that handle and distribute secondary datasets.

Tertiary sources are materials, such as books and articles, that are based on secondary sources or compiled information from research projects. They often provide an overview of the literature on a topic. Tertiary sources can be beneficial when researchers are developing research questions, or when they wish to have general support for an argument, but are usually limited in how much they help. Undergraduate student papers in social science classes often rely on tertiary sources to support their arguments, perhaps by citing a literature review ("Dufur's [2006] review of research on family structure shows that children from single-parent families are more likely to smoke cigarettes than children from stepparent families."). Textbooks provide perhaps the most common example of tertiary sources. However, many popular history books and general nonfiction books are also considered tertiary sources. These types of books are a good place to find references to secondary and primary sources, but should not be used as a substitute.

Tertiary sources seem best suited as part of the process of developing a research question. Social and behavioral scientists rely on primary and secondary sources of data to answer research questions and evaluate theories and claims (although warrants, when logically derived, are also important). For our purposes, a simple way of looking at the sources of data is to simply realize that most research projects use data that either (a) the researcher has collected (*primary data*) or (b) someone else has collected (*secondary data*).

Many researchers prefer to collect and utilize primary data. Why is this? By collecting primary data, researchers can tailor various aspects of the study so that it directly implicates the research question. There is usually (some) control over the sampling procedures, the measurement instruments (including questionnaires in survey research), and the data collection procedures (in-person, via the Internet). Consider a method that many researchers consider as the best way to determine whether one thing causes another: randomized controlled trials (RCT). These allow randomization of research participants into treatment and control groups, thus reducing or eliminating the influences of unobserved factors (Shadish et al. 2008). If the research question can be answered with an RCT and the researcher has the skills and resources to execute this type of design, then it can be quite effective as a tool for answering causal questions.

Yet even when designing a quasi-experimental or observational study—such as a survey of a sample of people in a community—researchers who collect primary data can develop a thorough set of questions to get at particular aspects of a concept, such as school attachment, stressful life events, voting behavior, or experiences of discrimination.

One of the drawbacks of many primary data collection efforts is that they are usually expensive and time-consuming. Think about collecting data from a representative sample of adults in the United States using a survey. It takes substantial time and money to draw a sample and develop and administer a questionnaire. You will likely have to employ a large staff to interview people in the sample. A much easier route has traditionally been for academic researchers to use what are known as WEIRD research participants. This refers to college students who are western (W), educated (E), and were raised in industrialized (I), rich (R), and democratic (D) countries (Henrich et al. 2010). College students often provide a captive audience for research projects and can be tempted into participating in studies with the promise of extra credit. Yet, they are not a good representation of most of the world. So should we trust the research findings of these studies if we wish to apply them in some way to other groups?

Therefore, it is quite common to find studies that use secondary data. Many secondary datasets are based on large, nationally representative samples of people, thus suggesting that the results of studies are not WEIRD. Most research projects that use secondary data are also much less expensive than those that collect primary data. In fact, as discussed in chapter 5, many secondary datasets may be acquired for free via the Internet. However, a key limitation is that since they were not designed specifically for a project, researchers must be willing to use data that may not be precisely suited for a particular research question or analysis. Perhaps the researcher wishes to study happiness, for example, but the secondary dataset available to conduct the study is limited to questions about life satisfaction (which is related to happiness, but is not the same thing). Therefore, there are important trade-offs for researchers when deciding whether to use primary or secondary data.

FROM CONCEPTS TO VARIABLES

In chapter 2, we discussed concepts, or general statements about classes of phenomena. For example, loneliness is a concept that is defined generally as a sense of sadness or melancholy due to the perception that one has no friends or acquaintances. The concept "stress" implies physical, mental, or emotional tension that individuals experience. The goal of many research projects in the social sciences is to use data to measure concepts. For example, what data might be needed to measure loneliness? Should they be derived from questions, observations of behaviors, biometric readings, or by asking friends and family members? The topic of *social measurement*, or how to measure social and personal phenomena, is vast and has generated its own particular set of research projects. In quantitative studies, researchers typically wish to translate a concept into a variable using a measuring tool of some kind, such as question or set of questions. Data are used in this translation process.

Measurement is a central task for science, but it can be difficult for social and behavioral research because many of the concepts used are imprecise or open to various interpretations. Take some of the education concepts listed in chapter 2: teacher quality, parental involvement, segregation, school attachment, and inequality. Or look at a list of concepts from sociology, political science, anthropology, social work, or economics. There are entries for alienation, deviant behavior, social conflict, social exclusion, worldview, exogamy, ritual, incentives, risk, and jingoism. Is it any wonder that many outside observers question whether these fields are scientific? Some of these concepts are difficult to pin down (perhaps we only know it when we see it!) and thus challenging to measure. Unfortunately, poor measures often lead to misleading results and dubious conclusions (Osborne 2013).

There are many useful resources that discuss measurement in the social and behavioral sciences. They provide guidance on how to develop good measuring instruments—such as by using questions, scales, indexes, and observational techniques (see Bradburn et al. 2004; DeVellis 2012; Smyth 2017). There are also books and other resources that discuss statistical methods for reducing errors in measures of social phenomena (Buonaccorsi 2010). This section provides just a few recommendations regarding social measurement, specifically some general advice to consider when collecting primary data or using secondary data to measure concepts and construct variables.

Measurement, in general, is concerned with assigning values (or *codes*) to the level of some quantity or quality of a phenomenon (Hand 2004). The values, which for our purposes will typically be numeric, are designed to label, indicate relative position, or provide a quantification that assesses where along a number line some phenomenon falls (Bulmer 2001). As with many approaches to research, much of the guidance on measurement in the social sciences is derived from the physical and natural sciences. Just as a physical science, such as chemistry, measures quantities of acids, compounds, or enzymes in terms of milliliters or microliters, many social and behavioral scientists strive to measure quantities of concepts, such as stressful life events, criminal activities, and even amorphous concepts such as alienation. Yet, this is complicated because many of our theoretical concepts have, a best, an ordinal quality: the phenomena they represent may be placed in relative positions. For example, if one is careful, then comparing how frequently two people use marijuana is feasible, but assigning a concrete number may not be. What does it mean for a person to say he has used marijuana twice in the past month? Does this mean two separate occasions, two marijuana cigarettes in succession at a party, or something else? It is often difficult to sort out the many possibilities. The social science disciplines do not have a standard system of measuring units, except for a few concepts (income, age), most of which are not particularly theoretically interesting.

Given these limitations, there are a few options. First, some disciplines are limited, in many situations, to concepts that are classified well by quantities and therefore the numbers assigned to them are, for the most part, meaningful. For example, economics is concerned primarily with concepts such as income, money supply, gross domestic product (GDP), prices, unemployment rates, and so forth. Although there are economic concepts that may be difficult to define precisely, such as demand, these are often assessed using simplifying assumptions. Demand might be measured, for example, using how much of a product was sold in the last quarter, even if this might have changed since the time it was measured.

Second, many researchers view their measures as approximations of concepts. These approximations may move closer to the actual concept by combining several items, such as by asking a series of questions that appear to indicate a concept such as loneliness. This is the approach that underlies *scale development*. Scales are a collection of items—such as answers to survey questions—that are combined into a single numeric score (DeVellis 2012).

The notion is that some concepts consist of several characteristics, so researchers must ask about each characteristic to measure the concept adequately. Of course, it is possible that if the approximations are not actually close to the concept or the list of characteristics is misguided, then combining them will simply result in a measure that is just as far away from the concept as any single item or question. In practice, the approximation approach underlies various types of measures, including nominal (unranked categories), ordinal (ordered categories), and interval/ratio (continuous, with the distance between categories meaningful in some presumed manner).

Third, social researchers may reject the quest for measurement analogous to what is found in the physical and natural sciences. Some argue that whereas measurement in the fashion of these sciences is useful, there is no suitable analogy in the social sciences. For many, this means we should look for patterns of social life through qualitative and ethnographic methods. Some descriptive information may be quantifiable, such as the ages of the research participants, but what is most important is what they do and how they do it as observed directly or indirectly by the researcher. Concepts are often constructed from these observations. This is part of the process of induction shown in figure 2.1.

Since this book is concerned primarily with quantitative data, the second option is considered in greater detail. However, it is important to keep in mind that most of the concepts you will work with will be measurable only approximately. This reinforces the principle that researchers should remember to carefully consider and repeatedly evaluate the concepts and data, and seek to replicate their research.

Operationalization

Operationalization involves the movement from a concept to a variable. The key question is, how is a concept measured? How does one move from a generalized statement of a class of phenomena to a quantifiable or qualitative variable? First, it is essential to define the concept clearly. What are its characteristics and how do these differ from the characteristics of a closely related concept? This concerns its *construct validity*. Take two concepts such as sadness and depression. Sadness is characterized by a personal sense of despair and feeling helpless, whereas depression is an extended period of anxiousness and feelings of despair that interfere with work, sleep, and interpersonal relationships. Yet, questions that ask a person whether he feels sad or helpless may indicate either of the concepts. Thus, measuring instruments, whether questions, observations, or something else, should begin with a clear *operational definition* of a concept. This will help determine if the measuring instrument satisfactorily discriminates between related concepts.

Once an appropriate operational definition is fashioned, it will take time to develop questions or observational techniques. It is best to consult with an expert on measurement before and during the development of measuring instruments. But there are also many resources available that either provide free access to sets of questions or charge a fee to gain access to them. Many of these instruments have been subjected to careful assessment to determine whether they are valid and reliable measures of various concepts (see sidebar 3.1).

If these do not provide instruments to measure a concept of interest, try an online search for the name of the concept in Google Scholar or an academic abstracting service (e.g., Pro-Quest), such as "how to measure [*name of concept*]." For instance, when I tried this with the concept *social distance*, I found a set of items called the *Bogardus social distance scale* that appeared suitable for some purposes.

Suppose, however, that there is little or no guidance regarding how to measure a concept. In this situation, a thorough understanding of the characteristics of the concept remains vital, but it is also a good idea to search for previous studies that have used it. As far as I have been able to ascertain, for instance, there is not a widely accepted set of questions that are designed to measure the concept *student cohesiveness* in secondary schools. However, a search of the research literature provided a list of several articles that have attempted to measure it. In one, the researchers utilized a subset of items from the Classroom

Environment Instrument (Pulvers and Diekhoff 1999). If I were developing my own questionnaire to measure this concept, I would consider including these questions. If I were using a secondary dataset, I would look for the same or closely related questions.

When relying on instruments that someone else has developed, such as when using secondary data, assessing their properties is critical. This usually requires some facility with social and behavioral measurement and assessment (Kline 2005), as well as careful consultation with an expert. However, many secondary datasets include sets of questions that have been subjected to careful screening and evaluation. If the concepts used in one's research are already measured with these questions, it is almost always a good idea to use them (although considering their properties yourself remains important). For example, many large-scale research projects attempt to measure depressive symptoms and *mastery* (feelings of control over one's life). The Add Health dataset (see http://www.cpc.unc.edu/projects /addhealth)—a frequently used resource utilized to study adolescents and young adults— includes two common sets of questions to measure these concepts: the Center for Epidemiological Studies Depression Scale (CESD-R; see www.cesd-r.com) and Leonard Pearlin and Carmi Schooler's (1978) mastery scale. If the Add Health is used to study, say, depression, mastery, and illegal behaviors, these questions will be useful. General instructions concerning ways to create scales from sets of questions may be found in DeVellis (2012).

Data and Variables

Once the careful work of defining the concept and determining how to measure it well is complete, or at least in a reasonable place (if ever!), the researcher then collects or accesses data and uses them to construct variables. Variables are empirical manifestations of concepts. Some people equate the term *variable* with the term *measure*. In data mining applications, variables are often called *features*. In any event, as taught in elementary statistics courses, a variable is a characteristic of something that has been observed and measured. It is called *variable* because it may have more than one value or characteristic; it differs for at least some cases. In practice, this might not occur, such as when a researcher collects data only on males, but biological sex remains a variable since it can take on other qualities besides male. The data that result from survey questions and scale construction are typically variables, but they also result from many observational and experimental techniques.

There are several ways of classifying variables and the data they represent. For example, a basic distinction is often made between qualitative and quantitative data. Yet, the differences are not always as clear as they may seem. Qualitative data consist of various forms of text and media, from descriptions based on direct observations of phenomena to photographs and video that document behaviors or events. These data are often descriptive and, as the name implies, provide the qualities rather than the quantity of a phenomenon. Quantitative data, on the other hand, are designed to quantify—measure the quantity of— some phenomenon. When speaking of qualitative versus quantitative data, a distinction is frequently made between textual and numeric data. However, this is not accurate since qualitative information can be measured with numeric codes: ethnic groups may be designated with different integer values; preferences for favorite ice cream may be assigned the numbers 1 through 5. Furthermore, quantitative data are often judged qualitatively, such as when a researcher places people in young, middle-aged, and older categories based on their age.

Qualitative data cover a much broader range of phenomena than quantitative data. Nevertheless, most research projects, certainly in the natural and physical sciences, but also in the social sciences (anthropology is an exception), utilize quantitative data, perhaps because statistics provides the analytic backbone for so much research. In any event, this book focuses on quantitative data because they are used so frequently, but some of the principles provided throughout this and the following chapters apply across many types of data and research projects.

There are actually several other ways to classify data, whether numeric or otherwise. For instance, in computer science some of these classifications include machine data, binary and Boolean (true/false) data, string data (numbers or characters), integer data, and metadata. This latter category consists of data that explain other data, such as information about a dataset: the source, the types of data and variables included in the set, creation and modification dates, and the size of the file.

The way data are classified directly influences the way variables are classified. Perhaps the most general way is to distinguish *discrete* and *continuous* variables. Discrete variables are those that take on only some sequence of values within a range of values; these values are typically represented by integers. They are often used to represent categories of some concept. Discrete variables are sometimes called qualitative variables, but we will avoid using this term since, as mentioned earlier, qualitative data include such a wide range of research objects. Continuous variables, on the other hand, may, theoretically speaking, take on any value within a range of values. Table 3.1 provides some examples of these variables. Note that there are several different types of discrete variables.

In each of these cases, the researcher must decide what number to assign to each possible outcome of the variable. For example, if a binary variable is designed to measure alcohol use in the past month, then what numbers should be assigned to each possibility: *no, did not use alcohol* versus *yes, did use alcohol*? This is an issue of *coding*, which is discussed later, but is also a key part of the measurement process in the social and behavioral sciences.

Another type of variable that is designed for convenience in some types of statistical analyses is known as a *dummy* or *indicator variable*. This is a set of binary variables that are used to denote nominal or ordinal variables. Each binary variable identifies membership of the units in one of the categories represented by the nominal or ordinal variable. For example, suppose a nominal variable represents political party affiliation in the United States: Democrat, Republican, and Independent. These categories may be represented by three indicator variables, each of which is binary: (1) Democrat: yes or no; (2) Republican: yes or no; and (3) Independent: yes or no. Note that these three variables must be mutually exclusive: if a person is placed in the *yes* category for the first binary variable (Republican = yes), then she must be placed in the *no* category for the other two binary variables (Democrat = no

TABLE 3.1 Types of variables

Type	Definition	Example
Continuous	May theoretically take on any value within a specific range of values	Age, which ranges from 18 to 88 (theoretically, age could be any real positive number)
Discrete/categorical	May take on only some values—usually integer values—within a range of values	Number of cars sold in the past week at a local automotive dealership; negative values may occur if we designate returns with negative numbers
Binary/dichotomous	Takes on only two values, representing two categories or conditions	Drank alcohol in the past week, no or yes
Ordinal/ordered	Takes on more than two values and the categories or conditions that may be ranked in some logical way	Education level grouped into high school graduate, college graduate, or graduate school degree
Nominal/unordered	Takes on more than two values and the categories or conditions are not ranked	Religious denominational affiliation, such as Catholic, Protestant, Jewish, or no affiliation
Count	Takes on only zero or positive integer values; designed to count some phenomenon	Number of traffic accidents at a particular intersection in the previous month
Multiple response	May take on more than one integer value	A checklist of ice cream flavors a person enjoys

and Independent = no). Table 3.8 that appears later in this chapter provides an example of a set of indicator variables (see also chapter 4).

Variables may also be defined based on their presumed probability distribution. For example, a *binomial variable* counts the number of "successes" (such as a six when throwing a die) in a particular number of "trials" (the number of throws of the die). If we extend this to more than two outcomes, such as shooting a basketball and (a) missing the basket, (b) making a two-point shot, and (c) making a three-point shot, then we are interested in a *multinomial variable*. However, probability distributions are beyond the scope of this presentation (see Rumsey 2006). In the next chapter, we'll learn more about how to handle data and the variables that they define.

FORMS OF DATA

In addition to classifying data and variables based on how they are defined and what they are designed to measure, it is also important, especially as we begin to think about data management, to consider some analytic categories of data. This has important implications for how data and variables are treated and represented as part of the research project workflow (see figure 1.2). The particular categories of data include those defined by the unit of observation, time, and space.

Unit of Observation

The unit of observation is the level at which the data are collected or represented. If a researcher collects information from people in order to determine whether those who experience higher levels of stress tend to fight more often, then the unit of observation is the individual. If someone wishes to compare the characteristics of more and less successful pharmaceutical companies and collects relevant data, then the unit of observation is the organization. The unit of observation dictates the form that the data will take. A similar term is the *unit of analysis*: this is based on what is analyzed and how the analysis is represented (Sedgwick 2014). Although data are often discussed in terms of the unit of analysis, it is more fitting at this point to focus on the unit of observation.

Many datasets conform to only one unit of observation. But this is not always the case. A common type of data is called *multilevel*. These are data that are hierarchical based on one level that is nested or contained in another level. For example, suppose a social scientist is interested in how much homework is actually assigned to elementary school children. She administers a questionnaire to a sample of these children who attend several schools in an attempt to measure how much homework they are given and some other characteristics (age, sex, ethnicity, academic motivation). But she also collects data from the schools, such as the percentage of students who passed the state mathematics exam, how many teachers there are per student, and so forth. In this situation, the student-level observations are nested within the school-level observations.

Time

Data may be collected over time. Economists frequently use *time-series data*, for example. These are data that represent information across a sequence of time points. Data on daily values or changes in the NASDAQ stock market, on annual homicide rates in Detroit from 1980 to 2010, or on Nebraska's monthly prevalence of influenza from January through December of 2016 are all time-series data. Time-series data tend to be collected on an aggregated unit, such as a particular stock market or a particular company. However, there are also time data that are collected among multiple units. This is actually a specific form of multilevel data—since time points are nested within individual units—that are called *longitudinal, panel*, or *cross-sectional time series* data. Imagine the researcher mentioned earlier is interested in not only how much homework students are assigned, but also whether this changes as they move up from grade to grade. She, therefore, returns each year and administers a questionnaire each time that asks about homework and other issues. Eventually, she has, say, six years of data on how much homework the students have been assigned from grades one through six. To complicate the data structure, she might even collect the school data each time. This creates a complex hierarchy of data, which are still considered multi-level. Longitudinal data are often distinguished from *cross-sectional data* or those that were gathered at only a single time point.

Space and Social Networks

Another type of data is referred to as *spatial data*. As the name implies, these are data that are collected across some defined space or area. A specific type of spatial data used mainly by geographers and cartographers is information on the location—typically using coordinates—of places on the Earth. We'll generalize this viewpoint a bit by defining spatial data as any that allow researchers to consider where the unit is located in relation to other units. Thus, data that include information on counties in the United States or countries of the world may be considered spatial since their location relative to other counties or countries is known.

It is not surprising that spatial data are often represented with maps. However, these data may also be shown in a structure much like cross-sectional or longitudinal data. Suppose, for example, that a researcher has data on county-level crime and mortality rates, such as the number of aggravated assaults and deaths due to heart disease for each county in the United States. The counties are identifiable by simply having their name or by having their coordinates. Lexington County, South Carolina, is located at 33.930965 North and 81.251883 West, whereas Maricopa County, Arizona, is located at 33.291797 North and 112.429146 West. These are data that may be used to specify location on a map.

A particular type of data that is concerned with conceptual space is *network data*. In the social sciences, these are typically data that map relationships among individuals. However, they can also map other entities, such as tweets, state-level legislation, or bibliographic information. They are frequently represented with network maps that include depictions of *actors* (usually individuals) and *nodes* (their relationship). Collecting network data can be challenging. Extending the earlier example, assume our researcher wishes to determine relationships among the elementary school children. She then might ask each student in the sample to identify his or her friends from among the other students in the school. When a friendship is found (which can be reciprocated or not), there is a node that links two students (actors).

Tables 3.2–3.7 provide some examples of these different forms of data. As is typically the case in research projects or when using statistical software, the data are displayed in a spreadsheet, or a table of rows and columns. This is also called a *data table*. However, as discussed later, datasets are often stored as text files since this makes it simpler to share data across software platforms (Gandrud 2015). Some researchers prefer the term *matrix* or *data matrix* for the spreadsheets to designate a rectangular array of numbers or characteristics of particular units. The rows of the spreadsheet or matrix typically represent the unit of observation, whereas columns represent *variables*: the different measures identified in the data (Wickham 2014). However, social network data are often represented with a square array to indicate the relationships and whether or not they are reciprocated.

TABLE 3.2 Individual-level data: cross-sectional

Name	Age	Years of education	Political party	Sex
John	25	12	Democrat	Male
Rebecca	31	16	Independent	Female
Norman	35	18	Republican	Male
Jessica	27	14	Independent	Female

TABLE 3.3 Multilevel data: cross-sectional

Name	Age	Years of education	Political party	Neighborhood
John	25	12	Democrat	The Heights
Rebecca	31	16	Independent	The Heights
Norman	35	18	Republican	The Heights
Jessica	27	14	Independent	The Heights
Leslie	23	16	Democrat	Longbranch
Peter	29	16	Independent	Longbranch
Amber	21	20	Independent	Longbranch
Mickey	34	18	Independent	Longbranch

Note: The individuals are nested within the two neighborhoods: The Heights and Longbranch.

TABLE 3.4. Multilevel data: longitudinal (long form)

Name	Age	Years of education	Political party	Time period
John	25	12	Democrat	1
Rebecca	31	16	Independent	1
Norman	35	18	Republican	1
Jessica	27	14	Independent	1
John	26	13	Independent	2
Rebecca	32	16	Independent	2
Norman	36	18	Democrat	2
Jessica	28	14	Independent	2

TABLE 3.5 Multilevel data: longitudinal (wide form)

Name	Age, time 1	Age, time 2	Political party, time 1	Political party, time 2
John	25	26	Democrat	Independent
Rebecca	31	32	Independent	Independent
Norman	35	36	Republican	Democrat
Jessica	27	28	Independent	Independent

TABLE 3.6   Spatial data: coordinates

County name	Latitude	Longitude	Assaults	Heart disease deaths
Albany, NY	42.575680	−73.935982	42.1	226.8
Lexington, SC	33.930965	−81.251883	12.1	170.8
Maricopa, AZ	33.291797	−112.429146	10.9	138.1
San Diego, CA	32.715730	−117.161097	25.9	126.0

Note: Assaults and deaths are the measured as the number per 100,000 population.

TABLE 3.7   Social network data: friendship ties

Chooser	Choice			
	John	Rebecca	Norman	Jessica
John	−	1	1	0
Rebecca	1	−	0	1
Norman	0	0	−	1
Jessica	0	1	1	−

Note: 1 indicates "Yes" and 0 indicates "No." For example, John reported Norman as a friend, but Norman did not report John as a friend.

There are some important aspects of tables 3.2–3.7. First, note that words rather than numbers represent sex and political party. Some software requires the user to replace the words with numbers, especially if they are to be used in a statistical model. Some principles for choosing numbers are discussed in chapter 4. Second, consider that there are two ways to set up the longitudinal data. In *long form*, each individual contributes as many rows of data as there are time points. For example, in table 3.4 Rebecca has two rows of data since her information is presented at two time points. In *wide form* (table 3.5), there is only one row for each unit of observation, but the variables are identified by their time point (actually, the unit of observation in longitudinal data with people is *person-time*). The multilevel data in table 3.3 may also be represented in either of these two ways, although only the long version is shown. Finally, the social network data in table 3.7 are shown as a square array, but may also be displayed as a rectangular data array that lists the number of ties that each individual has.

As mentioned earlier, a single nominal variable may also be represented by a set of indicator or dummy variables. For instance, table 3.2 includes a variable that assesses whether people say they are members of the Democratic or Republican parties, or are independents. Table 3.8 illustrates how this sort of variable may be represented as a set of indicator variables in a data table.

TABLE 3.8 How indicator variables are represented

Unit	Original variables	Indicator variables		
	Political party	*Republican*	*Democrat*	*Independent*
1	Republican	Yes	No	No
2	Republican	Yes	No	No
3	Democrat	No	Yes	No
4	Democrat	No	Yes	No
5	Independent	No	No	Yes
6	Independent	No	No	Yes

FINAL WORDS

We often assume that understanding data is simple, yet there are many important aspects that should be considered by any researcher, whether new or experienced. It is particularly important to consider their source, their quality, what they represent, and how they will be used. Understanding these aspects of data is critical as we move from concepts to variables. This chapter provides a number of ideas about how to approach and understand the fundamentals of data, including an appreciation for some key terms and issues:

- Data are defined as pieces of information, often collected for descriptive and analytic purposes.

- Data quality includes the completeness, accuracy, and timeliness of the data; as well as whether they are appropriate for a specific task.

- Validity refers generally to whether something is actually an indicator of what we think it is. Reliability concerns whether the data are consistent across different conditions.

- The issue of data integrity asks: are the data unaltered from their source or have they been modified in some way (intentionally or unintentionally)?

- Data used for research come from primary, secondary, and tertiary sources. Research in the social and behavioral sciences typically use either primary data that are collected by the researcher or secondary data that someone else has collected but are used by a researcher.

- Measurement is generally concerned with assigning values or codes to the level of some quantity or quality of a phenomenon, such as the concepts represented by variables in a dataset. Measurement in the social and behavioral sciences tends to be an approximation exercise given the types of concepts that are usually studied.

- Rather than attempting to come up with original ways to measure concepts, it is more efficient to rely on instruments that have undergone rigorous testing to determine whether they are reliable and valid indicators of the concepts.

- Data consist of numeric and qualitative characteristics of some unit, such as individuals or organizations. They may be classified based on the unit(s) of observation, time, space, and relations among units (such as social network data).

- Data are usually displayed in a spreadsheet, or a table of rows and columns. This is also called a data table or data matrix. The rows of the spreadsheet normally represent the unit of observation, whereas columns represent the variables: the different measures identified in the data.

EXERCISES FOR CHAPTER 3

1. Select one of the following concepts and do a literature review to determine how it has been measured in research studies. Try to determine if any studies have examined the validity and reliability of variables used to measure the concept.
   a. Self-control
   b. Impulsivity
   c. Authoritarianism
   d. Cognitive load
   e. Self-serving bias
   f. Perceived health
   g. Gender stereotype
   h. Role strain
   i. Disruptive technology

2. The Social Anxiety Scale for Adults was developed to operationalize the concept of social anxiety by asking a series of questions about social situations that people find themselves in. A description of the scale and the questions that make it up are available on the Measurement Instrument Database for the Social Sciences (MIDSS) website (see www.midss.org). Consider the following questions about this scale and its questions:
   a. What type of variable would each question be used to construct (see table 3.1)?
   b. The developers of this scale have published some articles in scientific journals that evaluated the validity of it for measuring social anxiety (hint: use Google Scholar or a journal abstracting database [e.g., ProQuest, Scopus] to search for one of these articles if those listed on the MIDSS website are not available). If you can gain access to one of these articles, what do the authors conclude in general about the validity of their scale?
   c. The developers of the scale published a research article in 2014 titled "Differences in Social Anxiety between Men and Women across 18 countries." If you can gain access to the article (or even a summary of it), what did they find regarding differences between men and women regarding their degree of social anxiety?

3. The following data are in a format known as *comma-separated values* (CSV), which are typically found in electronic files used to store quantitative and some types of qualitative data (chapter 4 provides more detail about these types of files). As the name implies, commas are used to separate the values of different variables. Like data tables, the unit of observation makes up the rows and the variables make up the columns. The first line is the name of the variable. Reformat these data so that they appear in a data table.

```
Name,age,year_in_school,major,GPA,employed,SAT
Andrew,21,3,philosophy,3.15,no,2000
Josephine,19,2,sociology,3.90,no,2100
Richard,23,3,psychology,2.91,,yes,1900
Rosemarie,20,2,economics,3.76,yes,2150
Esmerelda,24,3,philosophy,3.25,yes,1950
Randall,18,1,none,3.05,no,2200
Susan,20,3,math,3.20,yes,2330
Michael,24,engineering,2.90,yes,1875
Emma,19,chemistry,3.15,no,2000
Ethan,21,psychology,3.55,yes,1900
Madison,19,engineering,3.30,no,2175
Hunter,27,health,2.55,yes,1750
```

4. Consider the following data table. It lists a set of indicator variables from a sample of young adults who attend the same US West Coast college. Reconstruct the data table so that the three indicator variables are represented as one variable.

	School club affiliation		
Person	*Students for peace*	*Student gun club*	*Students for democratic action*
Marsha	Yes	No	No
Maggie	No	Yes	No
Magdalena	Yes	No	No
Roberta	No	No	Yes
Sue	Yes	No	No
Bob	No	No	Yes
Curtis	No	No	Yes
Hagar	No	Yes	No
Mathias	Yes	No	No
Zachary	No	Yes	No

5. Identify the type of data that each variable represents in the following data table (see table 3.1).

		Favorite television shows[a]				
Person	Family income in $	*Breaking Bad*	*Game of Thrones*	*NCIS*	Are you currently in school?	How many times did you visit a doctor in the past year?
Olivia	50,100	Yes	Yes	No	Yes	0
Emma	75,800	No	Yes	No	Yes	4
Abby	84,600	No	No	Yes	No	2
Sophia	72,300	Yes	Yes	Yes	Yes	0
Jacob	87,000	No	Yes	Yes	No	0
Adam	39,500	No	No	No	No	5
Tyler	65,200	Yes	No	Yes	Yes	3

a. This is based on a single question: "What were your favorite television shows in 2012?"

FOUR

Principles of Data Management

As mentioned in the previous chapter, data are an indispensable part of the research process. They are needed so that researchers can explicitly examine research questions, test hypotheses, and judge the validity of conceptual models. Given their status in the research process, it should be obvious that data need to be treated carefully at all stages in which they play a role. Consider, for example, what happens when researchers make mistakes in the way that data are used. In 2015, an interesting article about divorce appeared in the *Journal of Health and Social Behavior*. Using a large secondary dataset based on interviews with adults in the United States, the researchers compared various family situations to determine when a divorce is likely to occur. One key finding was that, when the wife becomes ill, the chances of divorce increase. However, after the article appeared, the authors attempted to reproduce this result, but they could not. Digging deeper into the steps they took as part of the research workflow (see figure 1.2), they discovered that "people who left the study were actually miscoded as getting divorced" (retractionwatch.com 2015). In other words, a number of people dropped out of the research project before it was completed, but they were inaccurately listed as going from marriage to divorce. As will become clear, correct coding of a variable's values is of utmost importance since subsequent steps depend on it to produce accurate results. Interestingly, once this coding error was corrected, the results only held up for marriages in which the wife had heart problems rather than illnesses in general. You should ask yourself why this might be the case. Is it a peculiarity of this particular research project or a more general phenomenon? But, for our purposes, the lesson is that the way the data are treated during project workflow—or the *data management* steps—is vital to a research project.

The previous chapter discussed data, including what they are and how they are usually characterized in the social and behavioral sciences. This chapter addresses what to do with data once they are available to the researcher. In other words, how does one manage the data? Data management refers to a series of steps, from putting together a dataset to importing it into a software package to ensuring there are no errors or duplications. The next chapter shows how to import existing data into relevant software. This chapter assumes that the data are already in an electronic file that has been read into a statistical software package, such as Stata, SPSS, SAS, or R, or a database management system such as MS Access, LibreOffice Base, or FileMaker. The goal is to present some principles and examples of data management.

Given the way the previous chapter defines variables, data management might also be called *variable management* since it concerns whether the variables are labeled and coded correctly. It has also been called *data wrangling* (Kandel et al. 2011). Regardless, we begin by considering some of the steps involved in *data preprocessing*. These are steps that should be completed after the data acquisition stage but before the analysis stage (see figures 1.1 and 1.2). However, in practice, there is often substantial interplay among the preprocessing steps and the analysis steps. It is not uncommon to discover errors during the analysis stage that need to be corrected by returning to the preprocessing stage (Wickham 2014). The preprocessing steps discussed next include codebooks, documentation, coding practices, data cleaning and screening, and naming conventions (Zhu et al. 2013).

CODEBOOKS

Let's assume that, although you may have been involved in designing the study and setting up the data collection procedures, you have now been given the raw data without any additional input into how the data were entered into an electronic file. Or suppose that you were provided with secondary data based on someone else's data collection project. What should you do first? The steps may vary, but an important early step is to examine the *codebook*. A codebook is a document that shows the structure and content of a data file. Well-designed codebooks provide some metadata, such as the source and types of data and variables included in the set. They also provide information about how the data were collected and on each of the variables in the dataset: names, type, a brief description (such as the survey question upon which they are based), categories of discrete variables and the frequency and percent in each category, relevant skip patterns, and information on missing data (ICPSR 2011). For instance, example 4.1 provides an excerpt from a sample codebook available through the Inter-University Consortium for Political and Social Research (ICPSR), a University of Michigan–affiliated data repository that makes data files from dozens of research projects available to researchers affiliated with many universities in the United States and elsewhere.

The codebook provides a brief description of the source of the data, notes how many data files are available (4), indicates that the data are available in SPSS format (a commonly used statistical package; see Appendix A), and provides some characteristics of the first parts of the data file. The codebook indicates that Part 1 has a rectangular file structure (similar to table 3.2), 11,879 cases or sample members (also known by the general term *units*), and

DESCRIPTORS AND MEASUREMENTS OF THE HEIGHT OF RUNAWAY SLAVES AND INDENTURED
SERVANTS IN THE UNITED STATES, 1700-1850
(ICPSR 9721)

Principal Investigator
University of Pittsburgh, Dept. of History

DATA COLLECTION DESCRIPTION
SUMMARY: The purpose of this data collection was to provide data about runaway
slaves and indentured servants in the colonial and antebellum period of United
States history. Data were taken from newspaper advertisements describing the
runaways. Variables include the state of the newspaper in which advertisement was listed, the year of the advertisement, the last and first names of the
runaway slave or indentured servant, race, sex, age, height, place of birth,
legal status (convict or in jail at time of advertisement), profession, and
knowledge of the English language.

EXTENT OF COLLECTION: 4 data files + SPSS Control Cards + machine-readable
                       documentation

DATA FORMAT:
Logical Record Length with SPSS Control Cards

Part 1: Runaway Slave   Part 2: Runaway Slave
Height Measurements   Height Descriptors
File Structure: rectangular   File Structure: rectangular
Cases: 11,879   Cases: 1,640
Variables: 14   Variables: 15
Record Length: 68   Record Length: 89
Records Per Case: 1   Records Per Case: 1

VARIABLE NAME AND POSITION		VARIABLE DESCRIPTION	EXPLANATION
STATE	1-2	STATE OF NEWSPAPER IN WHICH ADVERTISEMENT WAS LOCATED	USES STANDARD POST OFFICE STATE ABBREVIATIONS
YEAR	3-6	YEAR OF ADVERTISEMENT	
LNAME	7-21	LAST NAME OF RUNAWAY/SERVANT	
FNAME	22-40	FIRST NAME OF RUNAWAY/SERVANT	
RACE	42	RACE OF RUNAWAY/SERVANT	W = WHITE (NA) B = BLACK I = INDIAN M = MULATTO
SEX		SEX OF RUNAWAY/SERVANT	F = FEMALE M = MALE

Source: ICPSR (2011).

14 variables. The next portion of the codebook lists the variable names, their position in the data file, a brief description, and an explanation. The variable position is the columns that the raw data are placed in. For example, the variable YEAR is located in columns 3–6.

Understanding the location of the variables in a data file is crucial. As mentioned in chapter 3, data files are structured in different ways, but the most common for cross-sectional data, such as those described by this codebook, is with a rectangular data table or matrix (see table 3.2). Recall that the rows of the data table represent the unit of observation—such as people, states, or organizations—and the columns represent the variables. As discussed later in the chapter, data files are often available in plain text format. An advantage of this is that almost any software can read plain text files so that we may examine them in spreadsheet software, such as MS Excel or Google Sheets, or in statistical analysis software, such as SAS or Stata. A common and convenient type of plain text file for sharing data is known as a *comma-separated values* file, which has the file extension *.csv*. It consists of data provided as plain text but uses commas to separate the values of variables (see exercise 3 in chapter 3 for a brief example). In the codebook example, STATE and YEAR are two distinct variables, so they would appear as {*state,year*} in a csv file. Consider the following example in which the STATE is GA (Georgia) and the YEAR is 1841.

column	1	2	3	4	5	6	This implies that a line in the csv file appears as GA,1841,
entry	G	A,	1	8	4	1,	

The variable descriptions in a codebook may not be sufficient, so researchers often need to dig further into how the data were collected to fully understand what the variables and their values represent. Note that two of the variables, RACE and SEX of runaway/servant, are listed with the particular text that identifies each category. An artificial excerpt from the dataset is provided in table 4.1.

The codebook should be reviewed completely and carefully to understand the structure and contents of the data file. Another important step is to consider in more detail the context of the data:

- Where do they come from?
- Are they designed to represent a sample, a population, or neither?
- How were the data collected?
- Are they survey data, experimental data, data from official organizational or governmental records, or data based on qualitative observations?
- Are they cross-sectional, longitudinal, multilevel, or spatial?
- What were the goals of the study that collected the data? What information was the study designed to collect? What concepts are the data supposed to measure?
- How do these relate to the purposes that you may be putting the data to?

TABLE 4.1　Excerpt from dataset associated with the codebook shown in example 4.1

STATE	YEAR	LNAME	FNAME	RACE	SEX
VA	1854	JONES	JOHN	B	M
VA	1839	SMITH	MARY	M	F
NC	1959	DAYS	JAMES	B	M
GA	1841	COOPER	JOSEPH	W	M

Note: The data are fabricated.

- Were the data collected in order to test a particular theory or conceptual model? If yes, are you also planning to test a particular conceptual model?
- How similar is your model to the researchers' model who collected the data?

These questions are particularly relevant to the issues discussed in chapter 5, but are also important here because answering them helps us understand the data better. Other useful ways of examining the data files and variables are discussed later.

DOCUMENTATION

The codebook is a critical part of the documentation. The term *documentation* refers to written text that informs potential users about what the data files consist of or what has been done to the data prior to their arrival on a user's computer. Codebooks usually address only the first of these two issues. When managing data with software, the second documentation issue is satisfied by building text directly into the software instructions—which are also known as *program files* (or a computer *programs*)—such as by including explanatory notes in the script or syntax files used in software such as SPSS, Stata, SAS, R, or Python. Thus, program files are designed to tell users what steps are taken to process the data for analysis and to request that the software execute these steps. Since we've already seen an example of a codebook, let's first consider some principles regarding documentation in program files.

Recall that three statistical software packages are utilized in this book: Stata, SPSS, and SAS (see Appendix A for a brief introduction to each). Although commands to do various things—such as assigning codes to the values of variables or requesting a correlation coefficient—can be typed directly onto a command line, requested via drop-down menus, or even executed, in some cases, through a graphical user interface (GUI), it is rarely, if ever, good practice to use any of these options for executing data management steps. A key problem with using these approaches is that, without explicitly setting them up to do so, they fail to provide a clear record of the commands to execute. Thus, it is easy to forget the specific steps taken or to reproduce these steps. Recall from chapter 1 that a vital part of any research project is reproducibility (Kass et al. 2016).

The preferred alternative is to prepare text files, which, as noted earlier, are known generally as *program files*, that manage data and do many other data-driven tasks. Carefully preparing and documenting program files is essential for clear and consistent reproducibility. Recall the example at the beginning of the chapter. The researchers were unable to reproduce a key finding. Yet, because they were able to go back through the research workflow steps, the problem was identified and corrected.

Program files have different extensions in each software package. Stata uses *.do*, SPSS uses *.sps*, and SAS uses *.sas*. For example, a program file in Stata might be labeled *workflow.do*. A similarly purposed file in SPSS is *workflow.sps* and that in SAS is *workflow.sas*. Since each is simply a text file, though, any text editor may be used to prepare these programs. In fact, some researchers recommend that program files should always be written and available as text files so that any user with a computer—whether they have access to statistical software or not—will be able to read the file and understand what it is designed to do (Gandrud 2015). For example, Notepad++, a free text editing system for the MS Windows operating system, and TextEdit, the native text editing program for the OS X operating system used by Macs, are useful for writing and documenting program files for any of these statistical software packages (other text editing software may also be used, such as Vim, UltraEdit, or Sublime Text). This is the practice used in this chapter to prepare these files for data management.

Documentation within program files consists of notes—usually called *comments*—that provide some initial descriptive information and then specific reasoning for the decisions made by the author of the program. The initial documentation should include the following:

- A description of what the program file is designed to do (data management? combining data files? data analysis?);
- When the file was originally created;
- The date the file was last updated; and
- The name of the person who created the file and any others who contributed to it (Gandrud 2015, 23; citing Nagler 1995).

It is also a good idea to include comments for parts of the program file that do different things. For example, one part of the file might check the data for missing values, whereas another part might change the values of a set of variables. These parts of the file are called *blocks* and separating distinct parts of the file is called *blocking*. When creating a block, it is usually a good idea to have a comment describing what it is designed to do (Nagler 1995). Finally, if the program file creates another file (called an *output file*), include comments to indicate what its relationship is to the other file—for example, if it is a data management file that is executed before a data analysis file—and what version of the statistical package or data management software is used.

The following text provides an example of some initial documentation in Stata, SPSS, and SAS (see example 4.2). Notice that each uses a similar set of symbols to set off the

EXAMPLE 4.2   Example of file documentation

Stata	SPSS	SAS
/* 1. This file is de- signed to provide a frequency distribu- tion of the vari- able age 2. Creation date: 12 Jul 2017 3. Last updated: 21 Jul 2017 4. Creator: Hans Zim- merman, University of Rivendell 5. Stata version 14 */	/* 1. This file is de- signed to provide a frequency distribu- tion of the vari- able age 2. Creation date: 12 Jul 2017 3. Last updated: 21 Jul 2017 4. Creator: Hans Zim- merman, University of Rivendell 5. SPSS version 21 .	/* 1. This file is de- signed to provide a frequency distribu- tion of the vari- able age 2. Creation date: 12 Jul 2017 3. Last updated: 21 Jul 2017 4. Creator: Hans Zim- merman, University of Rivendell 5. SAS version 9.2 */
/* Executable lines begin next */ table age /* provides a table */	/* Executable lines . /* begin next . freq var = age . /* provides a table .	/* Executable lines begin next */ proc freq data=dataset; tables age; run; /* provides a table */

Note: More information about how to use Stata, SPSS, and SAS commands for data management is provided later.

comments so the software won't think it is supposed to execute the lines. However, in SPSS the "/*" at the beginning of a line is followed by a period (.) at the end of the line. The period in SPSS is also called the *command terminator* (Boslaugh 2005). All three packages offer others ways to identify comments. Stata, for instance, permits two slashes (//) at the beginning of a comment that appears on a single line of text. One may also use an asterisk (*) at the beginning of a line, but it will identify the comment as being on one line only and should be followed by a period (.) in SPSS or a semicolon (;) in SAS. The /* comment */ style also allows comments to be included within lines of text that list commands.

After the initial information about the file is addressed, additional comments should be placed liberally throughout the program file. If in doubt about whether some step should be described, err on the side of describing it. Comments should be used, in particular, to explain why you did something or what you did. Think about it from different users' perspectives: what would they need to know in order to reproduce the steps you took? What would happen if you had to go back and retrace your steps a year from now? What information would you require? It is also important to update comments if the file is revised in some way. In general, the documentation should provide a careful guide so that others can follow each of the steps taken by the analyst (Gentzkow and Shapiro 2014).

If visual appeal and esthetics are important to you, some experts recommend using more creative ways to identify comments. For example, in Stata, the initial documentation might appear as below:

```
/*********************************************/
*  1. This file is designed to provide a     *
*     frequency distribution of the variable *
*     age                                     *
*  2. Creation date: 12 Jul 2017             *
*  3. Last updated:  21 Jul 2017             *
*  4. Creator: Pallas Evander, University of *
*              Pallanteum                     *
*  5. Stata version 14                       *
/*********************************************/
```

This box style provides a bit more visual ease for identifying and reading comments in the file.

CODING

The term *coding* has become popular in recent years. It seems that young people across the globe are being encouraged to learn to code more often now than ever before. There are coding "boot camps," coding academies, massive open online courses (MOOCs), and many online resources and tutorials that promise to turn people into coders (we used to call them computer programmers). There are actually many types of coding, but our initial concern is with writing code to instruct the software to execute a set of commands. Fortunately, the statistical software packages shown thus far are considered very high-level programming languages that do not require much skill or background for code preparation.

In the social and behavioral sciences, there is another type of coding, however. This is the process of creating the variables that represent the concepts. As noted in chapter 3, this is part of the process of operationalization. In preparing the data, researchers designate one code to represent one category of a variable. These codes should make sense (always consider the audience and other data users!). For example, in table 3.2, years of education are coded into integer values, such as 12 and 16. Thus, 12 is the numeric code that identifies 12 years of education. This is reasonable. However, for some variables there is a certain arbitrariness to the codes. For instance, if a researcher needs to assign numeric codes to a variable such as religious affiliation—that is limited in this example to Hindu, Muslim, Catholic, and Protestant—what numbers should she choose? Since this type of variable is often converted to a set of indicator variables (which should be coded 0 and 1; see chapter 3), it may not matter. However, for an ordered discrete variable, such as "the United States should support the rebels in Syria," how should response options such as "Disagree," "Neutral," and "Agree" be coded? Again, there is some arbitrariness, but it is most common to use sequential integer values beginning with one: Disagree = 1; Neutral = 2; and Agree = 3.

There are various coding steps that are taken when preparing a dataset for analysis. Perhaps the analyst thinks that years of education should be placed into categories, such as

0–11, 12, 13–15, 16, and 17 or more. This corresponds in the United States to roughly (a) not a high school graduate, (b) high school graduate, (c) some college or vocational school, (d) college graduate, and (e) attended graduate school. Thus, she needs to *recode* the variable so that it matches this coding strategy. As suggested earlier, another common coding task is to represent a discrete variable with a set of indicator variables (see chapter 3). Recall that these are a set of binary (0,1) coded variables that are used to denote nominal or ordinal variables. Each binary variable identifies membership of the units in one of the categories represented by the discrete variable.

Some other common coding tasks include the following:

- Assigning names to variables
- Assigning descriptions to variables (these are *variable labels*)
- Assigning descriptions to values of variables (these are *value labels*)
- Changing codes that designate missing data
- Changing codes from one numeric value to another (this is known as *recoding*)
- Changing codes from characters to numeric values
- Checking and editing variables that are constructed improperly or that contain errors
- Identifying and modifying or removing implausible values
- Making sure there are no duplicate cases in the data file

Examples of several of these, as well as particular aspects of writing text to execute commands, are provided in this and subsequent chapters. However, just to give a flavor of what a coding task looks like, consider example 4.3. It shows a variable, *age*, which the codebook indicates has a range of 20–49. We wish to create a new variable, *catAge*, which places research participants into three categories: those in their 20s, those in their 30s, and those in their 40s.

Examine these commands for a moment. Stata uses the symbol / to represent the word "through." Stata and SPSS create the new variable after the new codes are assigned. In the SAS software, we first create the new variable, *ageCat*, and set it to missing (that is what the period (.) designates). This is followed by *if-then* statements and *less-than-equal-to* ($\leq$) symbols that may not be intuitive to some. However, it is a good idea to try to understand these better since they are used often for data management tasks. In coding jargon, *if-then* statements are a type of *conditional operator* and *less-than-equal-to* symbols are a type of *comparison operator* known as a *relational operator*. Notice also that the new numeric codes for the age groups are 20, 30, and 40. These may or may not be the best numbers to use, however. The researcher must decide how the variable will be used and then determine the most appropriate designations.

It seems that Stata and SPSS offer simpler ways to create the *ageCat* variable than does SAS. But it is important to point out at this time that most software includes many ways to execute various steps. *Efficient coding* refers to creating lines of code that execute the requisite

---

EXAMPLE 4.3   Using the codebook to guide a recoding task

```
Codebook
VARIABLE NAME &
  POSITION                    VARIABLE DESCRIPTION       EXPLANATION
age       8-9                 Age in years              Range:    20-49
                                                        Mean =    35.0
                                                        St.Dev. =  7.9
```

```
*  Stata

recode age (20/29=20) (30/39=30) (40/49=40), generate(catAge)
```

```
*  SPSS

recode age (20 thru 29=20) (30 thru 39=30) (40 thru 49=40) into catAge.
```

```
*  SAS
data dataset;
  set dataset;
  ageCat = .;
  if (20 <= age <= 29) then ageCat = 20;
  if (30 <= age <= 39) then ageCat = 30;
  if (40 <= age <= 49) then ageCat = 40;
run;
```

---

process quickly and without error. However, the most efficient code is not normally the most readable or intuitive code, so there is a trade-off. The examples in this book favor readability and easy comprehension over efficiency since it makes learning simpler, but as you become more accustomed to using statistical software, you will likely learn practices—such as loops and macros—that are highly efficient. In any event, there are more efficient ways to create the SAS code than is shown in this recoding example. Finally, don't forget the documentation: if these lines of code are part of a longer file that executes various tasks, then they should be placed into a block and preceded by a comment explaining why this new version of the age variable is created.

DATA CLEANING AND SCREENING

Data cleaning is a set of procedures designed to detect and correct errors in the dataset (Pohlabeln et al. 2014; Van den Broeck et al. 2005). Errors may occur at various stages of data acquisition and processing. Although some experts distinguish *data editing* and *data cleaning*, both serve a similar purpose: to ensure the integrity and quality of the data and variables. *Data screening* is intended to identify and designate appropriate identifiers for missing data, determine whether there are extreme values that might affect an analysis, and other approaches designed to determine if data have certain characteristics. Let's consider some steps from data collection in the field to having a dataset on your computer.

The initial data editing stage takes place in the field as the data are collected. Since data users tend to be the worst data editors (Sana and Weinreb 2008), it is important that those who collect the data are involved in the initial editing of the data. However, end users of data often have little control over what happens in the field, so they must consider methods to identify and correct errors within the dataset itself. What are some of these methods and how are they implemented using the software? Here are some issues and examples.

Check for Erroneous/Implausible Values

The codebook usually provides information on either the range of legitimate values (continuous variables) or the actual values of a variable (discrete variables). Moreover, if some data are missing—perhaps because a sample member refused to answer a question or was not asked a question for some reason—the codebook should also provide particular identifiers—which are usually numbers or a symbol such as a period—associated with them. Since missing data are special cases for coding and data management and analysis, a discussion of this issue is provided in chapter 7.

As emphasized earlier, it is critical that the data user consult the codebook to determine information about the dataset and each of the relevant variables. For example, the codebook in example 4.1 shows two legitimate character codes for the variable SEX: F = FEMALE and M = MALE. Suppose a review of the data table reveals a blank data cell, a symbol such as a period (.), or a letter such as T. In all likelihood, these are implausible or indicate that the datum was not available for this person. If it is a legitimate missing value, then there are methods to consider (see chapter 7). However, implausible characters such as a T are more difficult to rectify.

Another common example involves continuous variables such as age. If the data are from human beings, the age range is limited. If the data are from an adult sample, for instance, the age range is likely about 18 to some value close to 100 (but usually less). In addition, age is typically measured in years, so the values do not include decimals. It is also not uncommon to find large values that may indicate errors in data input or missing data. Suppose, for instance, that when a researcher examines a variable called *age* she finds the number 288. In all likelihood, a mistake occurred at the data entry stage when an 8 was keyed in twice by accident; age should be 28 rather than 288. However, it is not always clear. Here's a more difficult situation. In a study of fathers of children ages 1–6 a researcher finds that the age of one of the fathers has been recorded as 99. Although this is not an impossible value, it seems highly unlikely. Perhaps the number 99 has been reserved for a missing value, such as for those who refused to give their age. The codebook may provide a solution; perhaps it lists refusals as 99 or 999. If the latter occurs, the third 9 may have accidently been omitted. In any event, in either of these examples, the researcher should check the documentation on data collection, such as the original questionnaire (or talk to the people involved in data collection), to determine the true age value. But when using secondary data, this solution is rarely available. So careful judgment of the options is critical.

As suggested by the example of age, implausible values may often be identified in datasets by examining descriptive information about each relevant variable. Scrutinizing

```
┌─────────────────────────────────────────────────────────────────────────────┐
│                                                                             │
│   EXAMPLE 4.4   Examining some descriptive statistics                       │
│  ─────────────────────────────────────────────────────────────────────────  │
│                                                                             │
│   Codebook                                                                   │
│   VARIABLE NAME &                                                            │
│    POSITION              VARIABLE DESCRIPTION        EXPLANATION             │
│   age        8-9         Age in years               Range:      20-49       │
│                                                     Mean =       35.2        │
│                                                     St. Dev. =   6.1         │
│  ─────────────────────────────────────────────────────────────────────────  │
│   *  Stata                                                                   │
│   summarize age                                                              │
│                                                                             │
│     Variable |     Obs       Mean      Std. Dev.      Min        Max         │
│   -----------+---------------------------------------------------------      │
│        age   |     100      37.85      26.46109        21        288         │
│  ─────────────────────────────────────────────────────────────────────────  │
│   *  SPSS                                                                     │
│                                                                             │
│   descriptives age .                                                         │
│                                                                             │
│                      N        Minimum     Maximum       Mean                 │
│                  Statistic    Statistic   Statistic   Statistic             │
│         age         100          21         288        37.85                 │
│  ─────────────────────────────────────────────────────────────────────────  │
│   *  SAS                                                                      │
│                                                                             │
│   proc univariate data=dataset;                                             │
│    var age;                                                                  │
│   run;                                                                       │
│            Moments                                                           │
│   N                    100                                                   │
│   Mean                 37.85                                                 │
│   Std Deviation        8.46                                                  │
│                                                                             │
│   Quantile          Estimate                                                 │
│   100%  Max          288.0                                                   │
│   75%   Q3            42.0                                                    │
│   50%   Median        35.5                                                   │
│   25%   Q1            28.5                                                    │
│   0%    Min           21                                                     │
│                                                                             │
├─────────────────────────────────────────────────────────────────────────────┤
│   Note: The output is edited to show only the relevant parts. Other commands to consider are as follows: *univ*, │
│   *codebook*, *table* or *tabulate* (categorical), *list*—Stata; *freq* (categorical), *explore, list*—SPSS; and *proc freq* │
│   (categorical), *proc means, proc print*—SAS. Searching the software's help menu leads to more information │
│   about these commands.                                                     │
└─────────────────────────────────────────────────────────────────────────────┘
```

univariate statistics, especially the minimum and maximum values of variables, is useful. Graphical approaches are also helpful.

Example 4.4 provides an example, again using an age variable. Note that the codebook provides information on the variable as it should be, so we are looking for numbers in the actual dataset that are unlikely. In particular, find the maximum value listed in each printout. The commands—summarize, descriptives, and proc univariate—are commonly used to request simple univariate statistics. Consider that the numeric code assigned to this value is 288, which is implausible given the age range provided in the codebook.

Similar problems are common with variables that identify income, as well as with discrete variables. Income seems to be measured in a variety of ways in surveys and this sometimes leads to implausible values. Discrete variables, when coded numerically, should be identified with integers, but sometimes a stray decimal point is added so that, say, a 4 is listed as a 4.5.

As mentioned earlier, graphical techniques offer useful tools for exploring whether there are implausible or unusual values in the data. Although there are many techniques available, we consider only two: *box plots* and *scatter plots* (see Kandel et al. 2011, for some others). Recall that a box plot (also called a *box-and-whisker plot*) constructs a box based on the 25th and 75th percentiles and identifies the median within the box. It also shows observations that fall outside the box, including extreme values, in the so-called whiskers. Scatter plots show how two variables' values fall jointly using a coordinate system (see chapter 10 for more information). Example 4.5 displays commands to build box plots and scatter plots for age. The second variable in the scatter plot is occupational prestige (*OccPrest*), a measure of the perceived status of a person's occupation.

Figures 4.1 and 4.2 provide the box plot and the scatter plot that resulted from executing the Stata commands (the graphs are edited slightly). It should be easy to find the age value of 288. Note that it is quite a distance from the other data points. Since we are measuring age in an adult sample, it stands out as an error.

An extreme value such as age = 288 is known as an *influential observation* or an *outlier* since it can affect conclusions about the data and the statistical models by an inordinate amount. Examining variables for extreme values is an important part of data screening. However, when detected, it is essential to ask why they occur (Sabo and Boone 2013). Are they due to an input error, a respondent error, an unusual sample, or a natural occurrence (Osborne 2013)? Some analysts have been known to simply delete them since they can be inconvenient. But such an approach is unwise since they may be legitimate values and indicate something interesting about the data. You may recall that there are statistical procedures for examining data that have extreme values. Robust statistics, in particular, are affected less than other types of statistics by extreme values. For instance, the median is a robust statistic since it is affected much less than the mean (arithmetic average) in the presence of outliers. In addition to robust methods, transforming skewed variables or weighting the observations are other options available when extreme but legitimate values are present.

Although the codebook provides the most accessible information when using a new dataset, it may not be available, or, if you've collected the data, then a codebook needs to be prepared (see chapter 6). There are some useful commands that provide information similar to that provided in a codebook. These include the following:

- *codebook, describe* (Stata)
- *codebook* (SPSS)
- *proc contents* (SAS)

```
* Stata

graph box age

scatter OccPrest age
```

```
* SPSS

examine variables = age
  / plot = boxplot
  / statistics = none
  / nototal .

graph
  / scatterplot(bivar) = age with OccPrest .
```

```
* SAS

  /* First, create a constant for the proc boxplot command */
data dataset;
  set dataset;
  const=1 ;

run;

proc boxplot data=dataset ;
  plot age*const ;
run ;

proc gplot data=dataset ;
  plot OccPrest*age ;
run ;
```

Note: As of SPSS 14, there is also a suite of commands for creating graphs called *ggraph*. SAS also has a *proc sgplot* command that creates a variety of graphs.

It remains imperative, however, to examine each of the variables of interest in the dataset using some type of univariate and graphical analysis (Van den Broeck et al. 2005). Unfortunately, there are situations when implausible values cannot be detected with univariate statistics or graphical methods. You might find them only during the analysis stage. This reinforces the idea that data management and data analysis are not independent stages in the research project. Whenever questionable values are found, careful decisions must be reached regarding how to handle them.

Duplicates

Cases may appear more than once in a dataset. These are known as duplicates or *redundant observations* (Pohlabeln et al. 2014, 1006). It is not always clear why duplicates occur, but only one should be retained in the dataset. However, a serious problem is when the duplicates have different information, such as when two cases exist that are presumably from the

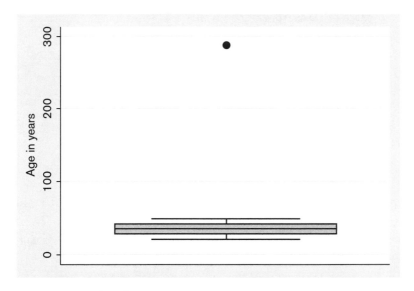

FIGURE 4.1 Box plot of age.

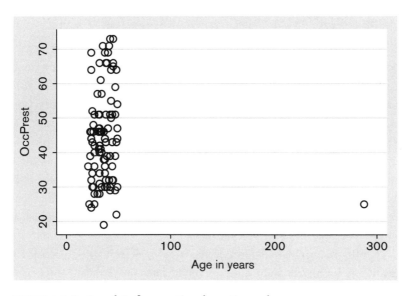

FIGURE 4.2 Scatter plot of occupational prestige and age.

TABLE 4.2 Data from six observations

ID	Age	Education	Party	Sex
1	25	12	1	0
2	31	16	1	1
3	35	18	2	1
4	27	14	1	1
1	25	12	1	0
2	31	16	2	1

same unit, person, or organization, but the values for particular variables differ. This usually occurs because an identification number has been entered incorrectly. When coming across such a situation, the best solution is to check with those who collected the data or examine the data collection instruments.

Checking for duplicates is not difficult in Stata or SAS. In SPSS, it takes a little more work. Consider the following example. Table 4.2 includes an identification (ID) variable and some demographic information from six rows of data derived from a larger dataset. Recall that identification numbers should uniquely distinguish the units of observation. But notice that two values of the ID variable are repeated, 1 and 2. The rows that include data from ID = 1 also have identical values, whereas the data from ID = 2 differ on political party. It is likely that the first case is a duplicate, but the second case may or may not be (perhaps the number associated with this ID is wrong). The software code shown in example 4.6 provides some commands for identifying and removing duplicates.

Inconsistencies between Variables and Values

Earlier, we discussed implausible values and mentioned that sometimes they are difficult to detect using univariate statistics. *Consistency checks* are designed to identify peculiar combinations of variables and their characteristics. For example, suppose that a survey question is intended to provide a screener for subsequent questions. A question such as "How many times have you used marijuana is the past year?" might be followed up with "How many times have you used marijuana in the past month?". Someone who responds "no times" or "zero" to the first question should also have a zero or a missing data code on the second question. But what if they do not? Consider the data in table 4.3. The variables *mjYear* and *mjMonth* reflect these two survey questions (assume that each has response options 0 = *none*, 1 = *one time*, and 2 = *more than one time*).

Can you identify the problems? Frankie has a zero for *mjYear* and a 2 for *mjMonth*, whereas Elga has a 1 for *mjYear* and a 2 for *mjMonth*. These are logically implausible. Computerized survey administration is supposed to prevent this by skipping the second question for those who responded zero to the first question, but errors are known to occur. Although it is best to find the original survey instrument to determine where the error occurred, sometimes it is appropriate to simply replace the entries in the dataset with plausible values

---

EXAMPLE 4.6   Checking for duplicates

```
*  Stata

duplicates tag ID, gen(dup_id)    /* creates new variable dup_id */
                                  /* coded 1=duplicate, 0=not duplicate */

list if dup_id == 1, sepby(ID)    /* shows duplicate rows for ID only */
duplicates drop                   /* removes duplicate ID=1 */
```

```
*  SPSS

/* identify duplicate IDs .
freq var = ID / format = dfreq

temp .
select if (ID = 1 or ID = 2)
list variables = all

/* these commands assume the last step identified ID=1&2 .
/* it lists each rows characteristics .

sort cases by ID Age Education Party Sex.
match files file = *
  / by all
  / first = first1

/* first1 is coded 1 for the first case and 0 for duplicate cases .


formats all (F3.0) .
select if first1 = 1 .

/* removes duplicate for ID=1 .
```

```
*  SAS

proc sort data=dataset nodup out=datasetnew;
  by ID;
run;

/* datasetnew is a new dataset that omits the duplicate ID=1
   to omit the second ID=2 row, use nodupkey in place of nodup
*/
```

Note: For more details on managing duplicate values, see Boslaugh (2005) for SPSS, Kelsey (2005) for SAS, or Mitchell (2010, chapter 3) for Stata.

---

by assuming that the response to the first question is valid. Hence, recoding is fitting, as shown in example 4.7.

There are other steps to data cleaning and other procedures that are useful (see Van den Broeck et al. 2005). For now, though, it is important to note that documentation and data cleaning are perhaps the least exciting part of the research process and often the most time-consuming, but they are also critical. In fact, the preceding examples provide only a small

TABLE 4.3   Example of data inconsistency

Name	Age	*mjYear*	*mjMonth*	Sex
Mike	15	0	0	M
Frankie	18	0	2	F
Stan	12	1	1	M
Elga	17	1	2	F
Axel	15	2	2	M

EXAMPLE 4.7   Checking for inconsistencies in the data

```
Codebook

VARIABLE NAME &
  POSITION            VARIABLE DESCRIPTION        EXPLANATION
mjYear    10          Marijuana use past year     0 = none
                                                  1 = once
                                                  2 = more than once

mjMonth   11          Marijuana use past month    0 = none
                                                  1 = once
                                                  2 = more than once
```

```
* Stata
replace mjMonth=0 if (mjYear==0 & mjMonth>0) /* note that > is used */
/* it's not clear what to do about Elga! */
/* perhaps her most plausible value is mjMonth=1 */
```

```
* SPSS
do if (mjYear = 0 and mjMonth > 0).
recode mjMonth = 0.
end if.
/* notice that SPSS uses a conditional operator .
/* known as if-end to execute the recode .
```

```
* SAS
data dataset;
  set dataset;
  if (mjYear=0) and (mjMonth>0) then mjMonth=0;
run;
```

window into the in-depth process that should go into the data screening and cleaning operations (Herzog 2016). Each of the steps outlined here is vital to the success of the project since—as the example at the beginning of the chapter shows—data errors frequently lead to suspect or invalid study results (Zhu et al. 2013). It is also important to document in the program file each of the data management steps. Furthermore, some researchers create *exception reports* that list questionable variables and values found during the data screening and cleaning process. This includes peculiar values and influential observations (Pohlabeln et al. 2014). Exceptions reports allow others to understand the data and the decisions better.

NAMING CONVENTIONS

Data management includes not only data screening and cleaning, but also naming and labeling variables, as well as their particular numeric or character codes. This is important because many datasets arrive with variables that have odd labels. An example is found in the ICPSR data repository introduced earlier in the chapter. The codebook for a school crime survey lists variables that are named Q1A through Q1V, along with many others. This is, of course, convenient since these names are relatively short and designate the question order in the survey. However, when preparing a data file, these variable names are not helpful and may cause errors in the analysis (it is difficult to keep track of what Q1C or Q1R measure!). Therefore, it is a good idea to provide descriptive names for variables, to use labels to provide additional context regarding what they are designed to measure, and to link words to codes for additional clarification.

Some principles to keep in mind include the following:

- Since different software treats symbols distinctly, it is not a good idea to use hyphens, underlines, or other common keyboard symbols ($, @, &) in variable names. Some researchers argue that if they are using only one program, then it is acceptable to use symbols that the software allows. However, you may use Stata, but a colleague might prefer the SAS software or R, so avoiding inconsistencies across software is good practice.

- For readability, use upper case and lower case letters, with no spaces, in variable names.

- Several years ago, variable names could only be up to eight characters. This is no longer the case as software now allows longer names. It is not a good idea to make names too long, though. But they should provide a good sense of what the variable is designed to measure. For instance, an earlier example included a variable called *OccPrest*. It is not clear whether this is descriptive enough, so perhaps it should be named *OccPrestige*. Decisions such as this often depend on who uses the data. Sociologists, for example, will likely understand the first version of this variable name, but a psychologist or a social worker might not.

- Do not use variable labels that are more than 50 characters; longer labels tend to run off the edge of the printout.

- Use brief value labels for the particular codes, perhaps no more than five words but less if feasible.

Example 4.8 shows a codebook and some variables from a data table. It is followed by example 4.9 that demonstrates how to assign names and labels in Stata, SPSS, and SAS

Name	Q10	Q20	Q30
Tom	0	0	31
Cizzy	1	1	29
Lisbeth	1	1	42
Dean	0	0	21
Harriet	2	0	37

(we'll assume that the dataset arrived with no labels). Note that the SAS software requires a different series of steps to assign value labels.

There are some potential problems with these labels that depend on the context of the project. For example, will your audience understand the term "drunk"? In the United States, I assume most people understand this to mean that someone used alcohol to the point of intoxication, but it might be understood differently elsewhere. Moreover, what does it mean to have "served in the military"? Do civilian employees count? The point is that the audience, as well as other data users, should continue to be on the researcher's mind throughout the project (see chapter 1).

PRINCIPLES OF FILE MANAGEMENT

Now that we have considered several data management steps, it is important to consider a related topic: file management. Researchers who discuss workflow (see chapter 1) emphasize the importance of using a system to handle the many programs and data files that are a standard part of a research project (Long 2009). Files may be developed, used, and updated by multiple members of a research team. Therefore, it is imperative that members of the team agree on a set of guidelines for naming, revising, and storing files. In the earlier example of documentation, the initial comment of a program file included who prepared the file and when it was last updated. This is a good procedure to follow and is essential to *version control:* a set of procedures designed to record changes to files so that those working with the

EXAMPLE 4.9 Renaming and labeling variables

```
* Stata

rename  Q10  DrunkMonth
rename  Q20  Veteran
rename  Q30  Age

label  variable  DrunkMonth "Times drunk in past month"
label  variable  Veteran "Served in the military"
label  variable  Age "Age in years"

label define   drunk 0 "0 times" 1 "1-2 times" 2 "more than 3 times"
label define   vet 0 "no" 1 "yes"
label values  DrunkMonth drunk   /* link drunk label to values */
label values  Veteran vet        /* link vet label to values */
```

```
* SPSS

rename  variables  Q10 = DrunkMonth.
rename  variables  Q20 = Veteran.
rename  variables  Q30 = Age.

variable labels
  DrunkMonth 'Times drunk in past month' /
  Veteran 'Served in the military' /
  Age 'Age in years' .

value  labels  DrunkMonth 0 '0 times' 1 '1-2 times' 2 'more than 3 times'
          / Veteran 0 'no' 1 'yes' .
```

```
* SAS

data dataset (rename Q10 = DrunkMonth Q20 = Veteran Q30 = Age));
  set dataset;
  label
    DrunkMonth = "Times drunk in past month"
    Veteran = "Served in the military"
    Age = "Age in years" ;

/* First, use proc format to create the value labels */
proc format;
  value drunk 0 ="0 times" 1 ="1-2 times" 2 ="more than 3 times" ;
  value vet 0 -"no" 1 ="yes"
run;

/* In SAS, value labels are assigned to variables for specific
   procedures rather than being linked to them in a dataset
   In the following the format option uses the variable name
   followed by the label name and a period to identify it as a
   value label and uses them in a frequency table

*/

proc freq data=dataset;
  format DrunkMonth drunk.
         Veteran vet. ;
  tables DrunkMonth Veteran ;
run;
```

files know when they were created and updated. An online version control system is called *git* (git.scm.com) and is widely used through the website *github* (github.com). Although it was designed initially for software developers, it has become popular among scientific researchers as an online location to collaborate on research projects and share files. Similar systems include Apache Subversion, Bazaar, and Mercurial.

Including comments that identify who and when a program file was created or updated is important. Here are some other principles of file management that are useful:

- As mentioned earlier, use a text editor and save program files as text files (which typically use the file extension *.txt*) so that others who use different statistical or data management software may read them. These may be converted easily into Stata, SPSS, or SAS program files. However, even if you use one of these statistical software packages to create program files, they are typically saved as text files even if their file extension is unique to the software. For example, a Stata do file (e.g., *workflow.do*) may be opened in a text editor.

- Keep the original version of the program and data files. Label them so that others will know they are the original files. For example, if I were using a file with secondary data called *KidHealth*, I might name the original, unedited data file as *KidHealthInitial* or *KidHealthOriginal*. Subsequent versions could then be designated as *KidHealthV1*, *KidHealthV2*, and so forth.

- Store the original data in a text file, such as a *csv* file. For example, it is a good idea to retain the original *KidHealth* data as a *KidHealth.csv* file. These types of text files can be read by most statistical software programs, as well as virtually all data management software. Therefore, collaborators and other users will be able to use the files regardless of the software they use. The text files for the original data should include the variable names in the first row. This makes it simpler to import them into statistical software.

- Place comments and notes in the data files (Long 2009). This is easy to do with Stata's *notes* command or SPSS's *document* command. For example, if I created a subset of the original data in the *KidHealthV2* data file, I could request that Stata include a comment stored within the data file: `note: this is a random 10% subset of data from KidHealthV1. It was originally created on 21 Dec 2016`. Comments may then be retrieved when the dataset is in memory by the Stata command: `notes`. SPSS works in a similar manner: execute the command `document [text of the comments]`. Then, `display documents` will list the comments.

- Use a clear directory structure for the files. This is more difficult than it sounds. Research teams should agree on the structure if they plan to share files. If not, then the person responsible for preparing and updating files should design a system that others could use (or she could use in the future) without much trouble. For instance, a different directory might be used for the data files, the program files, the output files, and the project presentation files (articles, graphics files, presentation software files). Each file should be dated and organized so the project flow is clear.

- Include comments in files that build off of one another to indicate how they are connected. Suppose I create a file called *KidHealthCleaning* that carries out the data management procedures discussed in this chapter. It reads the original *KidHealth* data and fixes a few errors and then labels the variables and their values. It then produces a new data file in, say, SPSS called *KidHealthDataV1.sav*. Next, I create a program file—call it *KidHealthGraphs*—that reads this SPSS data file and creates some graphs. The link between *KidHealthCleaning* and *KidHealthGraphs* should be clearly documented with a comment. It is not sufficient to simply rely on the commands in a program file to identify which other files it reads or otherwise uses. For example, consider the following comments:

```
/* File name: KidsHealthGraphs.sps  .
/* Creation date: 2 May 2017  .
/* Author: Shield Sheafson, University of Geatland  .

/* This file reads the data file KidHealthDataV1 and creates  .
/* box plots for the variables age, income, and SES            .
/* The data file was created by the program file              .
/* KidHealthCleaning on 15 April 2017                         .
```

- Although there are exceptions, include the data screening and cleaning, correction of duplicates, and labeling of variables and their codes in a single program file. Recoding may also appear in this file, but may need its own file to keep the workflow clear to other users. In some projects, each of these steps is so long that separate files are needed. These should be clearly documented regarding what they do and how they are related to the other data management files. It is also a good idea to learn to prepare *batch files* that can execute the commands from multiple files if there are several that build off of one another.

- Make sure you are aware of privacy issues that apply to any data that you share with others or place in an online version control system such as *git* or Apache Subversion. Many projects in the social and behavioral sciences have stringent safeguards to ensure that individuals who participate in research projects cannot be identified. In fact, many of those who are asked to participate in research projects are given a guarantee of confidentiality that their information will not be disclosed except for strict research purposes. Most organizations that collect and manage data—including universities—have Institutional Review Boards (IRB) that require detailed plans about how researchers will protect data from disclosure. It is, therefore, important to understand the requirements of your institution or of the organization from which the data are acquired to ensure that you follow these safeguards, especially when data are shared with other researchers or are potentially accessible to others.

- Back up the files! There are far too many tragic tales from the research world about researchers losing data and not being able to reproduce their results. So, find a reliable backup system. One way to think about these principles is by imagining that you spent several months on a research project, but then had to abandon it for a year as you went to study or teach on a tropical island. When you return, you must pick up where you left off and continue the project. Retracing your steps can be difficult without a clear directory structure, plain comments in each of the files, notes indicating how the files are connected, and the ability to locate the files since your company replaced your computer while you were away.

FINAL WORDS

Good data are critical to the social and behavioral sciences. Yet too often they are handled without sufficient care and this can lead to costly errors. It is never a pleasant experience when a researcher's work ends up on the website *Retraction Watch*! This chapter furnishes specific guidance about how to manage data. Its goal is to provide some principles that apply to how quantitative data are prepared for analysis. Some of the key terms and principles discussed include the following:

- Data management refers to a series of steps, from putting together a dataset to importing it into a software package to ensuring there are no errors or duplications (and correcting these if found).

- Data preprocessing is a key aspect of data management. It involves a number of steps that should be completed after the data acquisition stage but before the analysis stage begins. This includes reviewing the documentation and preparing and executing program files designed to clean and screen the data, rectify data errors, identify unusual observations, carefully code or recode variables, and assign names and labels. Thoroughly documenting each data management step helps others understand why certain decisions were made and how to reproduce them.

- Good data management practices should be accompanied by good file management practices. This includes using a comprehensible directory structure and a version control plan, especially when the project is a collaboration of researchers. It also includes making sure information about research participants remains confidential.

```
/*************************************************************/
* 1. This file is designed to complete the following        *
*    data management steps using the data file              *
*    KidHealthData                                           *
*    (a) examine the variable age for unusual observations   *
*    (b) recode unusual observations to reasonable           *
*        values if the error is obvious                      *
*    (c) assign a label to the age variable                 *
*
* 2. Creation date: 2 Apr 2017                              *
* 3. Last updated:  9 Apr 2017                              *
* 4. Creator: Peregrin Took, University of Numenor          *
* 5. Created for Stata version 14                           *
/*************************************************************/

/* Executable lines begin next */

/* Read the text file that includes the original data  */
*    [command to read a csv file - see chapter 5]

/* Examine age */
codebook age               /* shows characteristics of the variable */
summarize age, detail      /* detail provides extra information */

/* Examine a box plot of age */
graph box age, title(Boxplot of age)

/* Both of these procedures show an unusual value 288
   which is implausible in this sample
   Examining the original questionnaire indicates it
   should be replaced with age 28 */

recode age (288=28)

/* Check the recode */
summarize age, detail

/* label the variable */
label variable age "Age in Years"

/* create a new data file */
save KidHealthDataV1
```

Before moving on to examples of actual datasets, it must be reemphasized that thorough documentation is critical to the efficiency and success of a research project. Some recommend that a *research log*, updated as members of the team work on various aspects of the project, should be part of any research endeavor (Long 2009). Moreover, as this chapter has noted—perhaps to the point of exhaustion—providing comments for each task addressed in a program file is vital. To close, example 4.10 provides a summary of some of the data management steps shown in this chapter. It is written assuming that the file will be used in Stata but is simple to translate into SPSS or SAS.

The following exercises use a dataset called *firstyeargpa.csv*. It is a comma-separated values file that includes information on 20 college students. Information is provided on their sex, the number of clubs they belonged to in high school, their high school math and English grades, and their scores on the quantitative and verbal portions of the Scholastic Aptitude Test (SAT), a test required for admission to many colleges and universities in the United States. Finally, there is information on their first-year college grade point average (GPA).

The codebook in exercise 4.E1 provides the following information about the data file.

EXERCISE 4.E1   First-year GPA codebook

```
Study of First-Year GPA from a sample of students who attended the University
of Panem in the year 2198

Principal Investigator
Coriolanus Snow, School of Cultural Education, University of Panem

DATA COLLECTION DESCRIPTION
SUMMARY: The purpose of this data collection project was to provide data on
the first-year grade averages of students who attended the University of Panem.
It also gathered information on the students' high school records, including
their grades in English and mathematics and their SAT scores. The goal of the
research project was to develop a predictive model of first-year success at the
university to create a better class of students in the future.

File Structure: rectangular
Cases: 20
Variables: 7
Record Length: 19
Records Per Case: 1
```

VARIABLE NAME AND POSITION		VARIABLE DESCRIPTION	CODES/RANGE
Sex	1	Sex of student	0=male, 1=female
Clubs	2-3	Number of high school clubs	Range: 0-5 Mean: 2.3
SATVerbal	4-6	SAT-Verbal score	Range: 247-704 Mean: 478.3
SATQuant	7-9	SAT-Quantitative score	Range: 237-791 Mean: 511.6
HSMath	10-12	High school math average	Range: 1.65-3.76 Mean: 2.69
HSEnglish	13-15	High school English average	Range: 2.14-3.74 Mean: 3.01
GPA	16-19	First-year college grade average	Range: 1.65-3.9 Mean: 2.62

Source: University of Panem, 2198.

The dataset is available on this book's website (www.ucpress.edu/go/datamanagement). Complete the following exercises using this dataset.

1. Open up the file in a text editor of your choice (as mentioned earlier, some common options are Notepad, Notepad++, TextEdit, and Vim). Notice how the data are structured and where the commas appear.

2. Open up the data file in the spreadsheet software of your choice. Review the contents of the data file. Make sure you understand that the first row of the file contains the variable names. Do you notice any discrepant values? What are they?

3. Using statistical software of your choice (or as required by your instructor), check some descriptive statistics for the variables. Then, use a graphical approach, such as a box plot or scatter plot, to check the data for extreme values. Make sure you write a program file that takes these steps so you may replicate them if needed. What conclusions do you reach about any of the values that appear extreme? What should you do about them?

4. Write a program file that provides labels for the variables. For which variable(s) should you provide value labels? Depending on your answer to this question, create value labels for this/these variables.

5. If you haven't done this already, add comments to the program files you created in exercises 3 and 4 so that others will be able to follow what you were doing.

FIVE

Finding and Using Secondary Data

During the 1990s, the Harvard political scientist Robert Putnam made famous his thesis that social capital was declining in the United States. Based on various data sources, including a large survey that he managed, Putnam argued that people had become less trusting of others and their governments; there was a marked decrease in associational memberships such as bowling leagues, and people were increasingly disengaged from politics (see, e.g., Putnam 1995). All of this was a threat to democracy and predicted an apathetic and fragmented nation. His argument reached a high point with the publication of his best-selling book titled *Bowling Alone: The Collapse and Revival of American Community* (2000). However, sociologist Pamela Paxton pointed out that the concept *social capital* can mean several things and that Putnam's evidence was thin on each. She thought a more careful test of Putnam's thesis was needed. Therefore, she used data from the General Social Surveys (GSS), a set of national-level studies that are conducted in the United States every two years, to measure several aspects of social capital, including trust, spending time with friends, and membership in voluntary organizations. By examining the data over time, Paxton was able to chart changes in the variables that measured these concepts. The results of her careful analysis suggested that some types of trust were declining, such as general trust in other individuals, but that people continued to be involved with voluntary organizations (Paxton 1999). In general, they were not "bowling alone" but still "bowling together." An important point about this exchange of ideas is that Paxton did not need to collect her own data to test Putnam's thesis; rather, she used data that had been collected by others for more general purposes.

As mentioned in chapter 3, there are many different types of data and data sources. Recall that *secondary sources* are materials that someone else has collected or produced. For example, when a research team organizes and administers a survey and prepares the resulting data for analysis, but then makes a dataset available for others to use, this is considered a secondary source and is a common example of secondary data. Secondary data can be used to (re)examine the findings of the study for which the data were originally collected, extend them by considering additional variables or modeling strategies, or investigate new research questions and hypotheses (Greenhoot and Dowsett 2012). It is clear that secondary data are a valuable source of evidence in the social and behavioral sciences. Yet, even though some research methods books include chapters on secondary data (see, e.g., O'Leary 2014; Remler and Van Ryzin 2015), it is rare to find examples of how to locate and use this type of data to answer one's research questions. Thus, the main concern of this chapter is to learn about some sources of secondary datasets and consider how to use them in a research project. This includes issues such as locating, accessing, evaluating, and managing secondary datasets, as well as thinking through some key decisions about the analysis.

TYPES OF SECONDARY DATA

In addition to survey data that were collected by someone else, secondary data may also be classified into the following types:

- Official data, such as government or quasi-governmental information, cross-national data collected by international organizations such as the World Health Organization, and data published by private and nonprofit organizations. These fall under the general category of *administrative data* (see chapter 6).

- Material produced by individuals, such as blog posts, tweets, videos, photographs, journals, and various types of personal and household records.

- Online communities, such as message boards, community websites, chat rooms, and other online collectives.

- Research articles—if they are treated as individual units in a larger collective—that provide the material to conduct analyses, such as in a meta-analysis.

- Media, including films, commercials, books, newspaper and magazine articles, television programs, musical compositions, and artwork.

- Social and cultural artifacts, such as graffiti, rubbish, crafts, household items (such as from an archeological dig), and similar material (O'Leary 2014, 245–246).

Although there are likely others types, the line between primary and secondary sources is often obscured because many researchers combine data from different places. For example, suppose a research team is interested in whether nations that are industrializing quickly tend to lose animal species at a faster rate than other nations. Yet, they discover that there is no single data source that contains all the information needed to examine this issue. The team, therefore, combines data from four or five different organizations, such as the United Nations, the World Wildlife Fund, the International Union for Conservation of Nature, the World Bank, and so forth. Under a strict definition, such a dataset is considered secondary. Yet, it could also be considered primary since the researchers collected the data and organized them so they would be useful to the particular research project. In order to simplify things a bit, this type of compiled dataset is discussed in the next chapter that addresses primary and linked administrative data.

WHY USE SECONDARY DATA?

A large and perhaps even growing tendency in the social science community is to use secondary sources of data in research projects. Although it is difficult to find good information on the percentage of research articles in the social sciences that are based on secondary data, I looked at the last two years of a few journals in my academic field and found that about three-fourths of the articles used secondary data in one form or another.

But why is this so common? There are several advantages of secondary data, including the following:

- *Cost.* It is expensive to collect primary data. Even a modest survey of only 100 people can set researchers back several thousand dollars. Although there are some cost-efficient ways to conduct surveys—such as by utilizing online survey software—it is typically a high-cost endeavor, not only in terms of money, but also in terms of time. Many secondary datasets may be accessed via the Internet for free; others are available after paying relatively low fees. Moreover, since the data are already available and often in pretty good shape (but this needs careful evaluation), researchers may save quite a bit of time on their projects.

- *Longitudinal data.* Primary data collection tends to be expensive, but think about a project in which one collects data repeatedly for a number of years. This can be very expensive, even if the sample is restricted to a single community or school. Several publically available datasets are based on research projects that include data from samples of individuals or organizations collected over several years, thus allowing researchers to examine changes in outcomes of interest. For instance, the *National Longitudinal Survey of Youth – 1979* (NLSY79) has followed a sample of people in the United States for more than 30 years, from adolescence through adulthood. Hundreds of research projects have used these data to study economic, social, and behavioral outcomes, and how they change over the life course.

- *Representativeness.* The relatively high cost of primary data collection often necessitates collecting data locally or in a small area. Recall the matter of WEIRD research participants discussed in chapter 4. An important issue is whether our reliance on college students and other easily accessible samples is appropriate for answering research questions that are supposed to pertain to broader segments of the population. Many secondary data sources are based on international-, national-, or state-level samples, and their samples are rarely limited to WEIRD participants. For example, the *American Community Survey* (ACS), which is sponsored by the US Census Bureau, is based on a national sample of more 3 million households each year. The households are chosen through a careful sampling procedure and offer a good representation of adults and families in the United States.

- *Breadth.* Some of the large social and political surveys offer researchers the ability to study a considerable range of interesting research questions. For example, they allow researchers to examine broad questions about social processes, social policies, political behaviors, and understanding changes in society (Freese 2009). This is difficult to do with primary data unless a researcher is willing to spend a substantial part of his life collecting data. Although, when done well, this is impressive, it is difficult and, obviously, very time-consuming.

- *A variety of questions and variables.* Many large surveys ask numerous questions and thus contain an abundance of variables. For instance, the aforementioned GSS—a nationally representative data source that is based on information collected every two years—has more than 5,000 variables. Each time it is administered, it includes several hundred questions. Although measurement is a key concern, it is likely that a researcher can find relevant questions with which to measure social, political, or behavioral concepts of interest by relying on secondary data sources.

- *Reproducibility, replication, and extension.* As suggested earlier, one of the goals of a good research project is reproducibility: the ability to duplicate an entire study, such as an experiment, by an independent researcher. This requires access to the original data and detailed instructions about the methods used to produce the findings. Thus, researchers undertaking reproducibility projects use secondary data. Furthermore, replication does not necessarily require a new dataset since alternative questions might be used for a concept to determine the validity of a finding. Or another year of the data might be used for replication purposes. Secondary data are also useful for extending research findings. Perhaps the primary data were used to examine whether self-esteem affects success in school, but another researcher thinks that self-esteem and success in school are actually determined by the quality of parent-child relationships.

Thus, the model used in one project may be extended by considering additional concepts in a second model.

Although these advantages make secondary data attractive to many researchers, there are also some important limitations. These include the following:

- *Lack of control over who, what, how, and when.* A researcher who uses secondary data has no control over the sample. She might wish to study particular minority groups, but secondary data sources may include few of them in their samples. There is also no control over the concepts that are measured, including what questions are asked and how they are asked (Greenhoot and Dowsett 2012). For example, several large secondary datasets have been used to study adolescent drug use, with the goal of figuring out what percentage of youth in different groups use marijuana or other illicit substances. Yet, research suggests that the reliability of the data that result from some of these questions differs depending on the group (Johnson and Fendrich 2005). Therefore, comparing groups using these data may be futile. Moreover, a researcher may wish to study depression, but the questions in the secondary data source might not distinguish sadness from depressive symptoms.

- *When the data were collected.* Social and cultural phenomena and conditions change and thus research findings may depend on when the data were collected. For example, attitudes toward same-sex marriage have changed dramatically since the 1980s and 1990s (Baunach 2012), so using data from 20 or more years ago to examine associations between various concepts and these attitudes is a questionable practice, especially if one is interested in contemporary issues. It is up to the researcher to show why data from earlier years are useful for understanding what might be occurring more recently.

- *Thoroughness of measurement instruments.* Many large secondary datasets include sets of questions designed to measure particular concepts. For example, in chapter 3 we discussed the Add Health dataset and mentioned that it included sets of questions that assess depressive symptoms (the Center for Epidemiologic Studies Depression Scale) and mastery (Pearlin and Schooler's [1978] mastery scale). However, some large studies truncate sets of questions since each item included in a survey means some other item must be excluded. Yet, excluding items from a larger set may lead to validity problems.

- *Letting the data drive the research question.* As discussed in chapter 2, research is initiated and motivated by research questions, problems, and hypotheses. Often, there may not be data available to answer a particular research question, so the researcher should be prepared to collect her own data. The availability of secondary data, however, may motivate a researcher to design a study largely because the data are easily accessible (Vartanian 2010). This is usually not a good research practice.

- *Overestimating the time saved.* As the discussion in the previous chapter should have made clear, understanding and examining a dataset is time-consuming. There are many steps to be taken before an analysis is conducted. Merely reading the documentation and codebook of a dataset can take a long time, especially for the careful researcher. And this should be followed by a careful review of the relevant variables in the dataset. There may be a tendency to think that using secondary data is a simple matter of downloading data and then beginning an analysis using a few variables. But such haste must be avoided (Greenhoot and Dowsett 2012).

In general, researchers need to carefully consider how well a secondary dataset matches the requirements of their project (Hox and Boeije 2005). Are the sample, questions (including the way they were asked), and variables appropriate for the research question or the hypotheses that one's research project is designed to evaluate? What are some of the limitations of the dataset and how might they affect the results?

SOURCES OF SECONDARY DATA

There are many sources of secondary data. The most common include national government agencies and data repositories. Some of these allow virtually any user with the right software and an Internet connection to download data. Others are restricted to employees of organizations, such as colleges and universities, which purchase access to data repositories. Perhaps the largest of the latter is the *Inter-university Consortium for Political and Social Research* (ICPSR). As mentioned in chapter 4, this is an organization affiliated with the University of Michigan in the United States. Its holdings include hundreds of datasets from numerous research projects, but access to most of them is restricted to researchers affiliated with about 760 universities and government agencies that pay a membership fee. Some data repositories or project sites allow individual researchers access to their data, but charge a fee, require special permission, or mandate that they set up specific security protocols to protect the data.

Sidebar 5.1 includes the names and websites for several data repositories and project sites from which to obtain secondary data. Some of these allow direct downloads of data, whereas others require a user to first register and provide some personal information.

Although there is an abundance of choices, some of the larger repositories, such as the ICPSR, the National Center for Education Statistics (NCES), the Association of Religion Data Archives (ARDA), DataVerse, Pew Research Center, and the GESIS, are good places to begin to search for social and behavioral science data. For researchers who wish to use US government data, the open data website (www.data.gov) is especially useful since it includes

REPOSITORIES

Association of Religion Data Archives (ARDA), www.thearda.com

Awesome Public Datasets, https://github.com/caesar0301/awesome-public-datasets

Australian Bureau of Statistics, www.abs.gov.au

Bureau of Justice Statistics (BJS), US Department of Justice, bjs.gov/index.cfm?ty=dca

Bureau of Labor Statistics (BLS), US Department of Labor, stats.bls.gov

CDC Wonder (US Centers for Disease Control & Prevention), wonder.cdc.gov

Collaborative Psychiatric Epidemiological Surveys, http://www.icpsr.umich.edu/icpsrweb/CPES

Datasets for Empirical Development Economists, sites.google.com/site/medevecon/development-economics/devecondata

Data and Story Library (DLS), http://lib.stat.cmu.edu/DASL

Datahub, datahub.io/dataset

Dataverse, dataverse.org

Demographic and Health Surveys (DHS), www.dhsprogram.com

Dryad Digital Library, datadryad.org

Fedstats, fedstats.sites.usa.gov

Figshare, figshare.com

Gallup Analytics, http://www.gallup.com/products/170987/gallup-analytics.aspx

GESIS – Leibniz Institute for the Social Sciences (Europe), www.gesis.org/en/services/data-analysis

Google Public Data Explorer, www.google.com/publicdata/directory

The Guardian Datasets (United Kingdom), www.theguardian.com/data

InDepth Data Repository, www.indepth-ishare.org.index.php/home

Integrated Public Use Microdata Series (IPUMS), www.ipums.org

International Social Survey Programme (ISSP), www.issp.org

Inter-university Consortium for Political and Social Research (ICPSR), www.icpsr.michigan.edu

(continued on next page)

Kaggle – Home of Data Science, www.kaggle.com

Latin America Public Opinion Project, www.vanderbilt.edu/lapop/index.php

National Longitudinal Surveys (NLS), www.bls.gov/nls.home.htm

National Addiction & HIV Data Archive Program, www.icpsr.umich.edu
/icpsrweb/NAHDAP

National Center for Education Statistics (NCES), nces.ed.gov/surveys

Open Government Canada – Open Data, open.canada.ca/en

Pew Research Center, www.people-press.org

Roper Center Public Opinion Archives, www.ropercenter.uconn.edu

Social Science Data Analysis Network (SSDAN), www.ssdan.net

StatCrunch, www.statcrunch.com

Statistics Canada, www.statcan.gc.ca

Statlib, lib.stat.cmu.edu

Survey Documentation and Analysis (SDA), sda.berkeley.edu/index.htm

UCI Machine Learning Repository, archive.ics.uci.edu/ml/datasets

UK Data Service – ReShare, reshare.ukdataservice.ac.uk

United Nations Data, data.un.org/Explorer.aspx

US Census Bureau, www.census.gov

US Government's Open Data, www.data.gov

The World Bank, data.worldbank.org

DATASETS & SOURCES (US OR INTERNATIONAL)

American National Election Studies (ANES; United States),
www.electionstudies.org

Behavioral Risk Factor Surveillance System (BRFSS; United States),
www.cdc.gov.brfss

County Health Rankings (US Counties), www.countyhealthrankings.org

Consumer Expenditure Survey (CES; United States), www.bls.gov/cex

Fragile Families & Child Wellbeing Study (United States),
www.fragilefamilies.princeton.edu

General Social Surveys (GSS; United States), gss.norc.org

Health Behaviour in School-Aged Children (HBSC) (international), www.hbsc.org

(continued on next page)

International Social Survey Programme (international), www.issp.org

National Health Interview Survey (NHIS; United States), www.cdc.gov/nchs/nhis.htm

National Longitudinal Study of Adolescent to Adult Health (Add Health; United States), www.cpc.unc.edu/addhealth

National Statistics Online (UK data), www.statistics.gov.uk

Panel Study of Income Dynamics (PSID; United States), psidonline.isr.umich.edu

Religion Statistics and Geography (international), www.adherents.com

Sourcebook of Criminal Justice Statistics (United States), www.albany.edu/sourcebook

Sperling's Best Places (to Live; United States), www.bestplaces.net

Statistical Abstract (historical US data), www.census.gov/compendia/statab

Survey of Income and Program Participation (SIPP; United States), www.census.gov/sipp

Uniform Crime Reports (UCR), US Federal Bureau of Investigation (FBI; United States), www.fbi.gov/about-us/cjis/ucr/ucr-program-data-collections

World Factbook (international), www.cia.gov/library/publications/the-world-factbook/index.html

World Values Survey (WVS; international), www.worldvaluessurvey.org/wvs.jsp

Note: See Vartanian (2010) for a description of many more secondary datasets for the social sciences. Some of these sites may require the user to register before accessing their data holdings. A few are also restricted to members of organizations that pay annual fees for access. Check the websites for more information about the data holdings, such as their coverage, when they were collected, available variables, and so forth.

a portal to data from hundreds of federally funded research projects and data collection efforts.

As suggested earlier, a vital issue when choosing a secondary data source is to consider carefully why a particular dataset is useful for answering a specific research question. This requires a careful evaluation of the documentation that accompanies the dataset. The documentation should provide clear information about the sampling steps, the way the data were gathered, the questionnaire and its sources, how variables are constructed and coded, and other relevant material. It is also a good idea to conduct a literature review on the dataset to determine how it has been used by other researchers. How have the data been manipulated—such as through recoding or combining variables to measure

FIGURE 5.1 Education and gun control attitudes.

concepts—in previous studies? What limitations have other researchers brought up about the dataset? Are there any peculiarities regarding the sample that may raise issues or be seen as limitations? For instance, perhaps there is a disproportionate number of middle-class respondents. It is up to the researcher to have a clear rationale for using a particular secondary dataset. This requires a thorough understanding of the data's sources and uses in previous work.

EXAMPLES OF SEARCHING FOR, DOWNLOADING, AND IMPORTING DATA

Considering what was covered in the last chapter and the many choices for finding secondary data, let's see a couple of examples of the steps one might go through to find, download, and open a dataset. In chapter 4, we mentioned that it is a good idea to use text files, such as .csv files, for storing original datasets, if they are available. However, many repositories make datasets available for specific statistical software platforms. This can be convenient since the variables and their codes are usually labeled. Nevertheless, it's a good idea to know how to download datasets in various formats.

Before searching for a secondary dataset, it is vital to have a research topic in mind. Being too general or too abstract makes it much more difficult to find data and decide the best way to analyze them (Freese 2009). In the following example, assume that we are interested in the following topic: attitudes toward gun control. This is an important issue in the United States, especially given competing concerns with protecting Second Amendment rights relative to preventing mass shootings. Assume further that a careful review of previous studies led us to consider the conceptual model shown in figure 5.1. This is based on the hypothesis that people with higher levels of education are more likely to support gun control legislation (Kleck 1996). Thus, we should search for secondary datasets that are useful for measuring education and attitudes about gun control. It is also a good idea to include a few demographic variables, such as sex and age. This is because the research literature indicates that these are consistent predictors of attitudes about gun control and might affect the association suggested by figure 5.1. For instance, an additional hypothesis that is worth examining is whether the association between education and these attitudes is different for men and women. If it is, then sex is a *moderating* or *conditioning variable*.

Search for datasets here

FIGURE 5.2 Pew Research Center website.

The next step is to find a secondary data source that may be used to examine this conceptual model. Suppose that in reviewing the literature, we noticed that most of the studies of education and gun control attitudes had used regional or student surveys. We think, however, that it is important to consider this association at the national level. Thus, one step is to limit the search for datasets to those that are national in scope.

The next step is to determine where to look for secondary datasets. We might be tempted to conduct a general Internet search. However, a better place to start is usually at one of the large data repository sites (see sidebar 5.1). Looking over the choices and considering the type of social data—in this case, survey data—we likely need to examine the model, we decide to first look at the ICPSR and Pew Research Center websites. Both of these sites permit keyword searches. For example, as shown in figure 5.2, the Pew website (www .people-press.org) includes a search field in the top-right corner. Typing the term "gun control" revealed several surveys, including one conducted in 2015 titled "Gun Rights vs. Gun Control," that asked the question: "What do you think is more important—to protect the right of Americans to own guns or to control gun ownership?" The online Pew report from August 2015 includes a table that indicates that about 63% of those with a postgraduate degree, but only 47% of those who have not attended college, responded that controlling gun ownership was more important. However, since we would like to examine these data ourselves, the next step is to determine if they are available. Reading the information under the tab *Datasets* indicates that Pew data are released about five months after the surveys are conducted, so we might need to go back a few months earlier to see if there are data available (assuming our search is conducted in late 2015). After a bit of poking around, it turned out that the same question about guns was asked in a December 2014 survey. If one provides some general information, the dataset may then be downloaded for free (see *December 2014 Political Survey* at http://www.people-press.org/category/datasets/2014/ and click the download button to the right). This downloads a zipped file that includes the following: a methodology document, the questionnaire, the codebook, and an SPSS data file.

Rather than examining these files, let's consider another potential source of information on gun control attitudes. For example, recall that the ICPSR repository (www.icpsr.michigan.edu) includes hundreds of datasets. Figure 5.3 shows the ICPSR homepage. Browsing through the results of a keyword search for "gun control," this site (as mentioned earlier, its

FIGURE 5.3 Inter-university Consortium for Political and Social Research (ICPSR) website.

data are restricted to member institutions, which include many universities, that pay an annual fee) suggests that many news organizations conduct polls that ask people about this topic. There are also several large surveys, such as the *Survey of Gun Owners in the United States*, which have addressed gun control attitudes. However, some of these are 10–20 years old, and we would like more recent data. Therefore, a next step is to sort the results by time period. Again, there are several media polls, but there is also an entry for the *General Social Survey 1972–2012 [Cumulative File] (ICPSR 34802)*. Clicking the link reveals that the data are available in a variety of formats, including SAS, SPSS, Stata, R, and Delimited (a *.csv* file). And notice that these data cover a 40-year period. But suppose that our institution is not a member of the ICPSR network, yet we wish to use the GSS data? Are there other options? It turns out that yes, there are alternatives available.

The GSS, the American National Election Studies (ANES), and various other datasets are accessible from the *Survey Documentation and Analysis* (SDA) website (sda.berkeley.edu/index.htm), hosted by the University of California at Berkeley. The home page explains that this website includes codebooks, online analysis capabilities, and datasets that may be downloaded at no cost. The *Archive* option routes the user to a page that includes links to the various datasets. As of early 2017, this included the *GSS Cumulative Datafile, 1972–2014*. Clicking on the first GSS link brings up a page in which users may search for variables and download custom subsets (see figure 5.4). Let's consider the following steps:

1. Use the *Search* option to find variables relating to the term "gun."

2. Notice that there are several variables that involve guns, but two that seem most appropriate for gun control are called GUNLAW and GUNSALES. The

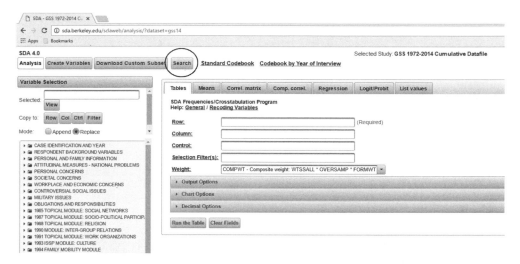

FIGURE 5.4 The General Social Surveys (GSS) on the Survey Documentation and Analysis (SDA) website.

variable GUNLAW looks promising. It is based on a survey question that asks: "Would you favor or oppose a law which would require a person to obtain a police permit before he or she could buy a gun?" The response options are "Favor" and "Oppose."

3. Click *Select* for GUNLAW and notice that it now appears in the box labeled *Selected*. Note also that if you click *View* a popup window shows the question text, the variable codes, and some frequency information. Does this appear to be an appropriate measure of gun control? (We'll assume it is for this illustration.)

4. Click *Analysis* in the upper left-hand corner of the page. When the new page opens, click *Col* to place the variable GUNLAW in the box labeled *Column*.

5. Then type YEAR in the box labeled *Row*, followed by *Run the Table*.

6. Browse the page that pops up. Notice that this question was included in the 2014 GSS, so it is relatively recent and seems to suit our purposes.

7. If we went through steps 3–6 for the variable GUNSALES, we would find that the question was asked only in 2006, so it is not as appropriate for studying recent attitudes.

Before deciding to use the GSS or the Pew data, however, it is a good idea to consider the two seemingly relevant questions about guns that our review has turned up. As a reminder, they are:

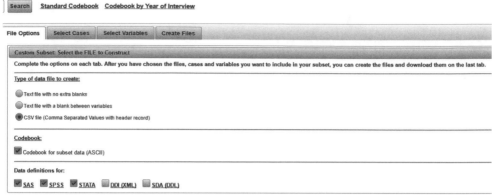

FIGURE 5.5 Creating a subset of General Social Survey (GSS) data on the Survey Documentation and Analysis (SDA) website.

- Pew, 2014: "What do you think is more important—to protect the right of Americans to own guns or to control gun ownership?"
- GSS, 2014: "Would you favor or oppose a law which would require a person to obtain a police permit before he or she could buy a gun?"

How do these questions compare? What are their similarities and differences? Has previous research used one or both of these questions to examine gun control attitudes? The GSS question has been used in several studies (e.g., Celinska 2007; Toch and Maguire 2014), but not to examine its association with education. The Pew question has also been used, though not as frequently (e.g., Schildkraut and Hernandez 2014). In addition, these studies do not discuss the questions' properties, such as validity and reliability. On its face, does the Pew or GSS question seem to be a good measure of gun control attitudes, or would you prefer a different question or measurement approach? This is a key question to ask when utilizing secondary data. There is usually not a straightforward answer, however.

Let's assume that we decide that the GSS question is appropriate for our research purposes. The next task is to create a custom dataset that includes the variables GUNLAW, EDUC, SEX, and AGE (try to find these variables using the *Search* option). The custom dataset may be requested using the Download Custom Subset option and the following steps:

1. Click *Download Custom Subset* at the top of the screen (see figure 5.5).
2. Under *Type of data file to create*, choose CSV file.
3. Under *Data definitions for*, choose SAS, SPSS, and Stata.

4. Click *Select Cases*. In the *Selection Filters* box, type *year(2014)*. This limits the data file to the 2014 GSS.

5. Click *Select Variables*. In the box that appears under *Specify individual variable names*, enter GUNLAW EDUC SEX AGE.

6. Click *Create Files* followed by selecting the *Create Files* button in the middle of the page.

7. Download the *Zip archive – ALL files* and save it to a local directory.

Assuming you were able to successfully download data from the Pew website, you should now have two zip files in your local directory, one of which includes the 2014 Pew data and another that includes the 2014 GSS data. The Pew data are provided in an SPSS file, whereas the GSS data are provided in a *.txt* file. Since we chose CSV file in the earlier step, these GSS data are in comma-delimited format. We'll start by considering how to import this file into the statistical software packages.

Importing the Data

We first examine the data in a spreadsheet such as Microsoft Excel or Google Sheets. Table 5.1 provides the first few rows of data.

Next, it is critical to examine the codebook that accompanied the data file. It provides information about the variables and the codes associated with each. Before beginning any data management step, be aware of how each of the variables is coded. Notice that each of them includes missing data codes. For example, the GUNLAW variable includes a 0 value that is labeled as IAP. A search of the GSS website (gss.norc.org) indicates that IAP is shorthand for "inapplicable." In other words, the question did not apply to some of the survey respondents. It is not always clear why this is the case and it is best to try to understand it a little better. Reviewing the documentation on its website that describes how the GSS is administered, it turns out that this survey uses a rotating set of questions. This means random subsets of GSS respondents are asked particular questions. It might be important to consider the ramifications of this when using the GSS data. Suppose we decide that it will not affect our project in any untoward way (but see

TABLE 5.1 General Social Survey data, 2014 extract

CASEID	GUNLAW	EDUC	SEX	AGE
57062	1	16	1	53
57063	1	16	2	26
57064	2	13	1	59
57065	0	16	2	56
57066	1	17	2	74

chapter 7 for more information about missing data). Nevertheless, this is another example of the need to thoroughly understand a secondary data source before using it in a research project.

Importing comma-delimited files is relatively straightforward in Stata, SPSS, and SAS. The following commands may be used (note that the GSS data file is renamed *GSS2014.txt*). However, it may be most convenient in SPSS to use the Import Wizard, which is available by choosing *File-Open-Data* or *File-Read Text Data* from the drop-down menu. The commands may then be copied from the Output window to a syntax file.

Importing text data files

```
* Stata

import delimited [pathname]\GSS2014.txt
```

```
* SPSS

get data / type=txt / file="[pathname]\GSS2014.txt"
  / delimiters=","
  / qualifier='"'
  / firstcase=2
  / variables=caseid F5.0 gunlaw F1.0 educ F2.0 sex F1.0 age F2.0 .
```

```
* SAS

proc import datafile="[pathname]GSS2014.txt"
  out=gss2014data /* creates an SAS dataset called gss2014data */
  dbms=csv replace ;
  getnames=yes ;
run ;
```

In Stata, the default is to look for the variable names in the first row of the data file, but in SPSS the subcommand firstcase=2 is interpreted as the data begin in the second row. In SAS, this information is provided with the getnames=yes subcommand. Moreover, SPSS and SAS are informed that the delimiter is a comma (delimiters="," and dbms=csv; *dbms* is the abbreviation for *database management system*).

Data Management

Suppose that the program files for Stata, SPSS, and SAS are not available. What initial data management steps should we take? Recall that in chapter 4 there were a number of steps, including cleaning, screening, and labeling the data and variables. Although a similar process should occur before undertaking any analyses of these data, the following program file example provides just a few of these steps. It assumes that the data documentation has been read thoroughly.

Data labeling and recoding

```
* Stata

/* This file is designed to import and show a few data management steps with
   the GSS 2014 data that include a question about attitudes toward gun laws

1. The steps include
     (a) recode the variable gunlaw to 0,1
     (b) recode the missing data
     (c) assign new names and labels to the variables

2. Creation date: 20 Jan 2017
3. Last updated: 20 Jan 2017
4. Creator: Penelope, University of Ithica
5. Created for Stata version 14

*/

/* import the data */
import delimited [pathname]\GSS2014.txt

/* rename the variables /*
/* note that Stata imports the names as lowercase */
rename gunlaw GunPermit
rename educ education
rename sex female

/* label the variables */
label variable GunPermit "Favor police permits for guns"
label variable education "Years of formal education"
label variable female "Sex of respondent"
label variable age "Age of respondent"

/* recode the variables */
recode GunPermit (1=1)(2=0) (else=.)
recode education (97/99=.)
recode female (1=0)(2=1) (else=.)
recode age (0=.)(98/99=.)

/* assign value labels */
label define gun 0 "oppose" 1 "favor"
label values GunPermit gun
label define fem 0 "male" 1 "female"
label values female fem

/* check the results */
tab1 GunPermit female
summarize education age, detail
```

```
* SPSS

/* This file is designed to import and show a few data management steps with .
/* the GSS 2014 data that include a question about attitudes toward gun laws .

/* 1. The steps include .
/*     (a) recode the variable gunlaw to 0,1 .
/*     (b) recode the missing data .
/*     (c) assign new names and labels to the variables .
```

```
/* 2. Creation date: 20 Jan 2017 .
/* 3. Last updated: 20 Jan 2017 .
/* 4. Creator: Penelope, University of Ithica .
/* 5. Created for SPSS version 21 .

/* import the data .
get data / type=txt / file="[pathname]\GSS2014.txt"
  / delimiters=","
  / firstcase=2
  /variables=caseid F5.0 gunlaw F1.0 educ F2.0 sex F1.0 age F2.0 .

/* rename the variables .
rename variables gunlaw = GunPermit.
rename variables educ = education.
rename variables sex = female.

/* label the variables .
variable labels GunPermit 'Favor police permits for guns' /
  education 'Years of formal education' /
  female 'Sex of respondent' /
  age 'Age of respondent'.

/* recode the variables .
recode GunPermit (0=8).
missing values GunPermit (8,9).
recode GunPermit (2=0) .
missing values education (97,98,99).
recode female (1=0)(2=1).
missing values age (0,98,99).

/* assign value labels .
value labels GunPermit 0
  'oppose' 1 'favor' /
  female 0 'male' 1 'female'.

/* check the results .
frequencies
  / variables = GunPermit female.

descriptives
  /   variables = education age.
```

```
SAS

/* This file is designed to import and show a few data management steps
   with the GSS 2014 data that include a question about attitudes toward
   gun laws

    1. The steps include
        (a) recode the variable gunlaw to 0,1
        (b) recode the missing data
        (c) assign new names and labels to the variables

    2. Creation date: 20 Jan 2017
    3. Last updated: 20 Jan 2017
    4. Creator: Penelope, University of Ithica
    5. Created for SAS version 9.2
*/
/* assign a library name where the data files reside
```

```
/* this is useful for saving SAS files to a local directory */
libname john "[pathname]" ;

/* import the data */
proc import datafile="[pathname]\GSS2014.txt" out=gss2014data replace ;
  delimiter=',';
  getnames=yes;
run ;

*/ rename and label the variables */
data gss2014data (rename=(GUNLAW=GunPermit EDUC=education SEX=female AGE=age));
  set gss2014data;
  label
    GunPermit = "Favor police permits for guns"
    education = "Years of formal education"
    female = "Sex of respondent"
    age = "Age of respondent" ;
run;

/* recode variables */
data gss2014data;
  set gss2014data;
  if (GunPermit=0) or (GunPermit>7) then GunPermit=. ;
  if (GunPermit=2) then GunPermit=0 ;
  if (education>96) then education=. ;
  if (female=0) then female=. ;
  if (female=1) then female=0 ;
  if (female=2) then female=1 ;
  if (age=0) or (age>97) then age=. ;
run;

/* assign value labels */
proc format;
  value gun 0 = "oppose" 1 = "favor"
  value fem 0 = "male" 1 = "female"
run;

/* check the results */
proc freq data=gss2014data;
  format GunPermit gun. female fem.;
  tables GunPermit female;
run;

proc univariate data=gss2014data;
  var education age;
run;
```

What other steps do you recommend? Are there any peculiar values for age or education? Is it feasible to have zero years of education in this dataset? What does the codebook suggest? It might be a good idea to check the GSS data more carefully, perhaps by visiting the GSS or the SDA website, to determine if zero years of education comprise a valid code.

There are other steps that might be useful to consider. For example, a common data management and analysis issue is to subset the data. This can mean a couple of things. First, a researcher may need to select only a particular subset of the data based on a variable.

For example, suppose one's interest in attitudes toward gun control concerns only those in the age group 20–50. Second, it is not uncommon to take a random subset of data. This might be done in a *split sample analysis*: one sample is used to estimate a statistical model, whereas the second sample is used to validate the model. This procedure is used often in data mining tasks and is considered one type of *cross-validation* (Attewell and Monaghan 2015). Both types of subsetting are relatively simple to execute. However, to select a random subset it is important to set a *seed* for the random number generator that is used in this process. A seed is simply a number that the user designates. This is so the results are reproducible (Gandrud 2015). Here are some ways to subset the GSS data.

Subsetting data

```
*  Stata

/* subset based on ages 20-50 */
tab1 GunPermit female if (age>19) & (age<51)
summarize education age if (age>19) & (age<51), detail
/* notice the way the if subcommand is used */

* random subset with 50% subsample
set seed 76543 /* this is the seed */
sample 50
tab1 GunPermit female
summarize education age, detail
/* be careful about saving the data since the remaining 50%
   might be lost */
```

```
* SPSS

/* subset based on ages 20-50 */.
temporary * create a temporary file */.
  select if (age gt 19 and age lt 51).
  frequencies
   / variables = GunPermit female.

/* do it again since the temporary file ends with the frequencies .
/* command .
temporary.
  select if (age gt 19 and age lt 51).
  descriptives
   / variables = education age.

* random subset with 50% subsample .
temporary.
  set seed = 76543.
  sample .50.
  frequencies
   / variables = GunPermit female.

temporary.
  set seed = 76543.
  sample .50.
```

```
    descriptives
      / variables = education age.
```

```
* SAS

/* subset based on ages 20-50 using the where command */
proc freq data = gss2014data;
  where age>19 and age<51;
  tables GunPermit female;
run;

proc univariate data = gss2014data;
  where age>19 and age<51;
  var education age ;
run;

/* random subset using the surveyselect procedure
   the 50% subsample is based on the sample size for the
   cases of the GunPermit variable that are not missing
   or 1,693 */
proc surveyselect data=gss2014data method=srs rep=1 sampsize=847
       seed=76543 out=subgss2014 ;
  id _all_ ;
run;

proc freq data = subgss2014;
  tables GunPermit female;
run;

proc univariate data = subgss2014;
  var education age;
run;
```

Don't forget to create a new data file once the data management stages are complete. As discussed in chapter 4, it is a good idea to keep the original data file in text format. This allows one to use the program files to reproduce all the steps in the workflow, a series of stages that are integral to the research project (see chapter 1).

A SIMPLE TEST OF THE CONCEPTUAL MODEL

Recall that the reason we located, downloaded, and (partially) cleaned the GSS data was to examine a simple conceptual model. The model, shown in figure 5.1, suggests that education is positively associated with support for gun control. Although the GSS survey question may not be an optimal measure of this concept, we will use it anyway to determine whether there is evidence to support the model. What are some simple statistical techniques that might be used? A cross-tabulation of *education* and *GunPermit* is not the best option since there are more than 20 education levels. Are you familiar with any measures of association that are appropriate for a continuous and a binary variable? Are there graphical approaches that might be useful? It is important to look at the data in different ways in order to make sound conclusions (Freese 2009).

Here are two ideas. First, we may compare average (mean) education levels among those who support and oppose gun permits. Second, box plots of education for these two groups might be useful for comparing their medians and distributions. This second step may also reveal any unusual observations. Try the following set of commands in one of the statistical software packages.

Testing the conceptual model

```
* Stata

/* means */
mean education, over(GunPermit)

/* boxplots */
graph box education, by(GunPermit)
```

```
* SPSS

/* means.
means
  / tables = education by GunPermit.

/* boxplots.
examine variables = education by GunPermit
  / plot boxplot.
```

```
* SAS

/* means */
proc means data= gss2014data mean ;
  class GunPermit ;
  var education;
run;

/* boxplots */
proc boxplots data= gss2014data;
  plot education*GunPermit ;
run;
```

What do the results indicate? There appear to be differences in the means and medians that suggest support for the model, but are they large enough to indicate that there are meaningful differences? Are you a statistics frequentist who uses p-values or similar inferential approaches to determine the "significance" of a difference? This might lead to other tests of the conceptual model. However, if you are a Bayesian, there are alternative approaches to consider. In any event, would you be comfortable presenting these results to an audience of your peers? Or are other analytic approaches needed? In later chapters, we will learn some useful principles for data presentation. For now, it is simply important to think about what the results of this elementary analysis suggest for the validity of the conceptual model. Chapters 8 and 9 provide additional ideas about how to test and present this model.

THE PEW RESEARCH CENTER DATA

Recall that we also downloaded data from a 2014 Pew Research Center survey that included a question about gun control: "What do you think is more important—to protect the right of Americans to own guns or to control gun ownership?" An important issue is whether this is a more valid question concerning gun control than the GSS question examined in the last section: "Would you favor or oppose a law which would require a person to obtain a police permit before he or she could buy a gun?" This is a difficult issue to resolve, and requires substantially more information about gun control attitudes, so we will not pursue it here.

However, an interesting question is whether the data from the Pew survey support the nominal differences by education shown in the GSS data. How would you determine whether or not the two datasets offer similar evidence regarding education and gun control attitudes? Diving into this problem is left as an exercise. This exercise is not only worthwhile in terms of learning to use secondary data, but also as a way to appreciate the promises and challenges of replication in fields where measurement is not standardized. A word of caution, however: make sure you review thoroughly the documentation that accompanies the Pew data to understand how the variable is constructed.

In addition, another research question mentioned earlier asked whether the presumed association between education and gun control attitudes is different for men and women. Think about some ways you might examine this research question with the GSS and the Pew survey datasets (hint: there are not notable differences).

FINAL WORDS

Secondary data are used in many research projects in the social and behavioral sciences. They offer a cost-effective alternative to primary data collection. Dozens of data repositories contain hundreds of datasets, many of which are free to use (see sidebar 5.1 and Vartanian 2010). However, there are several limitations to secondary data. One of the most consequential is that the researcher has no control over how the sample was chosen, the instruments constructed, and the data collected. Users may also need to compromise on the way concepts are measured.

This chapter has attempted to show some steps that researchers take to utilize secondary data. This includes finding a good match between the conceptual model and the data, in particular locating suitable variables to measure the concepts, and gaining a thorough understanding of the dataset, how it was constructed, and some of its potential limitations. It is also important to think about how to prepare these data for analysis by using good data management practices. In general, secondary data can provide an important source of evidence for many types of research projects. But recognizing the limitations that they may impose on the project is critical.

EXERCISES FOR CHAPTER 5

The US Presidential election of 2012 pitted the incumbent Barack Obama against former Massachusetts Governor Mitt Romney. This exercise is designed to explore people's feelings toward Mitt Romney in the election year. A common measurement tool in surveys is called a *feeling thermometer*. It asks people to respond along a scale from 0 to 100, where lower values indicate that the respondent doesn't care for the person ("cold" feelings) and higher values indicate the person likes the person ("warm" feelings). One research question is whether women and men felt differently about Mitt Romney during his campaign. Therefore, we will get some secondary data with which to test the following graphical model.

Although it is not always clear when using a binary variable like male versus female, the model proposes that males felt "warmer" than females about Mitt Romney. In other words, males are expected to report higher values, on average, on the feeling thermometer than females.

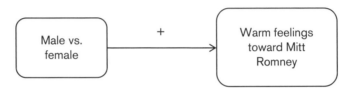

FIGURE 5.E1 Conceptual model of male and female feelings about Mitt Romney.

1. As a preliminary stage toward testing this model, go to the *Survey Documentation and Analysis (SDA)* website (http://sda.berkeley.edu/index.htm) from which the GSS data used earlier in the chapter were accessed. Then, complete the following steps:
   a. Select *American National Election Study (ANES) 2012 - released 7/1/13 (SDA 4.0)* from the list of data files available on the *Archive* web page.
   b. Select *Download Custom Subset*.
   c. Select the button *CSV file* under *Type of data file to create*, and check the *Codebook for subset data (ASCII)* button.
   d. Select *Variables* and, on this screen, place the following two variable names in the box: *FTPO_RPC* and *GENDER_RESPONDENT* (the first abbreviation designates "feeling thermometer presidential office—Republican Party candidate").
   e. Select *Create Files* and click *Create Files*. Once the two files are created, download them. You should now have two files titled something like *sub-data.txt* and *sub-cdbk.txt*.
   f. Review these two files using text editing software such as Notepad, Notepad++, or TextEdit (but don't save the data file in spreadsheet software such as MS Excel or Mac Numbers!). The first file should have the data separated by commas and the second file should be a codebook tailored for this subset of the 2012 ANES data.

2. Write a program file in Stata, SPSS, or SAS that does the following with the data file you downloaded in (1):
   a. Renames the variable so that *FTPO-RPC* is named *Romney* and *GENDER_RESPONDENT* is named *gender*.

b. Identifies for the software the missing values for the *Romney* variable (check the codebook for the missing value codes).

c. Creates a new variable called *female* that is coded as 0=male and 1=female.

d. Creates value labels for the variable *female*.

e. Provides the mean level of the *Romney* variable for males and females. (Hint: your code needs to provide the mean of the *Romney* variable for males and females separately.)

f. Include comments in the program file so that others will understand the steps you created.

g. Don't forget to save your program file so you may use it again if needed.

3. Please answer the following questions:

a. What are the mean responses on the *Romney* variable for males and females (there should be two means)? (Hint: the overall mean is 45.22.)

b. Do these means support the claim shown in the graphical model? Why or why not?

SIX

Primary and Administrative Data

On August 3, 1996, President Bill Clinton signed into law the National Gambling Impact Study (NGIS) Commission Act. Given the rapid growth of the gambling industry during the 1980s and 1990s, many policymakers saw a need for better information on the risks and promises of widespread gambling in the United States. Thus, the NGIS Commission was established to investigate. The committee quickly realized that, although various studies up until that point had provided some information on gambling behaviors and problems, there was a dire need to gather good, national-level data. The commission, therefore, contracted with the National Opinion Research Center (NORC) to conduct three studies: a national survey of adults in the United States., a survey of gambling facility customers, and a study of communities in which legal gambling activities (casinos, betting facilities) had recently arrived. These studies provided substantial information about the gambling behavior of adults in the United States, as well as the economic benefits and social costs of gambling facilities. For example, the primary data that resulted from the studies were used to estimate that (a) more than half of the adults in the United States gamble in some form and almost one-third gamble at casinos; (b) between 2 and 3 million adults are pathological gamblers, with another 15 million at risk for problem gambling; (c) pathological and problem gambling costs society about $5 billion per year due to lost wages, health-care costs, and other negative consequences; but (d) newly opened casinos do seem to reduce local unemployment (Gerstein et al. 1999).

Not many people like to lose their jobs. Getting fired or laid off can cause stress and anxiety, not to mention financial challenges. Economists Daniel Sullivan and Till von Wachter were curious to see if employees who were displaced from their jobs—which often occurs because companies close facilities, eliminate positions, or downsize their workforce—were at risk of dying! They combined two large administrative data sources: data on employment and earnings of Pennsylvania workers and US Social Security Administration death records. Sullivan and von Wachter (2009) determined that the risk of death among displaced high-seniority employees in the year following job loss was 50–100% higher compared to similar employees who did not lose their jobs. Even 20 years following displacement, the risk of death was 10–15% higher. Perhaps we should all be a little more compassionate when friends lose their jobs.

As discussed in chapter 3, primary sources are materials that researchers collect and use in their own analyses. Thus, when social scientists mention *primary data*, they are referring to information that was collected as part of a research project. These are original data, in some way, such as when a new survey on a topic is undertaken and the data consist of people's responses to a set of questions tailored specifically for the project. Primary data also consist of information gleaned from other sources, such as experiments, focus groups, qualitative interviews, ethnographic observations, and even the compilation of artifacts.

Many researchers prefer to collect primary data, even though it can be costly and time-consuming. In chapter 5, we discussed some of the advantages and disadvantages of secondary data. Reviewing this list should show equally the benefits and challenges of collecting primary data. Perhaps the most important benefit is that primary data collection, with certain constraints, can be designed to precisely fit the goals of a research project. For example, if a researcher wants to determine whether there is an association between owning an AR-15 semiautomatic rifle and views of federal and state gun control laws, it might be difficult to find a suitable secondary dataset that asks the direct questions needed to study this association. By designing and administering her own survey, she may craft specific questions that ask about the types of rifles people own and their views on gun control. The researcher will likely wish to ask multiple questions about gun control laws. How likely is it that a secondary data would include this type of information? Although collecting primary data can be expensive, it is often worth the cost if a researcher is taking an innovative approach to studying some topic. Nonetheless, as mentioned earlier primary data collection is time-consuming; it also requires a high level of training. Hence, it is best for those just beginning their research careers to work with an experienced team or rely on knowledgeable mentors when undertaking this type of research.

Research methods courses are often designed with primary data in mind. Reviewing the content of a few undergraduate courses in sociology, psychology, and political science shows that most of the time is spent on sampling, measurement concerns, interviewing and observational techniques, survey design, interpreting qualitative and quantitative data, using mixed methods, and summarizing findings. Psychology courses also tend to emphasize how to design and execute experiments. These topics are typically presented so that students gain skills to collect their own primary data.

Since I assume that most readers of this book have completed or are familiar with the content of a research methods course, this chapter avoids a recapitulation of the information covered there. Instead, it is designed mainly to provide some principles for working with primary data, with an emphasis on quantitative data. Moreover, as mentioned in the last chapter, a type of data collection effort that does not fit neatly into the primary-secondary divide involves *administrative data*: information compiled by organizations for record keeping purposes, but also because of reporting requirements, constitutional mandates (such as the decennial US census), and for other related reasons. Although administrative data may not be collected for research purposes, they are used regularly by social scientists in their projects. In fact, many researchers compile data from different sources, including administrative data and survey data, to create new datasets. Several of the data repository sites listed in table 5.1 include these types of datasets. Given how frequently this occurs in the social sciences, it is important to understand some principles for linking different data sources.

PRINCIPLES FOR PRIMARY DATA

As a reminder, here is a simplified list of the typical steps researchers go through to collect primary data:

1. Decide on a research question, set of questions, or hypotheses that motivate the project. Consider the specific concepts that need to be assessed.

2. Determine what types of data are needed to measure the concepts and answer the questions or test the hypotheses. What is the unit of observation?

3. Consider from whom or from what to gather the data. For example, if a sample is planned, what is the target population and how should sample members be drawn from it? Given the budget and analytic expectations, what is the appropriate sample size? There may not be a clear target population or the idea of a sample may not fit the assumptions of the project. In any event, establish the source of the data.

4. Decide on procedures for collecting the data, from sampling to administration. This includes when, where, and how to collect the data.

5. Develop the data collection instrument(s). This might include questionnaires, observational protocols, interview guides, or other approaches. Consider the best methods and instruments for measuring the concepts.

6. Pretest the instruments.

7. Administer the instruments to the sample of research participants. Or gather the relevant information in some fashion, such as by engaging in ethnographic observations and informal interviews.

8. Transfer the information gleaned from the instruments or other data gathering tools to electronic files.

There are obviously specific steps and variations that any project may need to consider—such as getting permission to do the study from review boards or responsible parties, as well as establishing how the data will be protected from disclosure—but this list provides a broad outline from which to understand primary data collection. There are several good books that provide practical details about the most common types of data collection efforts (see Groves et al. 2009 [survey research]; Harris 2008 [experiments]; Stake 2012 [qualitative research]; and Thomas 2011 [case studies]).

Data Entry and Integrity

Research data are typically placed in electronic files. This is certainly the case with quantitative data. Yet even most qualitative researchers now use electronic files to organize notes and identify thematic content from their interviews and observations. Thus, it is important for all researchers who collect primary data to adhere to some principles for handling data. Although computerized survey administration and data entry have reduced the need for some of the following, here are some specific principles regarding creating datasets and ensuring the quality and integrity of the data:

- Use double or triple data entry procedures. This involves comparing repeated entries to find any typos or input errors and then correcting them. If the resources are available, it is often helpful to have at least two people engaged in this task. Develop a plan to determine the correspondence of the data that are entered. For instance, suppose that research participant Rowan is identified as a male in one entry but a female in another. There should be clear guidelines to reconcile this discrepancy.

- Regularly check a specific number of entries after a certain number are entered. For example, a researcher might set up a system where a 10% sample of the entries is examined with each 100 entries or rows of data.

- If there are important coding tasks that need to be completed as the data are entered, create a program file designed to do this task and run it each time a certain number of cases are entered. For example, suppose you are entering data on football quarterbacks and an important variable is the *quarterback rating* (this is a common measure of the "quality" of quarterbacks). This variable is constructed using an algorithm that takes into account several variables. The algorithm may be programmed into a file and run as each, say, 10 rows of quarterback data are entered in the dataset.

- If feasible, consider completing data preprocessing steps each time a certain number of cases are entered (see chapter 4). This might be time-consuming and costly, but it helps improve data integrity as the data are being entered. It also makes it easier to correct errors since data entry is closer in time to data collection (ICPSR 2012, 21–22).

Fortunately, there is software designed specifically for moving data from a collection instrument to an electronic file. This obviates some of the concerns with manual entry of data. Survey software is typically suitable for instruments that are administered over the phone, via the Internet, or with a laptop or tablet computer or smartphone. Online survey tools such as SurveyMonkey, SurveyGizmo, and Qualtrics have the ability to create electronic files, typically in spreadsheet format, that contain data from their survey instruments. In addition, SPSS has a suite of software tools designed to integrate data collection, management, and analysis. Many large survey firms have developed their own software to similarly integrate these steps. This software often has built-in data consistency checks and other useful tools to ensure data integrity.

Data Files

Suppose, though, that we already have the primary data in electronic files or we need to build a data table or spreadsheet that organizes the data. What are some principles to follow when considering how to arrange and provide information about primary data? Some of these were discussed in earlier chapters. Recall the principles of file management outlined in chapter 4. Several of these apply to files that hold primary data. In particular,

- Keep a file that contains the original data. Preferably, some version of this should be a text file, such as a *csv* file, so that it may be read by various types of data management and analysis software.
- Add comments and notes to the file as appropriate. The capability to add these may not be available in text editing software, but they are easy to include when data are saved in a spreadsheet, Stata, SPSS, or SAS.
- Don't forget to have a reliable backup system. This cannot be emphasized enough. Furthermore, consider a data archiving plan for the long-term preservation of data (ICPSR 2012). Some of the data repositories listed in table 5.1 offer storage space and archiving at low cost. The widespread availability of cloud servers and repository hosting services such as *github* also makes data archiving relatively simple.

There are additional principles that have not yet been discussed. This includes what to do when data are contained in multiple files and the importance of data security.

- If the primary data span multiple files, use a clear directory structure. For example, suppose the primary data are contained in two files: the first has demographic information and the second has behavioral measures. Are they clearly labeled? Will another user be able to quickly determine which file holds which data?

TABLE 6.1 Student and school multilevel data

Person identifier	School identifier	GPA	Age of student	School graduation rate (%)
101	10	2.91	15	90
102	10	3.15	17	90
103	10	3.64	16	90
201	20	3.01	15	87
202	20	2.66	15	87
203	20	4.00	18	87
301	30	3.87	17	92
302	30	2.65	16	92
303	30	1.97	16	92

- Of utmost importance, if data are contained in multiple files, is to have a way to link the cases. This involves making sure that there is a unique identification number for each case. With multilevel data (see chapter 3), there should be as many identification variables as there are levels. For instance, for student data nested in schools, there should be a student-level identification variable and a school-level identification variable. Table 6.1 provides a brief example of a file that has data combined from two distinct files: a student-level file and a school-level file. Here we see that person 101 attended school 10, had a grade point average (GPA) of 2.91, was 15 years old, and attended a school that had a 90% graduation rate.

- Understand how to merge and concatenate files. Merging files generally involves adding variables, whereas concatenation involves adding cases. For example, if the demographic and behavioral data are in two separate files, then, at some point, they will need to be merged. However, suppose the data are from two different schools and each set is contained in a separate file. Combining these data involves concatenation since different cases are combined to form a larger data file. When concatenating files, it is helpful to have a variable that identifies which file contributed which cases. Here are some simple steps for merging and concatenating in Stata, SPSS, and SAS. In each example, *id* (shorthand for *identification*) is the unique identifier for the cases. Notice that each dataset needs to be sorted by the *id* variable prior to the merging step.

Merging and concatenating files

```
* Stata

/* sort the data */
use dataset1
sort id
save dataset1, replace

use dataset2
sort id
save dataset2, replace

/* merge the files */
merge 1:1 id dataset1 using dataset2   /* merge dataset1 and dataset2 */
                                       /* dataset1 is open in Stata */
/* concatenating files */
append using dataset1 dataset2, generate(newvar)

/* this works when neither dataset is open in Stata
   newvar is a variable that identifies the source
   of each case or observation
*/
```

```
* SPSS

/* sort the data .
get file = dataset1.sav.
sort cases by id.
save outfile = dataset1.sav.

get file = dataset2.sav.
sort cases by id.
save outfile = dataset2.sav.

/* merge the files .
match files
  / file = dataset1
  / file = dataset2
  / by id.
save outfile = dataset12.sav.

/* concatenating files .
add files file = "dataset1.sav" / in-ds1
  / file = "dataset2.sav" / in=ds2.

/* ds1 and ds2 are variables that identify the source of each case .
save outfile = dataset12.sav.
```

```
* SAS

/* sort the data */
data one;
  set dataset1;
run;

proc sort data=one;
  by id;
run;
```

```
data two;
  set dataset1;
run;

proc sort data=two;
  by id;
run;

/* merge the data */
data dataset12;
  merge one two;
  by id;
run;

/* concatenating files */
data dataset12;
  set dataset1 dataset2;
run;
```

There are some things to be careful about when merging and concatenating files. In particular, be aware of duplicates (see chapter 4). Moreover, when concatenating, make sure that the variables have the same names and are the same type across the two datasets. If one is a character variable and the other is a numeric variable, then the software will have a difficult time understanding how to combine the datasets. This also applies to the identification variable used to merge two or more files. In addition, be careful of variables that have the same name in two files designated for merging. If there are variables labeled *age* in each, but one measures age in months and the other measures age in years, rename them prior to merging.

- Data security. As mentioned earlier, many research projects that involve human participants offer a guarantee of confidentiality. This is designed to prevent others from identifying research participants. There is evidence that keeping information confidential improves the validity of data since participants may be more comfortable discussing sensitive and private issues. If the data do need to be kept confidential, then there should be a system of anonymizing the cases and keeping any personal identifiers secure. Once again, identification variables are important, but they should be generated in such a way that people interested in snooping around in the data cannot identify the participants. Thus, it is best to randomly assign identification codes to research participants.

When studies are designed to follow participants over time (longitudinal design), some personal identifiers need to be maintained. If this is the case, they should be kept in a secure location away from the data. And the files that link personal identifiers with the anonymized identification variables should also be kept safe and available only to a limited number of project personnel. In general, there should be a data protection plan associated with any data collection project. This includes using not only anonymous identification variables, but also secure data storage procedures.

Variables and Codes

Chapters 3 and 4 include extensive information about variables and coding. The principles outlined there are important for any quantitative data that are being prepared for analysis. Yet, when building primary datasets, there are some competing principles that should be considered. For example, chapter 4 discusses renaming variables so that they have descriptive names rather than names such as Q10 or Q25. However, it is common practice when preparing primary data files to name each variable so that it corresponds to the question number in a questionnaire. This makes it simpler to link the variable in the data file to the question asked during the survey. Nonetheless, when data are prepared for analysis, utilizing descriptive names is useful.

A vital coding issue involves missing data. More information on missing data is provided in chapter 7. When preparing primary datasets, it is important to include distinct codes for each variable that gives a sense of why the data are missing. This might include separate codes for the following situations:

- Some participants refused to answer.
- Some participants didn't know the answer to a question.
- Interviewer error (such as failure to mark an answer).
- Not applicable; recall that in the GSS dataset used in chapter 5 this was designated with the abbreviation IAP. A not applicable option is common when the questionnaire includes skip patterns and is frequently denoted as a "legitimate skip."
- No data were available (ICPSR 2012).

Consider that the reason a particular response is missing is important in the way researchers treat the data. For example, it is often a good idea to handle the first three situations as different from the fourth situation.

In some datasets, missing values are represented by blanks or empty cells. This is rarely an acceptable practice. Instead, missing data should be represented numerically or with a symbol that depends on the software (Stata and SAS use a period, whereas R uses the character *NA*). If numeric, the codes should be some value relatively distant from the legitimate values. For example, if age is missing, it might be coded with a negative integer (−9) or with a large three-digit number (999). The codebook should clearly identify this code as denoting a missing value.

Data Formatting

It is easy to think that there is never any reason to enter data yourself. There are such marvelous tools that place data into data tables or spreadsheets and so much data are already

TABLE 6.2 Data collapsed into frequencies

Sex	Age	Education	Drug use	Frequency
Male	30	12	No	20
Male	30	12	Yes	10
Male	40	12	No	15
Male	40	12	Yes	12
Female	30	12	No	24
Female	30	12	Yes	18
Female	40	12	No	11
Female	40	12	Yes	10
M	M	M	M	M

contained in electronic files that it is easy to forget that, on occasion, a researcher may actually need to enter some data. Regardless of whether this onerous task ever befalls a researcher, it is a good idea to reconsider some of the principles of data management and coding introduced in earlier chapters and understand some new ones.

Recall, for example, that most quantitative data, when represented in a data table or a spreadsheet, appear as a rectangular array. The rows normally represent the unit of observation, such as the individual cases, whereas the columns represent the variables: the different measures in the data. Unfortunately, data are not always provided in this way. There are many examples where datasets are exhibited with the variables in the rows or the data are collapsed into frequencies that represent combinations of cases. Table 6.2 provides an example of the latter.

In this table, the data have been aggregated to show, for instance, that there are 20 males in the dataset who are 30-years-old, have 12 years of education, and report no drug use. Although there is nothing inherently wrong with presenting datasets in this manner, it can be confusing to some people.

The statistician Hadley Wickham (2014) has coined the phrase *tidy data* to indicate that there should be a standardized approach to constructing and presenting primary datasets (although it applies just as well to any type of quantitative dataset). We have already discussed some aspects of tidy data, such as the principle that variables appear in columns and cases (observations) in rows. But Wickham also reviews some things to avoid, which are antithetical to good practices of representing primary data. These include the following:

· Column headers that provide values rather than variable names. Tables used in articles and presentations are often displayed in this way. Instead of columns representing distinct variables, they represent distinct values or codes of variables. Consider, for instance, table 6.3. In the table, there are, for example, 50 people aged 0–11 years and 5 people aged 26 and older in the Midway neighborhood.

TABLE 6.3   Columns as values

Neighborhood	Number of people in each age group			
	0–11 years	*12–15 years*	*16–25 years*	*26 years and older*
Midway	50	10	35	5
Arlington Heights	10	40	45	5
Lakeview	70	10	10	10
Maurytown	10	20	30	40
Southside	7	10	13	70
Crabtree	25	25	25	25

TABLE 6.4.   Multiple variables in a column

Variable	Average	Range
Age	45	20–60
Education	12	8–18
Income	$50K	$20–90K

Assuming that age is the key variable in this dataset, it should be represented differently. Even representing the data in a manner similar to table 6.2 is an improvement.

- Multiple variables are found in the columns. Observe the way table 6.4 is structured. Here, the average age in the dataset is 45, with an age range from 20 to 60 years.

  Once again, tables designed for presentation may be organized in this style, but datasets should not be.

- Variables are included in both rows and columns. This often occurs, for example, when data are collected over time or space. Some spatial data with this problem are illustrated in table 6.5. There are two rows for each observation, but the latitude and longitude are in a single column. For instance, the neighborhood of Midway is located at 12.0 latitude and -45.33 longitude. Its low and high temperatures in the month of May were 45°F and 70°F. This table should be reconfigured so that latitude and longitude are represented in separate columns (see table 3.6). Should the same issue apply to low and high temperature?

In all of these situations, there is confusion about how a dataset should be organized versus how research results should be displayed (Wickham 2014, 5–11). These are two distinct issues; confusing them will likely cause problems for those who attempt to manage the data and conduct the analyses.

TABLE 6.5   Variables in rows and columns

Neighborhood	Latitude/longitude	Month	Low and high temperature
Midway	12.0032	May	45
Midway	−45.3298	May	70
Recordville	11.9998	May	66
Recordville	−42.5467	May	80
Southside	14.2387	May	61
Southside	−40.2345	May	79
Willks	14.0001	May	75
Willks	−41.8769	May	82
M	M	M	M

TABLE 6.6   Collegiate Rugby Player Survey, 2016 (extract)

caseid	age	schoolyear	yearsplay	injuries
100	19	2	0	0
200	21	3	12	6
300	24	5	5	2
400	18	1	3	12
500	27	2	99	41

Documentation

Chapters 4 and 5 discuss the important role of documentation. One of the key issues involves codebooks. Recall that a codebook is a document that shows the structure and content of a data file, information about how the data were collected, and details about the variables contained in the data file. An essential task when constructing a primary dataset is to prepare a codebook and have it easily accessible to those who use the data. It is a good idea, for example, to have an electronic copy of the codebook in the same directory as the data file.

Codebooks should include metadata, including, at a minimum, the project title, the name of the principal investigator, the data collection organization (if applicable), the source of funding, a project description, the sampling procedures, coverage and time period of data collection, and the unit of observation (if it is not clear based on the other information). Moreover, each variable should be listed, along with its location in the data file, the question it is based on, the response options and codes, missing data codes, and frequencies or summary statistics. It is also helpful to have the instrument, such as an electronic copy of the questionnaire, available (ICPSR 2012). Example 6.1 provides a sample of a codebook based on a fictitious primary data collection project.

Table 6.6 provides a section of the dataset that accompanies this codebook.

EXAMPLE 6.1   Sample codebook

Title: Survey of Collegiate Rugby Players in the United States, 2016
Principal Investigator: Johan Laito, University of California at Wellington
Data collected by SurveyUnited, Inc., Fresno, CA, USA
Funded by the National Institute for the Spread of Rugby (NISR)

Project description
The purpose of this data collection project was to provide data on characteristics of collegiate rugby players and teams in the United States. It collected demographic data and information on when players began to participate in
rugby, their understanding of international rugby rules, and injuries experienced while playing rugby.

Sampling procedures
The athletic and intramural sports department of each public and private not-
for-profit college and university in the United States was contacted. Those
that indicated that they had a rugby program were placed on a list (only 5
of the 1,250 schools refused to provide information). A random sample (with
replacement) of the schools was then taken, with a yield of 100 schools. The
rugby coach and athletic director of each of these schools were contacted and
asked if the research team could contact the rugby players who were currently
on the team's roster. There were two refusals. Of the remaining 98, attempts
were made to contact all the players on the rosters. Those contacted (up to 5
letters and 10 telephone calls were used) were asked to participate in a survey of their experiences as rugby players. Of the 1,950 players listed on the
rosters, 1,900 were reached and 1,810 agreed to participate (92.8%). In all,
1,800 of these players completed a telephone survey during the data collection
period (response percentage: 92.3%).

Data collection period
January–August 2016

Variables: 12
Records Per Case: 1

Variable name and position		Variable description	Variable codes
caseid	1-5	identification variable	100 - 19987
age	5-7	age in years	17-25 (missing=99)
			(mean=21.5 sd=3.9)
schoolyear	8	year in school	1-6 (missing=9)
			(mean=3.2 sd=1.0)
yearsplay	9-10	length of time played rugby in years	0-12 (missing=99)
			(mean=3.9 sd=3.2)
injuries	11-12	number of rugby-related injuries in the last year	0-15 (missing=99)
			(mean=2.5 sd=3.9)
		etc.	

Suppose you were involved in this project, but your role was to manage the data and provide some analyses. Given what example 6.1 and table 6.6 show, what steps would you take to prepare the data for analysis? Consider the material from the previous two chapters to help you decide.

ADMINISTRATIVE DATA AND LINKING DATASETS

As mentioned earlier in this chapter and in chapter 5, administrative data can provide a good source of material for research projects. Administrative data are particularly useful for examining geographic variation and describing patterns of social and behavioral phenomena at the population level. However, there are also some limitations. First, administrative datasets are typically constructed with a narrow number of phenomena in mind, such as particular medical diagnoses or employment status. This often limits the number of other variables available to study associations and make comparisons. Thus, they are usually linked to other administrative data or to secondary data from surveys. However, this may present problems if the secondary data are restricted for confidentiality reasons. Second, there may be coverage problems, such as when US Social Security records are used to study older Americans, yet some people do not collect social security payments (Virnig and McBean 2001).

As an example of data linkage, recall the second example at the beginning of this chapter. The economists Daniel Sullivan and Till von Wachter (2009) linked two datasets, one that had employment information and the other that included mortality records, to study the risk of death among displaced workers. Other studies have linked various administrative data sources to investigate the association between types of health insurance and mortality, college attendance among young people raised in disadvantaged neighborhoods, and innovative drug development strategies in the pharmaceutical industry.

Administrative data are widely available. They may be found on websites and in many libraries. For instance, the World Bank has a wealth of data available on different nations throughout the world. Consider one of its data websites: datacatalog.worldbank.org. This site includes many administrative datasets. For example, there is a set of files labeled *GDP ranking (GDP)* that may be downloaded in MS Excel, as text (*csv*), or as a pdf document. Table 6.7 furnishes the first few rows of this dataset (as of early-2017).

Notice that the data are sorted from highest to lowest GDP. Now consider some other country-level data. The World Health Organization (WHO) maintains data files that list the health conditions and causes of death in most countries across the globe. For example, go to the following website: http://apps.who.int/gho/data/node.home. Find the page on the WHO website that lists *Child mortality* and then look for the data by country. Unfortunately, the data are listed for each country rather than in a single file (however, there are places to find this information in a single dataset). Locate the data for the countries listed in table 6.7. For each country, extract the most recent data on the *Neonatal mortality rate (per 1,000 live births)*. Adding these data to table 6.7 results in table 6.8.

There are several other sources of country-level data that might also be useful for creating a dataset with which to study various research questions about nations and the health

TABLE 6.7   Gross domestic product, by country, 2014 (extract)

	Ranking	Country	GDP (in millions of US$)
USA	1	United States	17,419,000
CHN	2	China	10,360,105
JPN	3	Japan	4,601,461
DEU	4	Germany	3,852,556
GBR	5	United Kingdom	2,941,886
FRA	6	France	2,829,192
BRA	7	Brazil	2,346,118
ITA	8	Italy	2,144,338

Note: The data were extracted in early-2017.

Source: The World Bank (data.worldbank.org).

TABLE 6.8   Gross domestic product (GDP) and neonatal mortality rate, 2014 (extract)

Country	GDP (in millions of US dollars)	Neonatal mortality rate (per 1,000 live births)
United States	17,419,000	3.7
China	10,360,105	5.9
Japan	4,601,461	1.0
Germany	3,852,556	2.2
United Kingdom	2,941,886	2.5
France	2,829,192	2.3
Brazil	2,346,118	9.6
Italy	2,144,338	2.1

Note: The data were extracted in early-2017.

Source: The World Bank (datacatalog.worldbank.org) and the World Health Organization (http://apps.who.int/gho/data/node.home).

and well-being of their residents. The point is that by combining administrative data we may make them useful for studying many topics of interest to the social science community.

Here is another example, but the data are provided in a more convenient manner. Researchers at Cornell University have assembled a dataset that includes child and family data, along with several other types of data, for each state in the United States. The website http://cms.mildredwarner.org/education_data_sources describes these data and provides a link to download them as an MS Excel file. The file is separated into worksheets that contain various types of data, such as business and employment data, US Census information, and Temporary Assistance for Needy Families (TANF) data. Table 6.9 combines data from several of these worksheets and from information on infant mortality available from the Kaiser

TABLE 6.9   Child and childcare statistics, 2002 (extract)

State	Percent of children in single parent families	Median annual pay of child care workers (in dollars)	TANF spent on childcare (in 1,000 dollars)	Population under 6 years of age	Infant mortality rate
Alabama	21.0	13,850	20,816	355,598	8.6
Alaska	19.9	17,730	5,977	57,034	5.8
Arizona	19.5	15,270	44,218	456,437	5.3
Arkansas	20.8	13,710	886	217,907	7.9
California	17.1	18,880	418,921	2,989,340	4.8
Colorado	16.8	17,380	6,340	354,594	5.1

Note: TANF, Temporary Assistance to Needy Families. The data were extracted in early-2017.

Sources: Cornell Linking Economic Development and Child Care 50 State Database and Henry J. Kaiser Family Foundation.

Family Foundation (www.kff.org). Perhaps these data would be useful for studying whether states that spend less per capita on childcare and needs-based family assistance also tend to have poorer health outcomes among their children.

There are numerous other administrative datasets that may be linked to provide data for research projects. For those studying public and private organizations, these include company reports, stock market information, nonprofit company records, business licensing and performance data, tax records, legal proceeding data, and employment and payroll information. For those studying health outcomes, there are mortality and morbidity data, health insurance information, and data on the number of physicians and other health-care workers per capita. And for those examining crime and the justice system, there are numerous sources of data on crime rates, jails, prisons, probationers, and expenditures for police departments and other crime control organizations.

A drawback to linking administrative data is that it can be time-consuming to locate and combine them. Suppose a researcher wished to determine the association between neighborhood racial/ethnic segregation and housing foreclosures. Although there might US Census Bureau data on segregation—or at least ways to measure it—foreclosure information is available mainly through municipal or local government agencies. Thus, a researcher might need to spend a substantial amount of time going to websites and contacting local government offices and courts to get this information for a reasonable sample of localities (Rugh and Massey 2010). Yet, the cost in time is worth it if the research is valuable and the information is not available in any other way.

A limitation suggested earlier is that administrative data do not usually provide individual-level data or measure many interesting social and psychological concepts (Jutte et al. 2011). One way that researchers have attempted to overcome this limitation is by combining administrative data and survey data. Consider the World Values Survey (WVS; www .worldvaluessurvey.org) that began in 1981 and is conducted about every five years. This survey has collected data from samples of people in almost 100 nations. The questions address numerous issues, including families, religion, children, neighbors, gender roles, trust, and politics. Survey responses from the WVS have been combined with country-level administrative data to answer interesting research questions. For example, Filipe Campante and Davin Chor (2012) were interested in why the Arab Spring occurred. This was a series of protest movements and riots that swept through several Middle Eastern nations in 2010 and 2011. The researchers first used World Bank administrative data to show that these nations had been experiencing not only increasing levels of educational attainment, but also higher unemployment rates over the previous decade. They reasoned that this combination made better-educated people more likely to join protest movements because of their dissatisfaction with the labor market. However, the aggregate data from the World Bank were insufficient to validate this hypothesis. They then used the WVS data to determine if well-educated people are especially likely to support public demonstrations if unemployment rates are relatively high. It turns out they are, thus supporting the notion that the Arab Spring was motivated by the combination of rising levels of education but poor employment prospects.

Other researchers link survey data with administrative data by requesting that their research participants allow them access to personal information collected by health-care organizations, such as medical records, data gathered by their employers, or court records, such as those concerning divorce, adoption, or other legal proceedings. Of course, as mentioned earlier, using secondary data may make this type of linkage difficult if there are confidentiality issues that prevent disclosure of personal or geographic identifiers.

Principles of Linking Datasets

We have already discussed the importance of having a proper identification variable to merge data so that different sets of variables are available for analysis. The same principle applies to linking administrative data with other sources of data. There must be a clear way to identify the unit of observation (or multiple units in a multilevel context) in both files. The principal question to ask is whether the entities to which the data apply are actually the same: are they the same family, company, neighborhood, or county (Herzog et al. 2007)? This is usually an easy question to answer when the unit of observation is a set of countries, states, or provinces. However, it is not so simple when the units are families, neighborhoods, or companies. There may not be standard identification numbers for these entities. Defining a neighborhood is also difficult if the geographic boundaries are not clear. Families may have the same common name (Smith, Jones, Kim) and thus be difficult to distinguish. Companies may also have similar names (Roberts Brothers, Inc., and Roberts Brothers, Ltd.), although tax identification numbers, if available, are standardized in the United States. A good practice is to consider using multiple data points to try to match entities, such as addresses, products sold, or types of services rendered (Roberts Brothers, Inc., is a plumbing company, whereas Roberts Brothers, Ltd., is an accounting firm).

Even when matches are successful, there tends to be a high likelihood of data duplication or discrepancies. For example, perhaps information on a family's health insurance comes from a database compiled by the company where one of the family members is employed and a health insurance database maintained by a state regulating board. In merging the data, there may end up being two variables with the same insurance information. On the other hand, the two data sources may disagree on what insurance the family actually has. Duplications are relatively simple to handle (see chapter 4), but discrepancies are not. It is often necessary to go back to the original records, if available, to reconcile discrepant data.

Disclosure Control

As mentioned earlier, confidentiality of participant data is a key part of many research projects. In this era of big data, there is a growing concern in the research community with protecting participants from being identified. This falls under the area of *statistical disclosure control*. Disclosure is when something about a research participant that would not otherwise be known is discovered because of released data (Hundepool et al. 2012). This assumes that such discovery occurs outside of the particular research project in which the data were utilized. Although the risk of identification is low in many projects, it increases when administrative data are linked. Suppose, for instance, that data from business tax records, publicly available company reports, and a survey of each company's employees are combined into a single dataset. In the survey, some of the employees report that a company had engaged in tax evasion. They also report the type of work they do and provide other information about the work environment. Even if the employee survey is designed to keep the companies' names anonymous, a clever analyst might be able to use information from the linked tax records and the company report data to identify the specific company mentioned by the employees. Although some may think this is acceptable—after all, who supports tax evasion—it violates the tenets of good research ethics.

There are a couple of approaches that are designed to protect research participants from being identified. First, the data may be changed in slight ways so that they are not as precise but maintain their general characteristics and relations to other data. Known as the *perturbative method*, this involves complex algorithms that are difficult to program but useful to implement. Second, data may be released only in aggregate or frequency form (see table 6.2) or certain data points, such as unusual or extreme observations, are simply omitted. These are known as *nonperturbative methods* (Hundepool et al. 2012). One particular approach is to use a sorting procedure to search for and identify rare combinations of variables that might make it easier to identify particular research participants. For example, assume that a survey conducted in one city includes a participant who is a younger minority male diagnosed with a rare form of cancer. The survey data are then linked to a hospital database that includes information on cancer diagnoses. The sorting procedure would likely identify this person as rather unique in the context of the dataset. Privacy concerns might then dictate that this person's records—or others similarly identified via the sorting procedure—be excluded from any data that are made publicly available. In any event, if administrative and other types of data are linked in a research project, it is important to consider the need to protect the confidentiality of research participants. Thus, some method of disclosure control to ensure data privacy should be part of most research projects (Torra and Navarro-Arribas 2014), whether they involve primary data collection or linked administrative data.

FINAL WORDS

Given the choice, many researchers favor primary data. However, some researchers prefer secondary and administrative data since they are usually less expensive to use and can save quite a bit of time. Nonetheless, a key advantage of primary data is that they may be tailored to strictly match the goals of the research project. From the sample drawn to the instruments used, primary data are a vital part of many sound studies. Since primary data collection is the focus of most research methods class, it is not necessary to repeat the general material that is taught in these courses. Thus, this chapter addresses a few principles regarding primary data and how they are managed.

For many purposes, administrative data—especially those that can be linked—are also useful for various types of research projects. This type of data offers an excellent source of information for answering a variety of research questions (Jutte et al. 2011). Administrative data can be particularly valuable for examining broad, macro-level research questions and for comparing phenomena across counties, provinces, states, and nations.

To summarize, the principles discussed in this chapter include the following:

- Employ data quality and integrity checks as the data are being entered into a database. This includes beginning the data preprocessing steps early.
- Utilize a reliable backup system and consider an archiving plan for the data.
- Whether using primary or administrative data, establish procedures to ensure the privacy of the data so that participants cannot be identified. A statistical disclosure control plan is essential.
- If the primary data span multiple files, use a clear directory structure, ensure there is a way to link the files with precise identification variables, and understand how to merge and concatenate files.
- Use multiple codes for missing data that indicate the reason the data are missing.
- Understand data formatting. Make sure that the cases and variables are organized in a consistent and clear way. Use tidy data principles.
- Prepare a clear and informative codebook that provides information about the study and each of the variables in the dataset.
- When linking administrative datasets or administrative data to survey data, have a plan to reconcile discrepancies that may arise. Carefully determine how to define and identify the cases. Make sure that the linking variable provides a valid match for the cases in all the datasets.

One of the sad things that the social sciences teach us is that there is usually a relationship between unfortunate social conditions. For example, states with high poverty rates also tend to have problems with homelessness and poor nutrition. The following exercises are designed to allow you to practice putting together a US state-level dataset that has measures of some problems, as well as some data on health-care costs. Note that this assignment may need to be modified depending on the time it is completed since data may be updated by organizations.

1. Using spreadsheet software (e.g., Apache OpenOffice Calc, MS Excel), create a data table with the following variables:

    a. *The percentage of children in poverty by state in 2009*. The source is datacenter.kidscount. org. Select *Economic Well-Being* under *Choose a Topic*. Scrolling down, you will find an entry under Poverty called *Children in poverty (100 percent poverty)*. On this page, make sure you select *By State, 2009*, and *Percent* from the left-hand side. You will need to change the data from percentages to numbers (in other words, we cannot use data with the % symbol; for example, if the datum reads 10%, ask the software to change it to 0.10 or 10).

    b. *Health-care costs per capita by state in 2009*. The source is http://kff.org/state-category /health-costs-budgets. Select *Health Care Expenditures per Capita by State of Residence*. Place these data alongside the poverty data that you have in the data table created in 1(a). You will need to change the data from currency to numbers (in other words, we cannot use data with the $ symbol or a comma).

    c. *The homelessness rate per 10,000 population*. The source is http://kff.org/state-category /demographics-and-the-economy. Scroll down to *Change in Overall Homelessness*. The data to place in your data table are in the column titled *2014 Homeless Rate per 10,000*.

    d. *Percent meeting government recommendations of fruit and vegetable consumption*. The source is http://www.cdc.gov/mmwr/preview/mmwrhtml/mm6426a1.htm. Use the data from the columns labeled *Fruit % and Vegetables* % (don't include the other data columns from this table).

2. Label the columns with the variable names provided in exercise 3(b) below. Save the file as a *csv* file (comma delimited) and call it *StateProblems.csv*.

3. Using SPSS, Stata, or SAS, write a program file that requests the following steps:

    a. Imports the *StateProblems.csv* file into SPSS, Stata, or SAS.

    b. Provides the following variable labels:

        i.   State = Name of State
        ii. Poverty = Children in poverty
        iii. HealthcareCosts = Per capita health-care costs
        iv. HomelessRate = Number of homeless per 10,000
        v.   Fruit = Meets recommended fruit consumption
        vi. Vegetables = Meets recommended vegetable consumption

    c. Requests the means for each of the numeric variables.

    d. Requests correlations for each pair of numeric variables.

4. Consider the conceptual model shown in figure 6.E1. Using the information from the correlations computed from the data table you've built, briefly describe whether there is evidence to support the model. Don't forget to describe why you reached this conclusion.

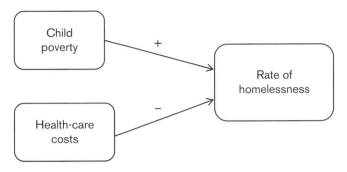

FIGURE 6.E1 Conceptual model predicting state-level rates of homelessness.

Here are a few rows of the data table that you should have created in the first part of the assignment.

State	Poverty	HealthcareCosts	HomelessRate	Fruit	Vegetables
Alabama	0.25	6,272.00	9.40	9.50	7.10
Alaska	0.13	9,128.00	24.30	13.50	10.50
Arizona	0.23	5,434.00	15.80	12.50	9.80
Arkansas	0.27	6,167.00	9.90	9.40	7.50
California	0.20	6,238.00	29.70	17.70	13.00
Colorado	0.17	5,994.00	19.00	14.10	10.10
Connecticut	0.12	8,654.00	12.40	14.80	8.70
Delaware	0.16	8,480.00	9.70	12.80	7.50
District of Columbia	0.29	10,349.00	119.90	15.20	9.20
More data should appear next					

Note: You may wish to delete the data from the District of Columbia since some of them comprise extreme observations.

SEVEN

Working with Missing Data

In 2000, the economist Paul Peterson published a research report in which he showed a positive impact of school voucher programs, especially for African-American children. School vouchers are funds provided by the government that pays for students' tuition at public and private schools. It is one of the cornerstone policies of the school choice movement: allowing parents to choose the schools their children attend rather than being assigned geographically. In any event, Peterson's research indicated that using vouchers improved the test scores among minority youth who had traditionally been underserved by the public education system. However, once the data used in his research were released, another economist, Paul Krueger, found that vouchers did not have an effect on test scores among any group. Digging deep into the data, Krueger discovered that the test scores of 292 African-American students were missing from Peterson's analysis, thus leading to the invalid conclusion that vouchers had a positive impact (Winerip 2003).

The medical field continues to be concerned with finding a way to prevent the transmission of the human immunodeficiency virus (HIV). Although HIV infection is not implicated in as many deaths annually as other health problems such as heart disease and lung cancer, it has still resulted in almost 40 million deaths worldwide, with an estimated 78 million people infected. The emphasis on finding a preventative has motivated hundreds of HIV prevention trials at the cost of millions of dollars. In 2012, the statistician Ofer Harel and his colleagues examined 57 of these trials and found that all of them had some data missing. They note, though, that few of the published reports of these trials said anything about how the missing data were treated in the analyses. According to Harel and his associates, this casts doubt on many of the findings: "the fact that approximately 88% of the studies reported possibly biased results is alarming" (Harel et al. 2012, 1391). These researchers also provide a pithy statement that is worth remembering: "Not thinking of the missing data problem does not mean the problem goes away" (1391).

One of the biggest challenges when collecting and managing data—whether they are quantitative or qualitative—involves what to do when data are missing. As they fill out questionnaires, for example, some research participants may not respond to certain questions. In open-ended interviews, respondents might refuse to answer questions about sensitive topics, such as sexual behaviors, illegal activities, or even their income. In chapters 4 and 6, we briefly discussed missing data, in particular how codes for missing data should be listed in codebooks and that researchers often need to assign particular symbols, such as periods, to the missing values of variables so that software recognizes them as such. In this chapter, we learn more about missing data, including the most common reasons data are missing, some types of missing data, and some methods designed to compensate for missing data prior to, or during, the analysis stage of a research project. The material presented here is at a slightly higher level than the material presented in other chapters. For those with little training in statistics, focusing on the first three sections may be most useful.

WHY ARE MISSING DATA A PROBLEM?

Most datasets, especially those that are based on surveys of people, include some missing data. These can occur for a number of reasons and most researchers wish to avoid them. But why are missing data a problem? Recall from elementary statistics and research methods that one of the goals of using a sample is to make inferences to a broader target population. External validity concerns the degree to which the results of a study can be applied to other situations or other people. External validity and our ability to infer to a target population may be compromised when data are missing, especially when they are missing more often for a particular group of people. For example, if older people in a survey are less likely than younger people to complete a questionnaire, it becomes difficult to compare older and younger people on some phenomenon of interest.

Moreover, from elementary statistics you may recall the issue of *statistical power*: the probability of detecting an association if there really is an association. In terms of hypothesis testing, this is the probability of rejecting the null hypothesis (H_0) when it is truly false. Statistical power depends on the size and the representativeness of the sample (Kraemer and Blasey 2016). When data are missing—especially when there is something systematic about why they are missing—statistical power is compromised and the validity of the study's conclusions are at risk.

REASONS FOR MISSING DATA

Data are missing for a variety of reasons. A common reason in survey research is that many projects in the social and behavioral sciences ask about sensitive topics or potentially embarrassing information. Many participants are uncomfortable answering inquiries about their sex lives or drug use. They may be concerned with the information getting out and revealing something they wish to keep secret about their lives. However, even well-designed experiments can suffer from missing data problems, such as when participants drop out of research projects that include follow-up data collection. There is actually a vibrant area of research that tries to solve the problem of missing data during the data collection stage. This includes a concern with how to ask questions or what data collection methods are best for gathering complete data. For example, is it better to have an interviewer fill in an answer sheet that is designed to elicit information about illegal behaviors or should participants fill in answers on a computer screen that only they can see? Studies indicate that the latter is better at minimizing missing and invalid data (Tourangeau and Yan 2007). In addition, what are the best ways to collect follow-up data? There is often a concern with locating research participants who may have moved or otherwise dropped out of a study.

But, in addition to sensitivity and embarrassment or dropout, there are several other reasons that data are invalid or missing. These include the following:

- Those responding to questions misunderstand the questions;
- They cannot retrieve the necessary information from their minds, such as when they cannot remember whether or when some event occurred or don't know how much money they made in the last month;
- They inaccurately estimate an answer, such as when they say they made $1,000 in the last month, but they really only made $800; or
- They have a difficult time figuring out how their answer matches a response option on a survey instrument (the question's responses include only "agree" and "disagree," yet a participant genuinely doesn't know; Tourangeau et al. 2000).

Some of these may result in missing data, whereas others lead to data errors. Which one of these occurs depends largely on characteristics of the research setting and how an instrument is administered. For instance, as the time to complete a questionnaire grows longer, participants are more likely to get tired and inaccuracies or simple refusals and omissions tend to increase. This is why it is imperative that instruments are pretested not only for content, but also for length. As mentioned in chapter 6, it is also important to identify the reason the data are missing with specific codes, such as "participant refused" or "legitimate skip." As we will learn later, most solutions proposed for missing data depend on understanding the cause and patterns of the "missingness."

TYPES OF MISSING DATA

As already suggested, there are several ways to categorize missing data. Here, we review two general ways. First, missing may be identified broadly by when they occur. This includes the following four situations.

Unit Nonresponse or Unit Missing Data

Potential research participants refuse to join the research project or they change their minds after initially agreeing to participate. One of the main problems with this type of missing data occurs when researchers wish to draw a random sample from some target population, but a subsample of people do not participate. When this subsample is not itself a random group from the original sample drawn, then problems arise. As suggested earlier, in this situation the external validity of the study is undermined. Say, for example, that a researcher has a list of people attending a Comic Con event (for convenience, we'll characterize this as a "population"). She wishes to draw a random sample to conduct a study that compares how many sessions of the conference males and females attend. However, a larger proportion of males than females refuses to participate because, if they do, they might miss some sessions! In other words, those who refuse are more likely to be males and more likely to attend the most sessions. This makes the results of the study suspect: they may not be as representative of males as of females.

Item Nonresponse or Missing Values

This occurs when participants refuse or forget to answer particular questions on a questionnaire or during an interview. Or they may give bad information intentionally and the data they provide cannot be used. Some of the issues discussed in the last section address this problem. For example, participants might skip an item accidently, not want to tell you something about their lives—such as how often they litter or cheat—or get tired of answering questions. Some participants might even get bored with the questions and thus provide some outlandish response or refuse to provide any more answers. Item nonresponse can also be caused by data entry problems, which are less likely now that computerized administration of survey instruments is so common.

Missing data due to item nonresponse create problems when using the data to estimate statistics, such as means or correlations. Suppose, for example, that a researcher conducts a small study to try to figure out the mean grade point average (GPA) among social work majors at his university. He gets a list of all social work majors, draws a random sample, and sends each of the sampled students an Internet survey that asks a few questions about their school experiences and their grades. One of the questions asks simply for their GPAs at the end of the previous semester. Table 7.1 provides the responses of each student to the GPA question, as well as their true GPA according to transcript data. Note the discrepancy.

Similar to extreme observations (see chapter 4), missing data can cause misleading conclusions to be drawn from the data analysis. In fact, the type of example provided in table 7.1 occurs all too often. People responding to survey questions who are on the "low end" of some well-known scale—such as GPA, income, or volunteering in the community—are more likely than others to not answer. This can also happen on the high end, such as when wealthy people are uncomfortable divulging their net worth. Or research participants may provide what they consider to be socially acceptable answers, such as that they volunteered more often than they actually did. This is known as *social desirability bias*. What should the researcher do in

TABLE 7.1 Reported and actual GPAs

Student	Reported GPA	Actual GPA
Jessie	3.2	3.2
Pamela	3.7	3.7
Robbie	2.8	2.8
Cassie	2.6	2.6
Chris	Refused	1.9
Average	3.08	2.84

these situations? In the GPA example, one solution to the refusal issue is to find another student for the sample through a random selection process. However, for many studies this is not feasible and researchers have to search for other ways to compensate for missing data.

A common problem in the social sciences that is difficult to address involves inquiries into personal income. Of course, some people do not have an income. However, as suggested earlier, questions about income, though they may not appear to involve a sensitive topic, tend to generate an inordinate amount of missing data. A perusal of various datasets based on surveys shows that missing values from income questions are frequent, with usually more than 10% of respondents refusing to answer. Yet many researchers are interested in the association between income and a host of concepts. Is it worth it to lose 10% of a sample so that income may be considered in a statistical model? Are people who refuse to answer income questions different from those who do answer? If they are systematically different, then the sample used in an analysis that omits them may no longer be a representative sample of a target population. In any event, it is important to pay close attention to questions and variables that involve participants' incomes. This is vital during the data collection, data management, and data analysis stages of a research project.

Missing Due to Follow-Up or Missing Wave Data

Assuming a longitudinal study design, people are initially part of a study and provide information at one time, but when they are asked to participate in a follow-up portion of the study, they refuse. A similar problem occurs when participants cannot be located, such as when they move or drop out of school, or are no longer available to participate in the study due to death, illness, or disability. This is also known as *loss to follow-up*. It is especially problematic when the reason for the loss is related to the phenomenon the study is designed to investigate.

Say that a researcher is trying to determine if participating in local government is associated with greater happiness. The conceptual model is shown in figure 7.1.

The researcher takes a random sample of community members and asks about their participation on local committees and boards, in elections, and so forth. One year later, she tries to ask the same group of people about their happiness. However, those who were not as involved in local government were more likely to have moved, but they are happier on average

FIGURE 7.1 Local government participation and happiness.

than those who were not involved and stayed. Think about what would happen to the presumed association between the variables that measure these concepts.

Missing Due to Design

Missing data might be generated because of the way the instrument is constructed. A common way this occurs in questionnaires involves skip patterns (see table 4.3 for an example). Skip patterns are a convenient way to make responding more efficient. For instance, suppose a researcher asks a sample of adolescents to fill out a questionnaire about their use of cigarettes. The questions ask details such as how often they smoke, how many cigarettes they smoke in a day or a week, from where do they obtain cigarettes, and so forth. A majority of adolescents don't smoke at all, so it is common to find initial questions such as the following:

Q1. Have you ever smoked cigarettes? (*circle one answer only*)
    a) No   [Go to question Q16]
    b) Yes   [Go to question Q2]

Q2. When was the last time you smoked a cigarette? (*circle one answer only*)
    a) Today
    b) In the last week
    c) More than a week ago but less than a month ago
    d) A month ago or longer

In contemporary surveys, these types of questions are often programmed into a computer so that those responding "no" to the first question are automatically asked question Q6 next.

The researcher might wish to examine responses to the second question, perhaps to determine how many adolescents have smoked in the last week. She could analyze data only from those who actually answered the question or from all of those in the sample. This is an essential issue to address since those who answered "no" to the first question are, to be specific, "missing" on the second question. If she decides to include those who never smoked in the analysis, then it is a simple matter to create a new variable that includes a code for "never smoked" along with others for those who smoked in the last day, week, or month. However, this type of skip sequence may still present a problem in a statistical analysis. Imagine that the researcher wishes to predict who smoked in the past week. So she compares some social and behavioral characteristics of those who smoked in the past week to those who did not.

But there are now three groups inherent in this analysis: (a) those who have never smoked, (b) those who have smoked but not in the past week, and (c) those who smoked in the past week. Problems arise when there are systematic differences between groups (a) and (b) since they are often lumped together during the analysis into a *did not smoke in the last week* category. This is known as a *selection issue*—there is a systematic but undetermined process that leads people to smoke or not smoke cigarettes—but it is beyond the scope of this presentation (see Remler and Van Ryzin 2015, chapter 11).

FORMS AND PATTERNS OF MISSING DATA

A second way to classify missing data is to consider how they are related to patterns of data and relationships among variables in a dataset. There are three general categories of missing data from this perspective (Little and Rubin 2014).

Missing Completely at Random

In this situation, the chance that a particular observation is missing is not related in a systematic way to the variable it is part of nor to the other variables under consideration. Consider a variable that measures happiness. Imagine that Julie, one of the research participants, does not answer the happiness question because she accidently skipped over it. Another participant, Fred, also did not answer this question because he was tired. An important issue is whether Julie's and Fred's other answers are related in some systematic way to the fact that they skipped the happiness question. Another question is whether Julie and Fred are more likely than other participants to have low or high happiness. In general terms, is the missing information on happiness related in a systematic way to responses to other questions or to the way the happiness variable is distributed? If those missing on happiness are, in general, just as likely to report being happy or unhappy as others in the study, then we may say that the missing data on happiness are random. Moreover, suppose that a researcher is interested in the association between happiness and grades in school. As long as missing data on happiness are not systematically related to grades in school, the missing data are random. When both of these conditions are met, we may claim that the data are missing completely at random (MCAR).

Problems arise when the missing data are systematically related to the variable to which they apply and to other variables. Recall an earlier statement that missing data on income are sometimes likely to come from wealthier people. Thus, the condition of "missingness" is related to the way income is distributed: wealth is positively related to the probability of a missing value. Furthermore, if a researcher is studying the association between income and, say, happiness, then, if there is truly an association, the missing data will likely affect the results of the analysis.

Missing at Random

Missing data may not be MCAR, but still be considered random in some sense. Data are considered as missing at random (MAR) if the "missingness" does not depend on the value of the variable that includes missing data after statistically adjusting for another variable. This can be quite complicated, however. Think about a study in which a researcher is interested in depression. Suppose people who are depressed are less inclined to report their income. In this situation, we would find that depression and the probability of having a missing value on income are positively related. Suppose, further, that depressed people, on average, have lower incomes than other people. In other words, there tends to be a high rate of missing data among depressed people and they tend to have lower incomes. In an analysis, the estimated average income is affected by the missing data on income: it will be lower than the actual average income. However, if, *within the depressed respondents*, the probability of reported income is unrelated to income level, then the data would be considered MAR, though not MCAR. In other words, if we take only those with depression and examine all their actual income levels, we would find that those with lower incomes are not more likely to have missing values than those with higher incomes. It should be clear that establishing MAR is challenging.

Missing Not at Random

If data are not MAR or completely at random, then they are classified as missing not at random (MNAR). Some observers call this *nonignorable missingness*. For example, if in a study of mental health people who have been diagnosed as depressed are less likely than others to report their mental status, the data are not MAR. When the data are MNAR, there is a serious problem. The only way to obtain accurate statistics, such as means or correlations, is to determine the "missingness" process. In other words, the researcher needs to determine how to predict when the data are missing and incorporate this into any analysis that uses the variables with missing data. This can entail a complex set of analytical steps.

A simple example is to imagine that, in a study of cigarette smokers, males with high education are less likely to answer a question that asks if they smoke. Moreover, even within smoking levels—such as daily smokers and weekend smokers—the more frequent smokers are less likely to answer the question about smoking. This is an MNAR situation that makes it difficult to predict who smokes. However, if the researcher can figure out how to predict who will be missing on the smoking questions —such as by noticing that highly educated males tend to be missing—then there are methods to compensate for the missing data and come up with a good predictive model of who smokes cigarettes. Methods of dealing with MNAR data are beyond the scope of this presentation, but Allison (2001, 2016) and Graham (2009) provide good overviews and advice.

ADDRESSING MISSING DATA IN THE ANALYSIS STAGE

As mentioned earlier, it is important to consider missing data at all phases of the research process, including the data collection, data management, and data analysis stages. We have already discussed—albeit briefly—minimizing missing data during data collection and how the instrument and the conditions of its administration are important. Chapters 4 and 6 also include recommendations regarding how to code missing data and the importance of distinguishing reasons the data are missing. This section concerns how to address missing data during the analysis stage. Unfortunately, the simplest methods are also the least accurate methods (Johnson and Young 2011). The state-of-the-art methods can be quite complicated to explain, yet are not too difficult to execute assuming the right statistical software is available.

There are several methods for dealing with missing data in the analysis stage (Widaman 2006). Most of these are called *imputation procedures* since they entail imputing or replacing missing values with some other values. Before describing some of these, consider the data in the following table. These are an excerpt from a US state-level dataset with various economic, crime, and suicide variables. The first dataset, called *USDataAll*, includes all the data, with no missing values. The second, called *USDataMiss*, includes a few missing values for three of the variables: robberies per 100,000, suicides per 100,000, and the unemployment rate. For instance, notice that, in the second panel of the table, robberies are missing for Alaska and the unemployment rate is missing for Arkansas. In the full dataset, there are other data points missing as well. Since the following methods should be used specifically for MCAR and MAR data, we will treat the missing values in the *USDataMiss* dataset as following one of these patterns.

US state-level data, 2005					
State	Robberies per 100,000	Suicides per 100,000	Unemployment rate	Gross state product	Poverty rate
Complete data (USDataAll)					
Alabama	185.75	12.1	5.1	.95	16.35
Alaska	155.13	17.1	7.8	.24	9.37
Arizona	173.76	17.5	5.5	1.04	14.45
Arkansas	125.68	14.1	5.4	.53	17.22
California	331.16	11.1	7.2	9.13	12.93
Colorado	96.18	16.4	4.2	1.08	11.63
Connecticut	163.21	9.2	5.7	1.19	8.46
Delaware	198.74	9.9	8.5	.27	10.24
Florida	299.91	13.4	5.1	3.39	12.88
Data with missing values (USDataMiss)					
Alabama	185.75	12.1	5.1	.95	16.35
Alaska	.	17.1	7.8	.24	9.37
Arizona	173.76	17.5	5.5	1.04	14.45
Arkansas	125.68	14.1	.	.53	17.22
California	331.16	11.1	7.2	9.13	12.93
Colorado	96.18	16.4	4.2	1.08	11.63
Connecticut	163.21	9.2	5.7	1.19	8.46
Delaware	198.74	9.9	8.5	.27	10.24
Florida	299.91	13.4	5.1	3.39	12.88

Logical Inference

Sometimes missing data can be replaced logically during the data management phase of a project (see chapter 4). For example, suppose that a female research participant did not answer a question about whether or not she had ever given birth. But her response to a later question indicated that she lived with her three biological children (not stepchildren or adopted children). In this situation, it is sensible to replace the missing code for the first question with the response "yes." The skip patterns discussed earlier may also allow logical inference. If a person has a missing value for "ever smoked cigarettes," but a responds with "smoked a cigarette in the last week," then it is logical to infer that the missing value code should be replaced with a "yes" code.

Listwise Deletion (also Called Casewise Deletion)

This is the default method used by most statistical software, including Stata, SPSS, and SAS. As shown in the data table above, Alaska has a missing code for robberies in the second panel, but it is not missing on the other variables. In an analysis that examined the correlation between robberies and unemployment, Alaska would be removed from consideration since it is missing on one of the variables. Thus, listwise deletion is also called *complete case analysis* since it includes only those cases with no missing data on the variables in the analysis. A key problem occurs when there are missing values for several variables and all are used in an analysis. In this situation, the number of cases can decrease by quite a bit. However, even though this may occur, it does not lead to invalid statistics assuming that the data are MCAR. If they are not, though, then the results will likely be incorrect (Allison 2001).

The correlation between robberies and unemployment is 0.35 in the full dataset and 0.32 in the dataset with missing values (using Stata's *corr*, SPSS's *correlations*, or SAS's *proc corr* command). Given this difference, might the missing data be something other than MCAR? If they are, then listwise deletion is not a wise choice. What additional analyses might be useful to test whether the missing values are MCAR? Attempting to answer this question is a useful exercise. For more advanced readers, search for documentation on the user-written Stata command *mcartest*, SPSS's *mva* command, or R's *LittleMCAR* option; each is designed to test whether missing data are MCAR.

Mean, Median, or Mode Substitution

Just as the name implies, this method replaces the missing values with the mean, median, or mode of the variable. The choice of which statistic to use depends on the type of variable. Continuous variables are replaced with the mean and categorical variables (or skewed continuous variables) with the median or mode. In the data in the table given earlier, this would entail replacing the missing values of robbery with the value 152.70, the missing values of suicide with 12.45, and the missing values of unemployment with 5.21. The code provided in chapter 4 that involves replacing values using, for instance, the *recode* command in Stata or SPSS, is useful for this purpose. In the SAS software, a simple *if-then* statement suffices.

Notice that the SPSS command *rmv (replace missing values)* generates a new variable that replaces the missing values with the mean, or *series mean (smean)*, of the variable.

Unfortunately, mean, median, or mode substitution is almost never suitable as a way to deal with missing data. One of the consequences is that they reduce the variability of the variable so that the standard deviation is smaller than it otherwise would be. For example, the standard deviation of robberies in the complete dataset is 100.3, whereas its standard deviation in the missing dataset when mean imputation is utilized is 97.0. These substitution methods can also cause problems for various statistical procedures, such as correlations and regression analyses. Thus, most experts recommend against their use.

Regression Substitution

This method develops a prediction model based on several other variables to predict some variable with missing data. It then uses the predicted values from this model to impute the missing data. Suppose we use the two variables that have no missing data, gross state product (GSP) and poverty rate, to predict robberies using a linear regression model. This implies the following equation:

robberies = $\alpha + \beta_1$ (GSP) + β_2 (poverty rate).

You might recall that α is the *y*-intercept and βs are called *regression slopes*. In any event, the observations of robbery that are not missing are predicted with this equation, but the intercept and slopes are then used to predict robberies for those observations where it is missing. For example, in the *USDataMiss* dataset the prediction equation for Alaska is

robberies = 101.8 + 37.67(0.24) − 0.71(9.37) = 104.18.

The numbers in parentheses are simply Alaska's values for GSP and unemployment. The value 104.18 replaces the missing value for Alaska robberies. In Stata, we do not have to construct a regression model directly; rather, a command called *impute* will do the work for us:

Regression substitution for missing data

```
* Stata

impute robberies gsprod povertyRate, generate(robberiesImputed)
/* creating a new variable is required */
```

In SPSS and SAS, a couple of steps are needed to perform regression substitution. However, this method for replacing missing data is not much better than mean substitution. In particular, it often overcompensates by creating a situation where statistically predicting some variable such as robberies, perhaps by relying on correlations, becomes overly precise.

A similar method is known as *stochastic regression substitution*. It is similar to the method just described except it adds a little bit of random variation to the imputed variable (*stochastic* is a synonym for *random*). This is supposed to reduce the tendency of regression substitution to overcompensate for patterns of missing data. We will see a preferred alternative to this method a bit later.

Hot Deck Imputation

This was a method used for many years by the US Census Bureau and many large survey firms. In fact, it was the subject of a lawsuit filed with the US Supreme Court by the State of Utah. Utah's representatives argued that the hot deck method—which was used to impute missing data in the 2000 census—resulted in an undercount of Utah's population, thus leading it to be underrepresented in its allotted number of congressional seats (Utah lost the case; see *Utah v. Evans*, 536 U.S. 452, 2002).

Hot deck imputation is based on the idea that people or other units (states, companies) that share many observed characteristics probably share others, too. So, if a value is missing for an observation, the hot deck algorithm looks for similar observations on a number of other variables and randomly selects a value from among these similar observations. For instance, in the state-level dataset, it might look for states with a similar pattern on the other variables as Alaska and then choose the robbery values for one of these states as the value for Alaska. There are user-written commands in Stata (type `findit hotdeck` in Stata's command window) and SPSS (Myers 2011) that will perform this type of missing data imputation. The SAS software has a procedure known as *SurveyImpute* that includes hot deck imputation. There is also a package called *HotDeckImpution* in R. However, it is no longer the preferred approach that it once was since, like some of the other methods described so far, it results in less variability in the target variable and leads to incorrect measures of association (Engels and Diehr 2003).

Maximum Likelihood Estimation

This is one of the two methods for missing data that are considered state of the art (Johnson and Young 2011). However, it is also probably the most difficult to understand without a good grounding in probability theory and statistics. In its most basic sense, maximum likelihood estimation (MLE) involves coming up with a statistical model that makes the patterns found in the data most likely. Say, for example, that I flip a coin 10 times and find that heads come up 3 times. If asked what the *most likely* probability of a head when a coin is flipped, I would have to respond 0.30 (or 30% of the time heads came up). Other probabilities—such as 0.2 or 0.4—would be less likely. Of course, we typically have other information with which to make such a judgment, but, in this crude statistical exercise, it turns out the *maximum likelihood*, or most likely value for the probability, is 0.3.

This is a simple example of a much more intricate undertaking. In the MLE approach to missing data, an algorithm finds the most likely pattern in the data irrespective of the missing data. The missing data are treated as another part of the statistical model to be estimated. A common algorithm used in missing data analysis is called the *expectation-maximization (EM) algorithm*. This involves a two-step interactive process that first develops a regression equation to impute the missing values (much like the regression substitution technique described earlier) and then uses a formula to fill in the missing data. It then returns to the first step and does the process again. The steps are repeated until a satisfactory solution is reached. This is an overly simplified description of a complex algorithm. Suffice it to say that MLE with the EM algorithm is an approach well suited to many datasets that have MCAR or MAR missing data problems (Allison 2012). Those interested in learning more about MLE for missing data may wish to consult Allison (2001) or Little and Rubin (2014).

The following shows how to estimate the means of some variables using MLE with the *USDataMiss* dataset. In Stata, the steps are different because we use a particular statistical technique called *structural equation modeling (sem)* to request the appropriate missing data method and compute the means. Whereas the SPSS and SAS routines use the EM algorithm, Stata uses another approach called *Full Information Maximum Likelihood* (FIML).

Multiple Imputation

This method combines a couple of different ideas about how to treat missing data. First, recall that regression substitution used a prediction equation to predict the variable that included missing data with some other variables. The stochastic regression version of this added a little random variation to compensate because regression substitution tends to make things overly precise. Multiple imputation (MI) uses a variation of stochastic regression as one part of its implementation. The second idea is that a single imputation model is unlikely to identify the different ways that data can be missing in a large set of variables. Thus, it is better to impute missing data multiple times in order to get a more accurate depiction of how missing data are generated. MI uses a type of the stochastic regression approach to come up with multiple imputed variables. Researchers using this technique then combine information from these multiple variables to compute statistics, such as means or correlations. Thus, here are the three steps used in MI:

1. Impute, or fill in, the missing values of the dataset, not once, but as many times as requested (as often as 25 times in some studies). This step results in a certain number of complete datasets.

2. Run the data analysis, such as computing means or correlations, with each dataset.

3. Combine the results of the analyses into a final result. There are rules that are followed to combine them, usually by taking the average of the separate results (Graham 2009).

MI has become so popular that most statistical software has specialized commands for it. Stata has a set of commands under its *mi* option, SPSS has a `multiple imputation` command, and, as shown in the previous example, SAS has a `proc mi` command. There are even standalone software programs that specialize in MI (see the list on the website http://www.stefvanbuuren.nl/mi/Software.html). There are several helpful online videos that show how to use MI in various statistical software packages.

In the following example, Stata, SPSS, and SAS are utilized to conduct an MI analysis with the *USDataMiss* dataset. As with the MLE example, our goal is simply to compute the means for the three variables that have missing data. We'll keep it simple by requesting only five imputed datasets, although it is easy to request more.

Multiple imputation (MI) for missing data

```
* Stata

set seed 5544     /* set a random seed so we may reproduce if needed */

mi set wide       /* tells Stata there are missing data */

mi register imputed robberies suicides unemploy     /* identifies the variables
                                                       with missing data */

mi impute mvn robberies suicides unemploy = gsprod povertyRate, add(5)
  /* requests 5 imputed datasets with add(5) subcommand */

mi estimate: mean robberies suicides unemploy /* requests means */
```

```
* SPSS

/* set a random seed so we may reproduce if needed */
set seed 5544 .

/* tell SPSS to create a new dataset .
/* from the dataset in active memory .
dataset declare mi_spss .

/* set up imputation model that requests 5 imputed datasets .
multiple imputation robberies suicides unemploy gsprod povertyRate
  /impute method=auto nimputations=5 maxpctmissing=none
  /constraints gsprod(role=ind)
  /constraints povertyRate(role=ind)
  /missingsummaries none
  /imputationsummaries models descriptives
  /outfile imputations=mi_spss .

/* open imputed dataset and request means .
dataset activate mi_spss .
descriptives variables = robberies suicides unemploy .
```

```
* SAS

/* the random seed is set within the command structure */
/* 5 imputed datasets are requested with the nimpute subcommand */
proc mi data=USDataMiss seed=5544 nimpute=5;
 var robberies suicides unemploy gsprod povertyRate;
run;
```

TABLE 7.2   Comparison of means from USDataAll and USDataMiss using MLE and MI

	Complete dataset	Stata		SPSS		SAS	
		MLE	MI	MLE	MI	MLE	MI
Robberies	152.70	149.10	151.60	149.09	147.33	149.10	152.16
Suicides	12.45	12.46	12.53	12.46	12.37	12.46	12.50
Unemployment	5.21	5.24	5.25	5.24	5.25	5.24	5.24

Note: MLE = maximum likelihood estimation; MI = multiple imputation.

Table 7.2 provides the means based on the complete dataset and those from the MLE and MI methods that used the *USDataMiss* dataset.

The means for *robberies* from the MI method in Stata and SAS are quite close to the actual mean in the full dataset. In addition, the means for *suicides* from the MLE method are almost identical to the actual mean. There is some variation across methods, though. This demonstrates that, even with sophisticated software, obtaining an accurate depiction of the actual mean from a complete dataset is not an easy task. Statistics is an uncertain sport and the notion of random variation implies that a high degree of accuracy is difficult to obtain. Nonetheless, the precision of the means estimated by both of these methods would probably please most researchers.

FINAL WORDS

Missing data are ubiquitous. Almost any dataset contains some missing data, especially when the data are from surveys or administrative sources. This is simply a condition that the social and behavioral sciences must live with. However, there are now sophisticated ways to deal with missing data that are within reach of most who are even modestly proficient with statistical software. Although this chapter has addressed only some basic principles and methods when confronted with missing data, this topic is a whole discipline unto itself and a single chapter cannot do it justice. Nonetheless, one thing to remember is that the type of missing data has important consequences for how the data are analyzed and what method is used to compensate for the incomplete data. The methods provided in this chapter focus on data that are MCAR or MAR. However, when data are systematically missing—when they are not MAR—then there are additional complications that require careful thought and the utilization of complex methods (Allison 2016; Graham 2009).

The following exercises use the data file *citydata.cvs* to consider some issues with missing data. The data are from US cities in the 1930s. The file is available on the book's website (www.ucpress.edu /go/datamanagement). There is also a text file, *citydata.txt*, that provides some additional information about the dataset, including the variable labels. The missing data for each variable are designated with a blank, rather than a number or symbol. Make sure that these missing data are read into the software correctly.

1. Write a program file (choose Stata, SAS, or SPSS) that completes the following steps:
   a. Reads the data file *citydata.csv*.
   b. Provides variable labels for each variable in the dataset.
   c. Creates a new variable called *CirrhosisMean* that uses mean substitution to impute the missing values for the variable *cirrhosis*.
   d. Creates a new variable called *CirrhosisMedian* that uses median substitution to impute the missing values for the variable *cirrhosis*.
   e. Creates a new variable called *SuicidesRegress* that uses regression substitution to impute the missing values for the variable *suicides*. Use the following variables as predictors in the regression model: *borninstate* and *popgrowth*.
   f. Requests descriptive statistics (means, standard deviations, minimum and maximum values) for the following variables: *church, cirrhosis, CirrhosisMean, CirrhosisMedian, suicides,* and *SuicidesRegress*.
   g. Uses MI to create 10 imputations for the variable *church*.
   h. Requests the mean of the multiply imputed version of the variable *church*.

2. After making sure the program file runs correctly, compare the means and standard deviations of the variables when there is missing data with those from their imputed versions. How do they compare? What limitations might there be to using the imputed versions of these variables?

3. Generate histograms or kernel density plots that compare the variables and their imputed versions (with the exception of the *church* variable). What do these suggest about how mean, median, or regression substitution affects the distribution of variables. (Hint: you may need to use the file generated by steps (a)–(f) rather than the MI file for this exercise. Thus, you should be prepared to run the program file more than once.)

EIGHT

Principles of Data Presentation

Perhaps the most famous nurse of the nineteenth century was Florence Nightingale. Born in Italy to a wealthy British family, she was trained as a nurse—against her parents' wishes—in Germany. While in her early 30s, she was asked by the British government to organize a team of nurses to care for sick and wounded soldiers fighting in the Crimean War (1853–1856). Upon arriving, she and her colleagues were horrified at the unsanitary conditions at the army base hospital. Nightingale quickly moved to clean the hospital and took care of hundreds of patients, carrying her celebrated lamp in the evening hours. Although she is most famous for her medical work during the Crimean War, she was also a methodical and skilled user of data. In particular, she assembled reams of data to show that soldiers were at risk of dying even during peacetime, due largely to the unsanitary conditions many lived under. Although her data were impressive and persuasive, she realized that bureaucrats and political leaders would not wish to study tables of information on health conditions. Thus, she cleverly devised more visually accessible ways to show them important findings regarding health problems. One of these visual techniques was called a *coxcomb*, which was a variation on the pie chart that had been developed several decades earlier by the Englishman William Playfair. Nightingale's coxcomb showed the year with circles and the pie slices or wedges as months. The larger slices indicated a greater number of deaths (Rehmeyer 2008). This coxcomb is presented in figure 8.1.

Note that the number of deaths decreased from 1854–1855 to 1855–1856, thus showing the salutary effects of improved sanitary conditions. Nightingale also used other graphical methods, such as bar charts, to demonstrate differences in death rates between soldiers and civilians. Although her coxcomb and other methods had some flaws (Wainer 2009), they

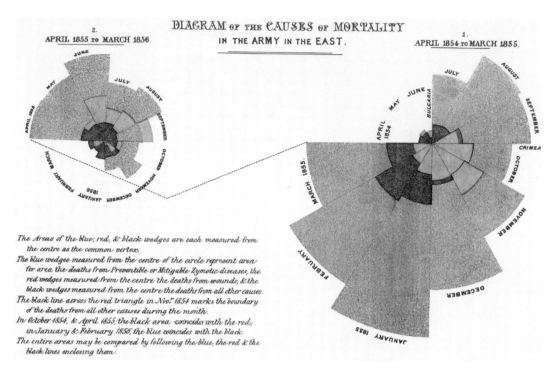

DIAGRAM of the CAUSES of MORTALITY
IN THE ARMY IN THE EAST.

2.
APRIL 1855 to MARCH 1856.

1.
APRIL 1854 to MARCH 1855.

The Areas of the blue, red, & black wedges are each measured from the centre as the common vertex.
The blue wedges measured from the centre of the circle represent area for area the deaths from Preventible or Mitigable Zymotic diseases, the red wedges measured from the centre the deaths from wounds, & the black wedges measured from the centre the deaths from all other causes.
The black line across the red triangle in Nov.r 1854 marks the boundary of the deaths from all other causes during the month.
In October 1854, & April 1855, the black area coincides with the red; in January & February 1856, the blue coincides with the black.
The entire areas may be compared by following the blue, the red & the black lines enclosing them.

FIGURE 8.1 Florence Nightingale's coxcomb.

still represent notable achievements in the history of data presentation. But can you think of alternative ways to present Ms. Nightingale's data?

The discipline of epidemiology largely began with the English physician John Snow, who was a contemporary of Florence Nightingale. But he began as a medical rebel because he thought that cholera, a deadly disease, was spread in the water supply rather than through the air. During an 1854 epidemic in London, he put his theory to the test. Snow utilized a variety of data to figure out how and to whom cholera was spread. His most famous data tool was a map of the area of London hardest hit by the epidemic (see figure 8.2). Not only did he place marks where cholera deaths occurred, but he also identified where water pumps were located. The map showed that the deaths clustered around pumps that drew water down river from where London's sewage was dumped. In particular, the Broad Street pump—circled in figure 8.2—was in an area with more deaths than in other areas (see the relatively long black bar the drops down from Broad Street). Snow convinced city officials to remove the handle from that pump and the epidemic subsided. Although we now know that cholera is caused by the waterborne bacterium *Vibrio cholerae*, it took a clever man presenting data in a creative way to save many lives from a deadly disease (Hempel 2007). Are there other ways you can think of to present Dr. Snow's data?

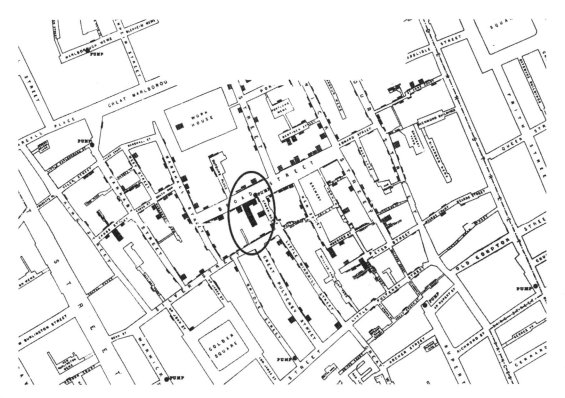

FIGURE 8.2 John Snow's London Cholera Map (1854).

Thus far, we have been concerned with developing research questions and acquiring data with which to examine these questions. There are several steps to take before the data are ready to be analyzed and presented—many of these are described in chapters 3, 4, and 7. The next step is to (1) recall your training in statistical analysis so that you may determine some ways to examine the data to see what answers they reveal for the research question and (2) consider ways to present the data and the results of the analysis to your audience. Since we presume that you are already well situated to take the first step, this and the next two chapters focus on the second step. This is because, as suggested in the Preface, data presentation is often not emphasized sufficiently in courses on the research process.

PRESENTING DATA

Data may be presented using a variety of techniques. And, given the abundance of data available, it is not surprising that they have been presented in some useful and not-so-useful ways (Wainer 2005, 2009). Pick up any newspaper or magazine, browse online images, or peruse government reports and you will likely find various forms of data presentation. Although some ways of presenting data are better than others, it is as much an art as a science to figure out the best methods for data presentation. It takes a mix of creativity, experience, and technical skills—along with good data—to determine the clearest route to reach an audience and communicate research findings.

To keep things simple, it is first important to make a distinction between two general categories of data presentation: *tables* and *graphics*. In the sciences, graphics are often referred to as *figures* and are further classified into *charts*, *graphs*, and *plots*, but may also include maps, diagrams, schematics, illustrations, and photographs. A term for these various types that is gaining in popularity is *data* or *information visualization (Infovis)*. However, the latter term is frequently used to denote a branch of computer science and design that deals with creating eye-catching images to get the viewer's attention (Gelman and Unwin 2013). Here, data visualization is simply a convenient term for the process of using a visual image to represent the results of an analysis. In general, the graphics discussed in this chapter are intended to provide visual depictions of data using symbolic representations. The representations appear in the form of bars, lines, points, or other geometric shapes. Data presented using graphics are contrasted to tables: the arrangement of data into rows and columns. Earlier chapters include several examples of tables. Moreover, chapter 4 includes two graphics, a box plot and a scatter plot, that are used to identify extreme values in a dataset (see figures 4.1 and 4.2).

Chapters 9 and 10 provide some specific principles for designing effective tables and graphics, as well as several examples of each. This chapter has slightly more general concerns: its purpose is to introduce some aspects of visualization and how these translate into the need for graphics and tables as part of the research process. It discusses some general design principles based on research on how people tend to see and interpret data when presented to them visually. Another goal is to get you, the reader, thinking about the most effective methods to present data to a particular audience.

VISUAL IMAGES

There's nothing quite like a memorable image to help us ponder some topic. Pictures of furry animals and cute babies evoke for many happy thoughts; a photograph of a calm beach can reduce anxiety and induce serenity. Images inflame, soothe, humor, teach, mislead, and motivate. But why is this so? Why do humans seem to be hardwired to respond to visual images, often more intensely than to auditory stimuli or words on a page? Neuroscience teaches that although about one-fifth of our brains process visual stimuli, those parts communicate with most other parts of the brain. In addition, animals are designed to sense movement, even when images are still (stare at the words on a piece of paper or screen long enough and they appear to move). Much of a person's early learning is visual and individuals tend to understand visual images quicker and with fewer errors than other sources of information, such as words on a page. Humans are also much better at remembering visual images than words or names of objects (Feinstein 2006).

However, people are also easily misled by visual images. We have a difficult time judging length, for instance, as demonstrated by the famous Müller-Lyer illusion, which compares

FIGURE 8.3 Muller-Lyer illusion.

two lines of the same length that have different styles of arrowheads at their ends (see figure 8.3). When the arrows are pointing toward the line, it appears longer (the website http:// dragon.uml.edu/psych/illusion.html has many other examples; see also Shepard 1990). Similarly, vertical lines seem longer than horizontal lines, even when they are the same length (Kosslyn 2006).

Unfortunately, some have selfish or unethical motives for designing misleading visual images. In this era of easy manipulation of photographs and questionable media messages, how often are images presented of products that don't live up to expectations? Find an advertisement of a fast food sandwich and then order one; the actual meal rarely stacks up well against its more robust image. Or consider the manipulation of celebrity or fashion model photos to make waistlines thinner and wrinkles and blemishes disappear (Reaves et al. 2004).

FIRST PRINCIPLES: CLARITY, PRECISION, AND EFFICIENCY

However, since researchers are—or should be—primarily interested in communicating results in a clear, concise, and accurate way, it is important to take steps that guarantee that the audience is not misled or deceived into reaching the wrong conclusion from the data. Thus, the first principle of data presentation is *clarity*: understand the message you wish to impart and provide it in a clear and concise manner (Tufte 2001). This is a key aspect of any data presentation, but it can be a challenge when using graphics or tables. One way to begin to think about this principle is to consider that data should be easy to identify and not be obscured by superfluous aspects of a graphic or a table. Don't be overly eager to impress or create a stunning image with bright colors, ornate typeface, or clever icons. Leave this task to the marketing and advertising departments. Instead, strive to provide a straightforward message about the results of the research.

Clarity is related to two other principles of good data presentation: *precision* and *efficiency*. Precision refers to ensuring that the data are presented accurately with minimal error. This is a topic that is equally important to data presentation as it is to data management (see chapter 4). Always keep in mind: *don't mislead the audience.* As already mentioned, people can be fooled by visual images, but they can also be misled by the *myth of the infallible graphic*. This refers to a tendency to believe there is an important association among concepts simply because they are correlated. The website *Spurious Correlations* (http://www.tylervigen.com /spurious-correlations) has many silly and amusing examples of phenomena that follow similar patterns over time, such as a graph of chicken consumption and US oil imports.

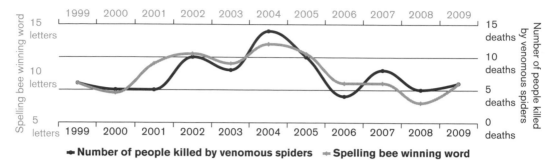

FIGURE 8.4 Letters in winning word of Scripps National Spelling Bee correlates with number of people killed by venomous spiders.

SOURCE: Wikipedia Commons. Licensed under the Creative Commons Attribution 2.0 Generic License.

Figure 8.4 provides one such amusing correlation. The types of data presentations illustrated in the following chapters assume that the research questions have a firm foundation (see chapters 1 and 2).

Efficiency refers to the ability to determine the point of the graphic or table quickly and clearly. As the cartographer Jacques Bertin (1983, 139) writes, "If, in order to obtain a correct and complete answer to a given question, all other things being equal, one construction requires a shorter observation time than another construction, we can say that it is more efficient for this question." A potential problem that arises in graphical presentations, in particular, is based on the *Ganzwelt effect* (Wainer 2005, 26). This is a visual phenomenon that occurs when someone stares at something long enough, such as a random scatter of points. Our minds try to make sense of the image and can fool us into thinking there is a pattern. The late paleontologist and evolutionary biologist Stephen Jay Gould captures this tendency well: "We think we see constellations because the stars are dispersed at random in the heavens, and therefore clump in our sight. Our error lies not in the perception of pattern but in automatically imbuing pattern with meaning, especially with meaning that can bring us comfort, or dispel confusion" (2010, 181–182). Thus, if a data presentation is not efficient, viewers, to "dispel confusion," run the risk of seeing patterns in an image that aren't really there because of the length of time it takes to try to figure out what the visual image represents.

How can data be presented in a clear, precise, and efficient manner? First, it is helpful to keep in mind that data presentation is fundamentally about *making comparisons* (Gelman 2014; see also chapter 1). Whenever data are presented, think about the comparisons that are explicitly or implicitly being made. Is the key comparison between males and females? The 2000 US census and the 2010 US census? California and New York? What is it about these units that is being compared? Crime rates? The probability of college attendance? The percentage of groups of citizens who voted in the last presidential election? Moreover, does the comparison make sense? Is it useful to compare trends in cheese consumption and the number of deaths due to bed sheet entanglement (see *Spurious Correlations*)? Regardless, even when comparisons may not seem evident, they are almost always there. Thus, keeping them in mind and considering the best way to present them throughout the data presentation process is critical.

Second, it is essential to consider the audience the researcher wishes to address. The audience of a data presentation must be able to *decode* the data. In computer science, decoding is the process of converting data from characters (symbols, letters) into a recognizable sequence or pattern. By creating a data presentation, the researcher has *encoded* the data—created an abstraction through the use of symbols, characters, and shapes—so the audience needs a way to decode the data: understand what message they are meant to convey. This process is also known as *graphical perception* (Cleveland and McGill 1985). Anything that impedes the decoding process, such as extraneous symbols or text, ought to be avoided. Extraneous information is known as *chartjunk* (Tufte 2001). Thus, the audience should be able to efficiently understand what the data presentation is meant to communicate without having to wade through chartjunk.

What are some issues to address when considering an audience? First, know something about the audience's skill level and educational background. Think of the typical people who are expected to see the data presentation. Do they have training in data analysis? Do they expect only descriptive results or those from an analytical approach (see chapter 1)? Along these lines, some audiences, such as those at academic conferences, may expect results based on a frequentist statistical framework. Thus, they want to see *p*-values, confidence intervals, and statements regarding whether the results generalize to a target population. Others might expect to see results in the context of a Bayesian framework and thus wish to understand what prior information was used and examine the credible intervals (Flam 2014). On the other hand, if the audience is made up of policymakers or the general public, they may not understand or care much about such matters. Rather, they will be concerned with concrete issues such as "how do these results help me understand an issue better or do my job better?" In the latter situation, some subscribe to the *grandparent rule*: if your grandparents can understand your data presentation, then it is satisfactorily clear and efficient.

Second, take into account the typical audience member's cultural background. For example, western readers are used to following text from left to right and the top to bottom of a page. Thus, they expect this pattern when reading or viewing data. But if the presentation is to members of another culture, such as native Chinese, Farsi, or Urdu speakers, then the data presentation may need to be modified, especially graphical depictions of data. Thus, an important principle is to *know your audience*.

Third, what do you want the audience to remember? Is it most important to understand a pattern, such as "the annual number of earthquakes in Nevada increased from 20 to 40 over a 20-year period"? Is a specific piece of the data important, such as "there were three earthquakes in Nevada in the past week; one of these measured 5.3 on the Richter scale (a moderate jolt)"? Or, should the audience take away a message about general geological conditions in Nevada over a 20-year time period? This suggests that the research objective must be clear or else the data presentation will be vague.

WHY WORDS ARE NOT ENOUGH

Although tables are a common form of data presentation, some researchers are wary of presenting data using graphics. Yet, as already mentioned, humans learn and retain information more efficiently through visual images than through words. Visual images are also useful for summarizing even complex information. Consider the following sentence that appears in a leading substance abuse journal: "This analysis revealed that impulsivity was associated positively with alcohol use severity at lower levels of P-AEQ positive expectancies; however, as expectancies increased, the relationship between impulsivity and alcohol use severity weakened" (Schaumberg et al. 2015, 43). Now think about how such a sentence could be translated into a table or a graph that would convey its content much more efficiently. If this is difficult to imagine, stay tuned.

There are two general purposes for tabular and graphical data presentation. First, both, but especially graphics, furnish researchers with information that may be obscured by the results provided by other statistical methods. As the famous twentieth-century statistician John Tukey said, "the greatest value of a graph is when it forces us to notice what we never expected to see" (cited in Wainer 2005, 123). Thus, Tukey and many others contend that exploratory data analysis (EDA), which is mainly a graphical approach to examining data, should be part of any research project. This aspect of data analysis was touched upon in chapter 4 when extreme values were examined using a box plot and a scatter plot.

A notable illustration of why graphical methods are valuable is known as Anscombe's Quartet. In a 1973 article, Francis Anscombe presented four small datasets with two variables each. The correlation between the two variables in each dataset is 0.82; however, graphing the data reveals something interesting. Figure 8.5 provides a version of the graphs from each dataset. Notice how different the patterns of points are, with extreme observations affecting some and curvature affecting others. Yet, a straightforward and widely used statistical test—the Pearson's correlation coefficient—might make one believe that the associations and their underlying patterns are the same.

Second, tabular and graphical data presentation is helpful—better yet, necessary—for the successful communication of research results. Of course, there may be other reasons to design tables and graphics, such as to sell products, impress an audience, send a message, illustrate a problem, for artistic reasons or just because creating visual images and spreadsheets is enjoyable. But this is not to say that these purposes, or others, cannot overlap. As mentioned in earlier chapters, the research process does not follow a straight line, but rather is interactive and often requires returning to an earlier stage as results emerge and motivate new ways of thinking about the data. Furthermore, presenting data graphically may serve exploratory and expository purposes, and be enjoyable, all at once!

But in the context of social science research, why are tables and especially graphics deemed indispensable—at least by some—as a medium of communication? A couple of answers were already provided: People tend to comprehend visual images quicker and with fewer errors than words on a page. Visual images also activate memories better than words. Tables presenting

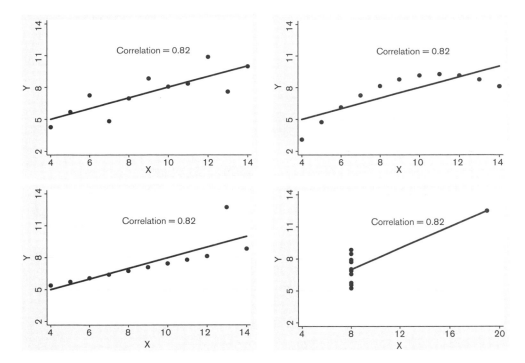

FIGURE 8.5 Anscombe's quartet.

SOURCE: Anscombe (1973).

research results are also expected by many of the arbiters of the research process, such as journal editors, university professors, and book publishers. In fact, some professional academic journals require that tables be used to present the results of statistical analyses. It is actually rare to find a research report or article that uses quantitative data but does not show results in a table.

In the social sciences, graphics are used less often than tables for presenting data. This is unfortunate since the information provided in a table can usually be transmitted more efficiently with a graphic (Gelman et al. 2002). In addition, whereas tables are suited best for providing precise information, several types of graphics are better at displaying trends and comparisons. It is not clear why graphics are not utilized more often, especially since most data presentations are designed to illustrate comparisons, but it may be that they are harder to construct than tables and often require proficiency with software that is difficult to acquire. Nonetheless, as demonstrated in chapter 10, it is worth the effort to learn to build data presentation graphics.

TYPES OF TABLES AND GRAPHICS

Before moving on to a discussion of some general aspects and additional principles of data presentation, this section provides a brief review of different types of tables and graphics. The next two chapters provide specific examples of several of these.

Tables

As mentioned earlier, tables are data that are arranged in rows and columns, usually represented by numbers. The data tables and spreadsheets from earlier chapters might be considered a type of table, although here we are interested in tables that are used to present research results (recall tables 6.3 and 6.4). In general, there are two types (Swires-Hennessy 2014):

- Reference tables show a lot of data with a high degree of precision. They are designed generally to provide users with a way to find particular pieces of data. For example, the US Census Bureau website includes hundreds of reference tables that show data on topics such as marital status and the number of children among adults in the United States (see www.census.gov). Other examples include US state-level data on crime rates or UK data on immigration by regions or council areas (see www.gov.uk).

- Summary tables provide some type of extraction of data from a reference table or a spreadsheet. The data are usually manipulated, analyzed, or summarized in some way, such as by sorting or providing summary statistics (means, percentages, ranges). The results of statistical models are usually presented in research reports using this type of table.

The main difference between a reference table and a summary table is that the latter should have an explicit goal: what is the audience supposed to learn from the table? What data summaries and comparisons are most relevant?

Graphics

There are various terms used for different types of graphics. Recall that, in general, graphics are visual representations of data that use symbols, such as geometric shapes. The seven types of graphics that are commonly used by the research community include the following (Kosslyn 2006).

Graph: a visual display that exhibits one or more relationships among data points. They are designed to show patterns and trends, and to allow the reader to quickly make comparisons.

Plot: a graphical technique that shows the association between two or more variables, of which at least two are typically continuous. Scatter plots are a common type.

Chart: it identifies qualitative associations among data or objects. Some common examples include family trees in genealogical research and flow charts in organizational studies.

Diagrams: pictures of objects or processes that use symbols to represent relationships. For instance, the models provided in earlier chapters to show hypothesized relationships among concepts are examples of diagrams. A particular type of diagram is a *schematic*. This is designed to provide elements of a system. A common example is a circuit diagram that shows connections among electrical units.

Maps: drawings that provide a representation of a physical layout, such as that of a city, county, province, or country. Maps are a frequently used data visualization tool, such as when depictions of US states are accompanied by data on life expectancy, poverty rates, unemployment, and other meaningful attributes. Recall John Snow's map of cholera victims that was shown at the beginning of the chapter (figure 8.2).

Illustrations: a visual depiction of an artist's rendering of some object of interest. In scientific research, illustrations are often used to show objects such as plants, molecules, electrical patterns in the brain, and so forth.

Photographs and video: an image created by light falling on a light-sensitive medium, such as photographic film or a pixel detection device (e.g., memory cards in cameras). An active area of social science research is visual studies that use photographs and video to document people, events, and environments (Tinkler 2013).

There is substantial overlap among these different types of graphics. For example, some consider plots as types of graphs; others use the term *chart* as a general category that includes plots and graphs (such as bar *charts*, line *graphs*, and scatter *plots*; Swires-Hennessy 2014). In chapter 10, the terms used to identify different types of visualizations rely on their most common names.

PRINCIPLES OF DATA PRESENTATION

It is useful to consider some characteristics and principles that apply to most types of data presentations in order to set the stage for specific discussions of tables and graphics. Some of these were outlined earlier. Recall the principles of clarity, precision, and efficiency, as well as the importance of knowing the audience. Furthermore, do not forget that clear research objectives and sensible comparisons allow for straightforward and efficient data presentations.

A useful way to think about tables and graphics is to visualize layers. Just as photographic files may be manipulated in photo editing software using layers, data presentations are constructed by imagining that layers of an image are placed one on top of another. There are three general layers that apply to visual data presentations: (a) a frame that is typically a rectangle or matrix, (b) axes and coordinate systems (for graphics), and (c) data presented as numbers or geometric objects (Wickham 2010). For example, figure 8.6 provides illustrations of each separate layer of a graphic that represents a series of points ordered from left to

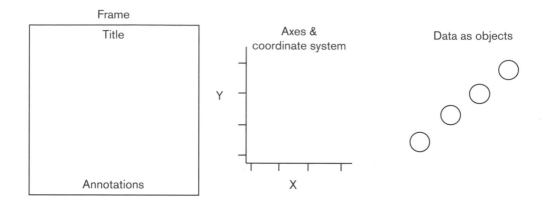

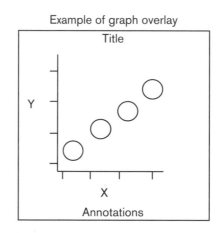

FIGURE 8.6 Layers of a graphic.

SOURCE: Adapted from Wickham (2010, 6).

right. These might represent data that change over time. The geometric object is a hollow circle, which is layered on a rectangular frame with a coordinate system consisting of axes representing, say, time along the horizontal axis (X) and the scale of the data values identified by the vertical axis (Y). The layers are then overlaid to make up the final graphic.

Given this type of layering scheme, what are some principles that should be followed in order to keep the message of the graphic or table clear and avoid distracting elements? Here are several general principles.

Identify the Comparisons of Interest

Although this was mentioned earlier in the chapter, it is worth reiterating. Too often, those who present data and research results do not attend to this issue. The result is a confusing data presentation (Gelman et al. 2002). For example, suppose a researcher wishes to examine the association between educational attainment and support for the death penalty. She, therefore, presents the average years of formal education among those who support and do not support the death penalty, which is, say 12.5 and 12.8 years. This method focuses on comparing education. A clearer approach is to look at the percentage of support among those in different educational groups, such as those who graduated from high school, but not college, and those who graduated from college: {Support | graduated from high school} = 75% versus {Support | graduated from college} = 60%. This comparison is easier for the audience to understand. See tables 9.9 and 9.10 in chapter 9 for an example of this issue.

Be Aware of Software Defaults

Software used for data presentation includes default options. For example, when creating a table in word processing software, the default is usually to include gridlines that distinguish each cell. When creating a graphic in presentation or statistical software, the default is to use color to distinguish different parts of the image. These defaults may or may not be appropriate, but more often they are not (Niemi and Gelman 2011). In fact, in my experience default options frequently get in the way of clarity and efficiency. Thus, it is important to learn how to specify options in the software, such as through commands in statistical software or by varying them in presentation or word processing software.

Emphasize the Data, Not the Nondata

Many data presentations spice up the image with background images, embedded visuals, ornate typeface, and bright colors. Our eyes may be drawn to these aspects, rather than to the patterns in the data, thus breaking the principles of clarity and efficiency. It is usually best to take out the clutter: remove the chartjunk. Consider the graphic represented in figure 8.7. What do you see when you first look at it? Perhaps you think it would be more visually appealing if the background photo were in color. This may be true, but think about the main message the graphic is trying to impart. It's a rather simple message: children were more likely to attend National Parks across the four-year time period. Is the background photo needed or is it simply distracting? It is rarely a good idea to include background photos since they obscure the data (Kosslyn 2006). What about the statement that is embedded in the graphic? Is it located in the appropriate place? As suggested later, there are other aspects of this graphic that need improvement. I have also seen background photos used in tables. Are these needed or are they merely distracting?

Aspect Ratio

This refers to the dimensions of the table or graphic. The ratio is calculated by dividing the width by the height but is often represented as W·H. For example, a square has an aspect ratio of 1:1. Many televisions and computer monitors have an aspect ratio of 16:9, or a width of 16 units and a height of 9 units. The frame of a table or graphic also has an aspect ratio. For instance, figure 8.7 has an aspect ratio of approximately 16:11, a bit taller, relatively speaking, than most television screens. One of the keys is to make sure that the aspect ratio is the correct size so that the comparisons can be made easily. For example, when using bars

FIGURE 8.7 A cluttered graphic.

for comparison purposes, where the height of the bars represents some quantity such as cost or number of items sold, create an aspect ratio so that those representing different items or stores are close together (but not overlapping; Kosslyn 2006). This allows the audience to quickly grasp what is being compared. The same principle applies to tables: make sure the audience can detect the comparison by keeping the relevant numbers near one another.

Figure 8.8 provides an example of the same data in graphs using two different aspect ratios. The first has an aspect ratio of about 3:4, whereas the second is about 10:3. Notice how different the trend line appears in the two graphs. What message does each convey? Is it the same message? It is best to avoid extreme aspect ratios. In figure 8.8, a good idea is to redesign the graph so the aspect ratio is somewhere between the two.

When creating a table, consider whether it is best to represent the data in portrait or landscape orientation. Landscape has a larger aspect ratio than portrait and this will affect how the table is read by the audience. Moreover, since people raised in western cultures tend to view images from left to right first and then down the page, a larger aspect ratio affects what the audience sees first and how long it takes to get to data that are farther down the page. In

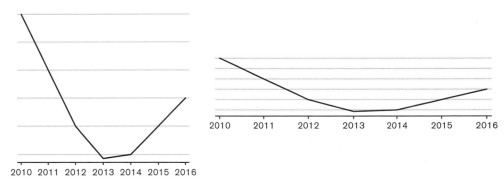

FIGURE 8.8 Aspect ratio example.

TABLE 8.1 Data ordering example

County name	Heart disease death rate	County name	Heart disease death rate
Adams	226	Triumph	423
Bluestone	171	Adams	226
Greer	92	Bluestone	171
San Angeles	126	Westbrook	139
Triumph	423	San Angeles	126
Westbrook	139	Greer	92

any event, there's no hard rule about which aspect ratio is best; it depends on the context of the data presentation. Regardless, it is vital to consider what comparison or data points the audience is supposed to see and focus on.

Data Ordering

Data in tables and graphics are often ordered alphabetically. This is not a good general practice and should only be used in limited circumstances. It is better to order data from largest to smallest (Cleveland 1993). This makes it easier for the audience to compare key parts of the data. Consider the two data displays in table 8.1. Which one provides a more efficient way to compare data? Many reports provide data in the style of the left-hand side of this table, with the counties in alphabetical order. However, recall that a key goal of data presentation is to make comparisons, with the principle of efficiency in force. By ordering the data from largest to smallest, comparisons are much simpler to make. In the right-hand portion of table 8.1, it is easy to see that Triumph County has a substantially higher death rate than the other counties, whereas the lowest death rate is in Greer. Now imagine if these data were presented in a bar chart or a dot plot (see chapter 10). In a bar chart, it is best to sort the bars from longest to shortest.

An exception to the principle of data ordering by size is when there is a more naturally occurring order to the cases or when the cases are grouped conceptually (expenditures on household items vs. leisure activities; Miller 2007a). Perhaps the most frequent example involves time. When data are presented across time, such as by year or decade, it is important to keep the time dimension clear. Thus, if the data presented in table 8.1 were available across several years, then they should be sorted by year before they are sorted from highest to lowest death rates.

Keep the Format of Tables and Graphs Consistent

It is important to keep the formatting and style consistent across tables and graphs (Wainer 2008). This follows the principle of clarity. The audience will likely get confused if a graphic on one page shows trends of stomach cancer death rates with a line graph, but on the next page trends of brain cancer death rates are shown in a bar chart. Similarly, if one row of data in a table lists percentages, it may be confusing if the next row presents rates for a similar phenomenon.

Labels and Annotations

In order to create a clear data presentation, it is a good idea to use well-thought-out labels and annotations (see figure 8.6). Labels are used as titles, to identify axes, and to designate symbols used to represent the data—such as lines that signify changes over time in some phenomenon. Annotations include legends, footnotes, sources, and other explanatory text. Some important aspects of labels include the following:

- Titles should clearly specify the content of the table or the graphic. What is being presented? Means and standard deviations? Confidence intervals? Percentages? Trends over time? Furthermore, consider the context, such as when and where the data were gathered, as well as the name of the dataset if using secondary data (although the dataset may also be identified in a source note). For example, rather than using "Table 1. Population Data," consider "Table 1. Total Population of South American Countries, in Millions, 2010."

- Keep the axes labels horizontal rather than vertical or diagonal (Wong 2010). Some presentation software shifts the labels to a diagonal when they are lengthy; this is rarely a good idea since the audience is then forced to read in an awkward position. Examine figure 8.9. The years are not as easy to read as when the text is aligned horizontally.

Annotations are designed to illuminate various aspects of the table or graphic. For instance, providing the source of the data in a caption at the bottom of a table or graphic is important to show the audience from where the data were obtained. Explanatory notes

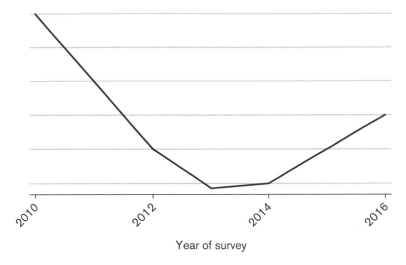

FIGURE 8.9 Axis label alignment example.

provide extra information about the data, such as definitions of concepts, the meaning of abbreviations, and the statistical procedures used to generate the content of the table or graphic. Information from statistical procedures, such as significance levels, are usually provided in footnotes.

Typeface

This term is often confused with the term *font*. The font is the particular text style that is used in a document, such as Garamond or Times New Roman; the typeface is how it appears on the screen or the page. Since we are concerned here with visual images, the term typeface is more appropriate. In any event, as any user of word processing or presentation software knows, there are dozens of choices when it comes to fonts and typefaces. Design experts recommend that a sans serif style be used when graphical or tabular data are intended to be read on computer screens. Some of the more common sans serif fonts include Cambria, Helvetica, Verdana, and Arial. More important, though, is that the temptation to use multiple fonts and stylized typefaces in documents and graphics should be resisted. No more than three fonts should be used in any work (Evergreen 2014). Exposing the audience to too many typefaces reduces clarity and efficiency. In addition, be careful of the types of fonts chosen for a presentation. If you expect that the presentation will be photocopied, for instance, make sure the typeface has easily distinguishable letters, numbers, and symbols, such as F and F or ! and 1.

In addition, try to avoid using italics and be careful with the use of bold typeface. Titles are often bolded and this is generally acceptable. But varying the size of the typeface may be more effective (especially in graphics), with slightly larger text identifying titles (Kosslyn 2006). Larger text is also useful for drawing attention to more important parts of a visual image.

Using Color

Many people expect to see color rather than only shades of gray in graphics. Most graphics online and many of those that appear in reports use color to highlight various aspects of the data. Color is utilized less often in tables, but is found on occasion. The careful use of color can be valuable for aiding clarity and efficiency. However, without sufficient knowledge of its strength and weaknesses, it is also easy to abuse the use of color. Thus, if data are presented using color, here are some suggestions that will help it aid rather than detract from data presentations (Evergreen 2014; Silva et al. 2011).

- Contrasts can be a help or a hindrance. Our eyes are drawn to bright colors on muted backgrounds. In addition, warm colors, such as red, are more likely to get attention than cool colors (although the relative brightness affects this phenomenon). Objects in color that are included in black and white or grayscale visuals are quite effective at drawing the eye. Thus, using color to highlight certain parts of a graphic or table can be valuable. However, avoid using these strategies if they will draw attention to extraneous or trivial parts of the data presentation.

- Do not use dark color backgrounds in graphics; use white or a subdued color. Be careful of using blue on red layers. People tend to get confused by a depth effect since red is viewed as visually "closer" than blue.

- Be aware that some viewers may be colorblind. The most common type of colorblindness is red-green followed by blue-green. Thus, be careful when considering the use of reds and greens as background or foreground. The same goes for blues.

- If colors are used for different bars in a graphic, use distinguishable shades of the same color rather than distinct colors. If lines are in color in a graph, use those that are easy to discriminate, such as red and blue. But be careful of lines that cross since a red line is perceived as in front of a blue line. If colors are employed in a table, used them to highlight the relevant comparisons you wish to make.

- Use colors to highlight important parts of the graphic. For example, it is effective to use a different color for an important line in a line graph since it draws the viewer's attention. This reinforces the efficiency of the graphic. Similarly, if a particular number or numeric comparison is important, use color to emphasize it. But be careful because this practice is easily abused.

- Avoid blue and yellow if the table or graphic will be photocopied. Don't use yellow if the visual image will be converted to black and white or a grayscale.

- Consider the website www.vischeck.com for helpful advice regarding the use of color in visual images.

Many data presentations, especially those designed for print, are limited to black and white or grayscale (including this book). Black text on a white or light gray background is the most legible combination, so avoid dark gray or black backgrounds with light text (Wong 2010). An interesting phenomenon is that people tend to see darker grays as larger in magnitude than lighter grays (Silva et al. 2011). Thus, when using different shades of gray for a bar or to distinguish numbers, be aware of this effect. Light shades of gray are effective as subtle gridlines in graphics; darker shades or blacks tend to be distracting.

Data in the Context of the Overall Presentation

Finally, it is important to think about how to discuss the tables or graphics in the context of the overall presentation, whether this is an article, research paper, report, or talk before an audience. The key is to accurately describe the purpose of the data presentation and its most important aspects. Some advice that researchers often hear is that the data presentation—whether it consists of a table or a graphic—should "stand on its own." In other words, someone with a reasonable amount of understanding should be able to pick up the table or the graphic and determine its context and meaning. Although this is good advice and can lead to improvements in data presentations, it is often empty because it is rare that they are asked to "stand alone."

Unfortunately, there is no fixed principle regarding how to integrate text and data presentations. It tends to be discipline specific and established by practices that have been used for many years. However, Miller (2004) and Swires-Hennessy (2014) provide valuable advice about this issue for social scientists. Research has demonstrated, though, that efficiency is higher when graphics are combined with text than when tables are combined with text (Gelman et al. 2002). This is likely because, as suggested earlier, people tend to understand visual images quicker and with fewer errors than numbers on a page.

FINAL WORDS

This chapter describes some principles of data presentation. It is designed to complement information from earlier chapters on developing research ideas and gaining access to and managing data. The next two chapters build on this one by providing specific examples of creating tables and graphics to present research results.

The basic message of this chapter boils down to the following: research results should be presented in a clear, precise, and efficient manner. Think about the audience: what message are you trying to communicate? Will they understand a technical presentation or should it be simplified? It may be necessary to design data presentations in more than one way to reach different audiences. Moreover, it is a good idea to create, say, a graphic in a couple of different ways and determine—perhaps by asking others to review them—whether one is clearer and more efficient than the other. By always keeping the audience in mind, as well as by following some of the principles introduced in this chapter, researchers may design data presentations appropriate for audiences ranging from novices to experts.

To summarize, here is a list of some of the specific principles outlined in this chapter:

- Before creating a table or graphic, think carefully about which comparisons it is designed to communicate to the audience.
- Beware of software defaults when creating tables and graphics. They often detract from the goals of clarity and efficiency, so it is important to learn now to vary aspects of the data presentation.
- Emphasize the data, not the nondata; remove extraneous information and chartjunk.
- Use the appropriate aspect ratio for the data presentation.
- Although there are exceptional circumstances, order the data from largest to smallest.
- Be consistent in how the presented data are measured and in the design of tables and graphics.
- Use clear and concise labeling and annotations so the purpose of the presentation and the context of the data are clear.
- Avoid italicized text and be judicious in the use of bold typeface. Choose a small number of fonts that are easy to read and not overly ornate or stylized. Use sans serif fonts if the data presentation will be viewed on a computer screen.
- Understand the most effective ways to use color in data presentations.

EXERCISES FOR CHAPTER 8

1. Find a graph and a table from an online media source. Evaluate it based on the principles outlined in this chapter.

2. Go to the website www.gapminder.org/data. Choose a couple of data visualizations that interest you (find an *Indicator name* and click *Visualize*). You will notice that *Gapminder* prefers to present data as colorful and dynamic bubble charts. Discuss the strengths and weaknesses of the data visualizations. What are some principles of data presentation that the visualizations do a good job of following? What are some areas they could improve upon?

3. Consider the following two ways to present data on the US murder rate (murders per 100,000) over time. Table 8.E1 provides a tabular presentation of the data and figure 8.E1 presents a graphical presentation of the data.
   a. Thinking about the principles outlined in this chapter, what are some ways you might improve each data presentation?
   b. Compare the two ways of presenting trends in the murder rate. Discuss which mode of presentation you prefer and why.

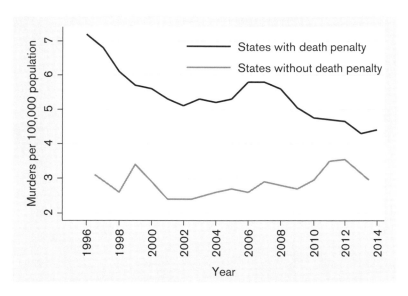

FIGURE 8.E1 Trends in murder rates, 1996–2014.

TABLE 8.E1 Trends in murder rates, 1996–2014

Year	States with death penalty	States with no death penalty
1996	6.98	3.73
1997	6.44	3.65
1998	6.11	3.32
1999	5.42	3.77
2000	5.06	2.97
2001	5.13	3.05
2002	5.10	2.98
2003	5.22	3.04
2004	5.07	3.08
2005	5.21	2.95
2006	5.24	3.10
2007	5.38	3.24
2008	5.15	3.01
2009	4.78	3.39
2010	4.47	3.21
2011	4.55	3.53
2012	4.59	3.54
2013	4.32	3.46
2014	4.41	3.40

NINE

Designing Tables for Data Presentations

Tables are probably the most frequently utilized data presentation tool. In fact, they have been around for centuries, with one of the earliest known data presentations found in an ancient Sumerian tablet from about 3,500 BCE. It showed what appeared to be the yield of two crops—perhaps wheat and barley—over a three-year period in a 2 × 3 table (Stigler 2016). Even this early, data presentation was concerned with comparisons. Modern-day journal articles and research reports continue to present data with a tabular display. Unfortunately, many researchers fail to think carefully about how to translate data or statistical results from software to presentation. For instance, I have often read research papers by students and professionals alike that present tables formatted in a manner similar to table 9.1. It is obvious that these tables were produced directly by some statistical software. I wonder if they have become so habituated to the use of software that they fail to realize that the tables produced as output are not designed for publication or presentation to the typical audience. Rather, statistical software is designed for the researcher, who then needs to translate the output for the audience.

What are some problems with these two ways of presenting data? As discussed later, an overemphasis on precise values takes away from the clarity and efficiency of the presentation. Notice the output that lists average wages: there are six digits after the decimal place! Given that the variable measures average wages per hour, is there ever a situation where such a high degree of accuracy is appropriate? It is highly doubtful. Are the occupational names comprehensible? Consider the set of data that concerns average age in years. Are the data presented clearly? Are all the gridlines necessary or are they distracting? What does the word "Mean" mean? "Std. Deviation?" Will an audience understand these terms? I hope it is obvious that these tables are poor ways to present data.

TABLE 9.1A   Output table from statistical software

	Average wages per hour	
occupation	nonunion worker	union worker
Professional/technical	9.836149	10.333510
Managers/admin	10.077551	9.708871
Sales	6.575510	8.235933
Clerical/unskilled	7.723552	6.371978
Craftsmen	7.027660	8.483089
Operatives	4.760546	7.224349
Transport	3.030422	3.637123
Laborers	4.704118	6.935729
Farmers	8.051530	NA
Farm laborers	2.935092	3.454104
Service	5.762595	7.288839
Household workers	NA	6.610305
Other	7.226227	10.402010

TABLE 9.1B   Output table from statistical software

Average age in years, by sex

SEX	Mean	N	Std. deviation
Males	48.91	1,141	17.315
Females	49.42	1,397	17.892
Total	49.19	2,538	17.633

This chapter uses the principles introduced in the last chapter to develop examples of tables that are better suited for data presentation than shown in table 9.1. It also presents a few additional principles of data presentation that apply specifically to tables. One of its goals is to integrate the material in earlier chapters to begin to demonstrate how a process that starts with a research question concludes with the presentation of the research results. Again, the point is not to show how to prepare a research report from start to finish, for there are already several fine resources about this more general issue (Baglione 2016; White 2005), but rather to provide some examples of how to present data that have been compiled to answer a research question or test a hypothesis. Whereas this chapter focuses on tables, the next chapter addresses on graphics. However, before considering the tabular display of data, it is useful to return to an issue introduced in chapter 8: tables versus graphics.

TABLE OR GRAPHIC?

Some experts argue that data presentations rarely, if ever, need tables (Gelman 2011a). Instead, the results of quantitative research studies are almost always communicated better using graphics. Others claim that tables provide valuable information, especially when the audience needs to be aware of specific pieces of data and particular results from an analysis (Koschat 2005). Although I am partial to the first point of view, tables continue to be ubiquitous in research presentations. They are also required by many of those who manage the research process and control the flow of research products, such as course instructors, thesis advisors, managers of research organizations and government agencies, and journal editors. Thus, this chapter describes some principles and provides illustrations of a few tables.

Recall from chapter 8 that tables are suited best for providing precise information, whereas graphics are better at displaying trends and comparisons. Since most research presentations focus on comparisons of one sort or another (see, e.g., figure 10.2), graphics serve a critical role in the research process. However, because of the many types of graphics available to the researcher and the many nuances involved in visual communication, they can present challenges. This may not seem to be the case given the pervasiveness of graphical presentations of data online and in the print media. Nevertheless, popularity does not equal quality. Thus, after furnishing a few more principles and some examples of tables that adhere to these principles, the next chapter provides advice about designing graphics.

TABLES

Recall from chapter 8 that tables are defined as an arrangement of data into rows and columns. Generally, the two types of tables used for data presentation are as follows:

- *Reference tables*: designed to provide a lot of data with a high degree of precision; and

- *Summary tables*: typically intended to furnish the results of some type of data manipulation, analysis, or summary.

Most quantitative research articles include summary tables. Often, the size of the table is designated as row-by-column, such as a 2 × 3 table that has two rows and three columns. Summary tables usually present numeric data in their cells that represent some statistic, although there are exceptions. The unit of observation or set of variables is normally represented by the rows. The columns are usually designated for particular statistics, such as means and standard deviations, or something about the variable that is accounted for or predicted in the conceptual model. For example, recall that figure 5.1 presented a conceptual model in which education was presumed to predict gun control attitudes. Gun control

TABLE 9.2   Data precision example: population and percentage

Country name	Total population (in millions)	Country name	Percentage of engineers with PhDs
Brazil	205	Brazil	0.67%
Colombia	48	Colombia	0.45
Argentina	43	Argentina	0.41
Peru	31	Peru	0.39
Venezuela	30	Venezuela	0.34
Chile	18	Chile	0.33

Note: The PhD data are fabricated.

attitudes comprise the variable we wish to predict. A couple of tables later in the chapter provide information with which to judge this model.

Before discussing some principles that apply to tables, it is vital to reiterate that data presentation is one of the last steps in the research process. Creating an informative and well-organized table (or graph) requires a clear research question or hypothesis, suitable data, and good analytic skills. The data that go into a table should be based on the principles outlined in earlier chapters. If these principles are not followed, it will not matter if a table is perfectly formatted and organized since the data that they present will likely be flawed and the message they impart erroneous.

How Precise Should the Numbers Be?

The first principle involves the number of digits used in a table. For numeric data, use a small number of digits before and after the decimal point to ensure clarity and minimize clutter. Some experts recommend that no more than two or three should be used; any additional digits are difficult for an audience to process (Wainer 1997). Thus, $27,276 should be written as *$27 thousand* or *$27* with a note indicating that dollars are represented in thousands. Or a population of 15,940,008 can be displayed as 16 million without loss of clarity in most situations. Moreover, if a set of numbers can be represented adequately with no decimal places, then the principle of clarity will usually be satisfied.

For some measurements, there is a tradition of using three digits after the decimal point, such as baseball batting averages or basketball field goal percentages (Klass 2012). It is best to follow these conventions in data presentations. However, the total number of digits, whether before or after the decimal, should never exceed five (Koschat 2005). Look back at table 9.1 and notice how severely this principle is broken.

As is usually the case with data presentation, context matters. For example, suppose data are presented in two parts of a table. The first part of table 9.2 includes population data for several South American nations; the second provides the percentage of engineers in each nation who have a PhD degree (the latter are fabricated).

It would not be particularly illuminating to most readers to see the actual totals in the population column. However, the two decimal places are important in the percentage of engineers column (but, as discussed later, there may be better ways to present this information). Notice there is less than 1% in each nation.

Understanding the Numbers

The audience should know what each number in the table means. Thus, titles, headers, and annotations should, in some way, allow the viewer to understand each number. This is related to the earlier principles, but it is important to reiterate it.

A zero before a decimal point is called a *leading zero*. A simple rule of thumb regarding whether to include leading zeros is the following: if the number can exceed 1.0, then use the leading zero; otherwise, omit it. For instance, suppose that a table presents rather small percentages, such as 1.2% and 0.8%. Since the first of these exceeds 1.0, the leading zero in the second should be included. However, proportions and some other measurements have a maximum value of 1.0; thus, leading zeros are not necessary.

Include totals or averages for columns and rows (Wainer 1997). For example, if a table includes the population of the 10 largest cities in Virginia, include a row that shows the total population. Or if a table provides the average age of survey respondents from four different ethnic groups, provide the average age of all respondents. Notice that this principle is not followed in table 9.2.

Given a concern with understanding numbers in a table, is there another way to present the data in table 9.2? Is there a way to eliminate the need for the decimal places? After all, some readers may be confused by a quantity like 0.67%. This leads to the issue of how data should be scaled when presented in tables. Small percentages, for instance, are often presented better by translating them into a different scale. If 0.33% of Chile's engineers have PhDs and, let's say, there are 50,000 engineers in Chile, then the number of engineers with a PhD is 165. This translates into 33 PhDs per 10,000 engineers. Thus, it might be better to present this type of measurement scale than to display the percentage with decimals. Is table 9.3 easier to understand than table 9.2? Again, think of the audience. Are they more comfortable with percentages or with prevalence measures? The psychologist Gerd Gigerenzer (2002) argues that lay audiences—and even many experts—are more comfortable with frequencies, such as the prevalence measure presented in table 9.3. Probabilities, proportions, and even small percentages can be difficult to comprehend. Thus, claiming that out of every 10,000 engineers in Brazil, 67 have a PhD (or about 7 out of every 1,000) is easier to understand than 0.67%. In addition, comparing this to Chile's estimate of 33 out of every 10,000 is simple to grasp.

Whichever scale is used to represent the data, it is important to keep it consistent in data presentations. The principles of clarity, precision, and efficiency are rarely met if the measurement scales change within tables. For example, it would not be a good idea to add another column to table 9.3 that lists the percentage of accountants in each nation who have advanced degrees. Moreover, don't confuse absolute and relative percentages or rates and frequencies (Wong 2010).

Finally, many tables provide information using monetary units or percentages. If confident that the audience will understand symbols for these units, they will help clarify what

TABLE 9.3   Data precision example

Country name	Number of engineers with a PhD per 10,000 engineers
Brazil	67
Colombia	45
Argentina	41
Peru	39
Venezuela	34
Chile	33

Note: The data are fabricated.

particular numbers mean. However, when using symbols to identify measurements, such as dollar signs ($) or percent signs (%), use them only once per column or panel. Otherwise, they can quickly clutter up a table. Notice that in table 9.2, the percent sign appears only after the first number in the column.

Titles and Other Labels

Recall that chapter 8 included advice about labels. A critical label in a table is the title, which should provide a sense of the context, measurements, and data coverage. This includes the year or years if the data have a time dimension. It also includes what the data represent or their coverage, such as "US adults ages 18–75" or "Adult residents of the Isle of Wight in 2017." If titles become too long, move some of this information to an explanatory note.

Row and column labels should provide information on each particular phenomenon addressed. Remember to use words. Some tables in social science journals use crude variable names or abbreviations to label the rows, such as Q4 or HHI (for the *Herfindahl-Hirschman index*). This should be avoided. Instead, tell the reader what the variable measures, such as "Age in years" or "Total annual family income." If the name is too long to serve as a row or column label, make sure that its abbreviation is spelled out in a note. Use explanatory notes, if needed, to indicate sources, clarify the statistical model, and identify important aspects of the data. Finally, if footnotes are needed to explain an abbreviation, indicate some comparison, or otherwise elucidate something about the table, it is best to use Roman lowercase letters rather than numbers. For instance, use a system of superscripted a, b, c, etc., rather than a 1, 2, 3, etc. It is too easy for the audience to confuse numbers identifying footnotes with numbers representing data.

Typeface, Shading, and Lines in Tables

Recall that typeface refers to how the fonts appear on the screen or the page. In tables it is not uncommon to see an italicized typeface used to set off different categories of text. It is easier on the audience to use spacing and indenting to draw attention to groups of items. For example, consider table 9.4 that presents two ways to identify groups of nations. The use of

TABLE 9.4 Italics versus indenting

Country name	Total population (in millions)	Country name	Total population (in millions)
South America		South America	
Brazil	205	Brazil	205
Colombia	48	Colombia	48
Argentina	43	Argentina	43
North America		North America	
United States	325	United States	325
Mexico	125	Mexico	125
Canada	35	Canada	35

Source: Statisticstimes.com.

TABLE 9.5 Column shading example: songs and platinum records by members of the Benjamin family

Name	Birth year	Sex	Platinum records	Songs released 1965–2005
Michael	1962	M	52	89
Jesse	1966	F	27	75
Hal	1954	M	5	36
Jackie	1952	M	2	10
Hailey	1956	F	1	8
Lexie	1959	F	1	21

Note: The data are fictitious.

indented text is more efficient. The extra space that precedes the North America row also helps distinguish the two groups.

Groups of rows are known as *panels*. For example, table 9.2 includes two panels, one that represents South America and the other that represents North America.

A common practice is to use shading to highlight various parts of a table. A modest gray shade may be used to identify an important row or column in a table (Wong 2010). Shading is also useful for distinguishing rows in large tables (Swires-Hennessy 2014). It allows the eye to track distinct rows better. But it is important to be careful about misleading or confusing the audience by overusing shading. Table 9.5 provides an example in which shading may be helpful to highlight a particular aspect of the data presentation. What do you think?

It is generally a good idea to avoid gridlines, vertical lines, and double lines. Use single horizontal lines to separate the title, headers, and content. Lines are also employed to identify *column spanners*, which are used to group particular columns of data.

Alignment

Alignment of text and numbers is important in tables. Some general rules are that titles are left- or center-aligned. The far left column header, which typically identifies the unit of observation or represents a column of variable names, is left-aligned, whereas the remaining column headers are center-aligned. Row headers are left aligned. Numbers should be decimal aligned if the software allows it. If not, then use center-alignment if the number of digits for each number is identical or right-alignment if they are not (use right indenting to align the numbers beneath the column label). Right-alignment is also useful for whole numbers. Table 9.5 illustrates the use of alignment. Be aware, though, that some typefaces change the way alignment appears on screen or in print.

Statistical Software Output

Do not use the output of statistical software as tables (Miller 2004). This is a problem highlighted by table 9.1. Although there are some specialized programs that create reasonable tables, such as the user-written Stata commands *tabout* and *estout*, the output delivery system (ODS) in SAS, the *TableLooks* option in SPSS, or the *xtable* package and *Sweave* tool in R, most of them limit the amount of control that one has over some important formatting issues. Although these program options may increase precision, it is often better—unless the researcher is technically proficient with statistical software—to use tools designed to produce tables. For example, OpenOffice, Numbers for Mac, MS Word, MS Excel, and similar word processing and spreadsheet software are quite simple to use and offer control over spacing, lines, alignment, and other features of the table. The software LaTeX is utilized by many in the scientific community to create publication quality tables. Though it has a steep learning curve, it produces impressive tables. There is also print and digital publishing software available for the technically proficient.

If there is a concern with precision, such as when many data points are reported, develop a system for importing statistical software output into word processing or spreadsheet software. But, even if you have such a system, it is still good practice to complete additional formatting work to ensure that table design principles are satisfied.

Style Guides

Many academic disciplines and their professional associations publish their own style guides. For example, there is the *American Sociological Association (ASA) Style Guide*, the *Publication Manual of the American Psychological Association (APA)*, and the *American Political Science Association (APSA) Style Manual*. These publications include instructions about how to format tables. Similarly, most professional journals provide instructions about how tables should appear. Some of these journals follow the guidelines promulgated by the main professional associations that they represent. Although a few of the standards found in these sources may be at odds with some of the principles presented in this chapter, it is best to follow them when you are working in a particular discipline or submitting a manuscript to a professional journal.

TABLE 9.6   Percentage of youth, ages 12–17, who report alcohol use in the past month, by selected European and North American countries, 2010

Country	Alcohol use in the past month	Minimum legal drinking age
Europe		
Bulgaria	47.3%	18
Czech Republic	46.8	18
United Kingdom	46.4	18
Croatia	41.2	18
Italy	41.1	18
Estonia	38.7	18
Greece	36.9	18
Denmark	31.6	16
France	28.7	18
Germany	26.4	16
Ireland	25.9	18
Finland	24.9	18
Norway	22.0	18
Sweden	21.3	18
Iceland	13.9	20
North America		
Canada	34.6%	19[a]
Mexico	30.1	18
United States	22.6	21
Total	33.1%	

Source: Survey of youth alcohol use (fabricated), 2010 (alcohol use), and http://drinkingage.procon.org (minimum drinking age). The total sample size is 22,387.

a. The minimum age is 18 in Alberta, Manitoba, and Quebec, but 19 elsewhere in Canada.

EXAMPLES OF TABLES

The following tables show some of these principles at work. Table 9.6 presents some fabricated data that compare the prevalence of alcohol use among youth from several European and North American countries. It also includes data on the minimum drinking age in each country. Since the title is relatively long, the source is listed in an annotation below the table. However, the title is incomplete since it does not mention the far-right column. Should this be rectified? How?

Table 9.6 utilizes shading since there are so many rows. It also uses indenting and spacing to distinguish European and North American countries, includes percentage signs only once in each panel, and utilizes decimal alignment for the numbers. Moreover, since Canada's

TABLE 9.7   Percentage of youth, ages 12–17, who report alcohol use in the past month, by selected North and South American countries and sex, 2010

	Alcohol use in the past month		
Country	Female	Male	Total
North America			
Canada	24.6%	33.5%	29.1%
Panama	23.6	30.7	27.2
Mexico	19.1	21.1	20.1
United States	17.6	20.9	19.3
Nicaragua	15.7	18.9	17.3
Jamaica	12.0	15.2	13.6
South America			
Brazil	20.3%	25.0%	22.7%
Peru	20.1	22.9	21.5
Colombia	19.6	22.1	20.9
Paraguay	18.9	19.7	19.2
Chile	17.0	18.3	17.7
Suriname	15.1	16.0	15.6
Total	18.6%	22.0%	20.3%

Note: The survey question from which the data were derived was "Have you had an alcoholic beverage in the past month, besides using for religious services or at family meals?"

Source: The fabricated survey of youth alcohol use in the Americas (FSYAA), 2010. The sample size is 20,020.

minimum legal drinking age depends on the province, there is a footnote that indicates the three provinces where the age is younger. The footnote symbol is a letter (a) so as not to confuse the audience with another number. Now, consider the additional principles outlined earlier. Does this table require any modifications? If yes, what do you recommend? For instance, will the audience gain anything of value from the digit after the decimal place in the alcohol use column? Some experts will likely argue no (Wainer 1997), whereas others might claim yes (Swires-Hennessy 2014). Importantly, what is the purpose of the table? Can you imagine the conceptual model it might be used to examine? (Hint: what concept is accounted for?)

Table 9.7 displays a three-way table that includes a column spanner ("Alcohol use in the past month"). Three-way tables are useful for representing three variables, in this case alcohol use by nation and sex of the youth. Note that there is now a column total and a row total. This is a simple table since there are only two columns under a single category. However, it is easy to incorporate more information, such as if one wished to include other types of drug or alcohol use. Do you notice any patterns represented in this table? Consider a couple of comparisons.

One of the most common types of table found in research articles provides summary statistics from a sample. As noted earlier, these tables usually provide averages, percentages, and measures of variation in the data. Although one can expect the audience of a research article or professional presentation to be comfortable with such a table, others may not be. Thus, the

TABLE 9.8   Means, standard deviations, minimum, and maximum values for selected demographic and time use variables, Nebraska state employees' survey, 2015

Variable	Mean	SD	Minimum	Maximum
Demographics				
Age in years	41	10	18	66
Years of formal education	13	4	11	20
Family income in $1,000s	54	17	21	109
Time use—typical day				
Hours of sleep per night	7.1	1.6	4	10
Hours of commuting time per work day	0.8	0.8	0.2	2
Hours of work/employment per day	8.5	1.1	6	11
Hours of recreation per day	0.5	0.2	0	1

Note: SD, standard deviation. The total sample size is 987. The data are fictitious.

terms and explanatory notes should be tailored with the audience in mind. But let's assume that table 9.8 is designed for an audience of social scientists who understand basic statistics. Are there aspects of it that should be modified so that it satisfies the principles discussed earlier?

Using Tables to Answer a Research Question

Recall that chapter 5 provides an example of how to download some secondary data. These data might be useful for examining whether higher levels of education are associated with support for gun control (see figure 5.1). An additional research question is whether the association between education and support for gun control—if it exists—differs among males and females. Thus, sex is examined as a *moderator* or a variable that *conditions* the association between education and gun control. One way to envision such a potential association is provided in figure 9.1. The vertical arrow that points from sex to the horizontal line represents a moderating effect.

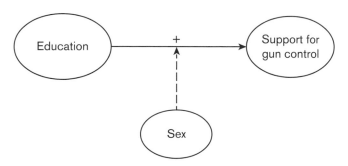

FIGURE 9.1 Conceptual model of education, sex, and gun control attitudes.

Chapter 5 includes some code that imports data from the 2014 General Social Survey (GSS), completes some data management steps, and then examines the association between education and support for gun control using means and box plots. The gun control variable is based on a survey question that asks: "Would you favor or oppose a law which would require a person to obtain a police permit before he or she could buy a gun?" The response options are coded as 1 = "Favor" and 0 = "Oppose."

After revisiting and running the data management steps of the code, execute the following code that requests average (mean) education levels overall and by sex.

Code to obtain means for table 9.9

```
* Stata

/* means */
mean education, over(GunPermit)

/* means by sex */
mean education, over(GunPermit female)
```

```
* SPSS

/* means.
means tables = education by GunPermit.

/* means by sex.
means tables = education by GunPermit by female.
```

```
* SAS

/* means */
proc means data=gss2014data mean;
  format GunPermit gun.;
  class GunPermit;
  var education;
run;

/* means by sex */
proc means data=gss2014data mean;
  format GunPermit gun. female fem.;
  class GunPermit female;
  var education;
run;
```

Given the results, consider table 9.9. First, is there a difference by education in attitudes toward gun permits (Kleck 1996)? Second, if there are differences, are they noticeably distinct for males and females? More importantly for our purposes, though, is whether the table does a good job of representing evidence that can be used to evaluate the conceptual model in figure 9.1. It seems that it suffers from a lack of efficiency and perhaps too much precision. Is using two digits after the decimal place overdoing it or is it needed since the differences are

TABLE 9.9 Average years of schooling for those who oppose and favor gun permits, by sex, General Social Survey (GSS), 2014

| Gun permits | Sex of respondent | | Total |
	Male	*Female*	
Oppose	13.47	13.26	13.37
Favor	13.92	13.73	13.82
Total	13.76	13.63	13.69
Sample size	766	927	1,693

Note: The gun permit variable is based on the following survey question: "Would you favor or oppose a law which would require a person to obtain a police permit before he or she could buy a gun?"

Source: General Social Survey, 2014 (http://www3.norc.org/GSS+Website).

relatively small? Should we use statistical significance tests for these results? Or are they problematic given the data, the research question, and the assumptions of frequentist statistics? Is there additional information from prior studies that might be brought to bear in a Bayesian statistical framework? In general, are there better ways to present this information?

Table 9.9 provides a good illustration of a principle needs to be addressed before the analysis is conducted and the table is created: identify the key comparisons of interest (see chapter 8). Although education is important in the conceptual model, the key comparison is attitudes toward gun permits. Thus, this should be the focus of the comparison. Placing education levels in the columns is not the best was to organize this table.

A more common way to evaluate this type of evidence is to reexamine the way that education is represented. One approach is to recode the education variable—which ranges from 0 to 20 to represent years of formal education—so that it denotes a discrete number of categories. For example, educational achievement in the United States is often divided into high school graduate, some college, and college graduate. Table 9.10 provides an alternative way to examine the model by considering this measurement strategy for education. Using some of the tools discussed in chapter 5, try to reproduce the information displayed in this table (hint: use the *recode* commands in Stata and SPSS or *if-then* commands in SAS to create a new variable that categorizes education).

Does table 9.10 provide evidence with which to evaluate the conceptual model? It is certainly clearer and more efficient than the evidence in table 9.9. The most obvious pattern is that a higher percentage of females than males favor gun permits in each education category. However, the conceptual model suggests that education is associated with attitudes toward gun control. Is this accurate? Perhaps, but there appears to be a threshold effect for females, with only those who graduated from college more likely than others to be in favor of gun permits. Can you think of additional ways to test the conceptual model using these results? One idea is to compute relative differences in the percentage of males and females who favor gun permits in each education category. For example, the relative sex difference between high school

TABLE 9.10 Percent of respondents who favor police permits to purchase a gun, by sex and education, General Social Survey (GSS), 2014

Educational attainment	Sex of respondent		Total
	Male	Female	
Less than high school	67.9%	75.6%	72.5%
High school graduate	59.7	75.0	67.6
Attended college	66.7	74.1	70.8
Graduated from college	71.1	82.2	77.2
Total	66.3%	77.2%	72.3%
Sample size	766	927	1,693

Note: The permit variable is based on the following survey question: "Would you favor or oppose a law which would require a person to obtain a police permit before he or she could buy a gun?"

Source: General Social Survey, 2014 (http://www3.norc.org/GSS+Website).

graduates is $(75.0 - 59.7)/59.7 = 0.26$, whereas among college graduates it is $(82.2 - 71.1)/71.1 = 0.16$. (Do you think it would be helpful to include these relative differences in the table? Should they be presented as percentages?) This suggests a modest moderating effect of sex, but additional information is required to reach any conclusions, especially if a frequentist or a Bayesian statistical framework is used. For example, those following a frequentist approach would likely wish to see confidence intervals and significance tests regarding the differences across the sex and education groups. Those who prefer a Bayesian approach might want to know what prior information was used and examine credible intervals.

An additional question is whether this is the best way to illustrate these results. Presenting moderating effects using a table, in particular, is not an efficient approach; many audience members find them difficult to understand. Thus, these types of effects are often represented using graphics. This increases the clarity and efficiency of the message provided by statistical results. We return to the conceptual model regarding gun control and the evidence in the next chapter and show how it can be represented with graphics.

FINAL WORDS

Tables are a frequently used medium to represent research results. Although some argue that graphics are preferable because they are clearer and more efficient, it is unlikely that tables as a data presentation tool will fall out of favor anytime soon. Thus, this chapter is intended to provide some guidance in designing tables that display the results of the research process. Several important principles should be heeded. Rather than recapitulate each of these, perhaps the most vital may be thought of as follows: be clear and consistent in the way the data are presented. Use labels and other identifiers that the audience will understand. The most important of all is to make sure the comparisons provided in the table are appropriate given the research questions that motivated the work in the first place.

1. Consider, once again, the table that appears in the chapter 8 exercises (see table below). Now that you have learned some additional principles regarding tables, what improvements would you make to the table?

Year	States with death penalty	States with no death penalty
1996	6.98	3.73
1997	6.44	3.65
1998	6.11	3.32
1999	5.42	3.77
2000	5.06	2.97
2001	5.13	3.05
2002	5.10	2.98
2003	5.22	3.04
2004	5.07	3.08
2005	5.21	2.95
2006	5.24	3.10
2007	5.38	3.24
2008	5.15	3.01
2009	4.78	3.39
2010	4.47	3.21
2011	4.55	3.53
2012	4.59	3.54
2013	4.32	3.46
2014	4.41	3.40

2. The chapter 3 exercises include a slightly different version of the following table.

| Person | Family income in $ | Favorite television shows[1] | | | Are you currently in school? | How many times did you visit a doctor in the past year? |
		Breaking Bad	Game of Thrones	NCIS		
Olivia	50,100	Yes	Yes	No	Yes	0
Emma	75,800	No	Yes	No	Yes	4
Abby	84,600	No	No	Yes	No	2
Sophia	72,300	Yes	Yes	Yes	Yes	0
Jacob	87,000	No	Yes	Yes	No	0
Adam	39,500	No	No	No	No	5
Tyler	65,200	Yes	No	Yes	Yes	3

1. This is based on a single question: "What were your favorite television shows in 2012?"

Reformat this table so that it satisfies the principles regarding tables discussed in this chapter.

3. In the chapter 4 exercises, you used a data file called *firstyeargpa.csv*. The program file you wrote was designed to label the variables and provide some descriptive statistics. Revisit this data and program file. Request the means, standard deviations, and minimum and maximum values for each variable. Using the principles outlined in this chapter, construct a summary table that provides these statistics.

4. In the chapter 6 exercises, you created a data table that had US state-level information on various issues. You then read the data file into statistical software and completed some data management steps. Using the data table and this file, complete the following.
   a. Use the data table you created to construct a reference table with the data for each state. Rely on the principles presented in this chapter to format the table.
   b. Using the data file and statistical software of your choice, construct a summary table with the following information: the median, mean, and standard deviation for the variables children in poverty, per capita health-care costs, the number of homeless per 10,000, and the percentage who meet recommended daily vegetable consumption.

TEN

Designing Graphics
for Data Presentations

On most mornings as I am going to my office, I follow a path that takes me past a display of research posters. One of the posters that has been on the wall for quite a while presents the results of a study on children's perceptions of their parents. Figure 10.1 provides a slightly modified version of one of the graphics that is part of the poster. Given what was discussed in chapter 8, do you see problems with this visual display of data? Is the message of the data presentation clear? I hope your answer was "yes" to the first question and "no" to the second. This is an example of a data presentation that, with a little thought and consideration of some principles outlined in chapter 8 and in this chapter, can be avoided or, better yet, improved.

In late 2015, a surprising research finding was reported in news media across the globe. Economists Anne Case and Nobel Prize winner Angus Deaton published a study that compared the death rates among middle-aged Caucasians—roughly aged 45–54—to those of other age groups in the United States and to similar age groups in several western nations. The surprising finding is that, although these rates for most groups have decreased over the last 20 years, middle-aged Caucasians experienced a slight increase in death rates. The authors attributed this to a rise among these adults in drug overdoses, suicides, and alcohol-related diseases (Case and Deaton 2015). Figure 10.2—which is reformatted from the original to make it suitable for this page—appeared in many media outlets.

Although this is an interesting graphic that, for the most part, satisfies the principles of clarity and efficiency, Andrew Gelman (2015)—responding to an earlier announcement about this finding—pointed out that adults in this age group were actually older, on average, in 2010 than in 1990 by about half a year. And this slight increase in the average age is sufficient to account for the observed trend in death rates. The point is that even well-designed

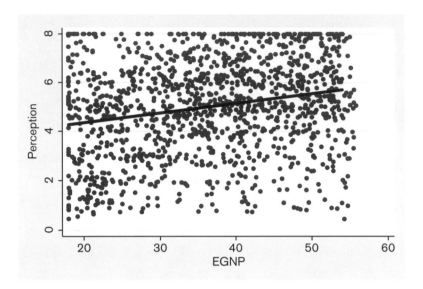

FIGURE 10.1 An obscure graphic.

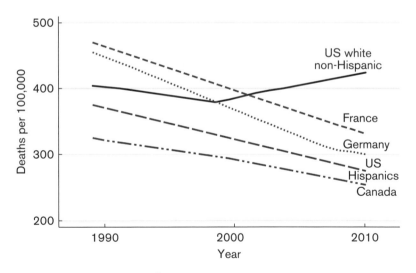

FIGURE 10.2 All-cause mortality, ages 45–54.

SOURCE: Adapted from Case and Deaton (2015).

graphics based on carefully chosen data and sophisticated statistical analyses can deliver a questionable message. To be fair, though, it is unclear whether the other nations in the graphic also saw the average age of 45- to 54-year-olds increase. If they did, then the main result of the graphic is important. There has also been a documented increase in suicides and alcohol-related liver diseases among middle-aged adults in the United States, so a tragic public health problem is evident and is a significant research topic.

This chapter addresses some principles of data presentation that, if followed, improve the design of graphics. As mentioned in chapter 8, one argument that has merit is that the results of quantitative data analyses are ideally communicated with graphics, such as graphs, plots, and charts (Gelman 2011a; Wainer 2009). Thus, similar to chapter 9's emphasis on tables, one of the key goals of this chapter is to integrate material from the previous chapters to demonstrate how the research process that begins with a question ends with a presentation. It does this by providing examples of some common types of graphics used by social scientists. This is accompanied by a few illustrations of using graphics to communicate research findings.

GRAPHICS

Recall that graphics are designed to provide visual depictions of data using symbolic representations. The symbols used in graphics include bars, points, lines, and other geometric shapes. Most graphical depictions of data also include text in the form of titles, labels, and annotations. Although some experts defend the use of tables (Koschat 2005), there is a substantial movement in the research world advocating for the use of graphical methods in data presentation (Wainer 2009; Ware 2013). In particular, the field of data graphics and visualization is growing, with books, journals, and websites devoted to encouraging the use of visual images in academic research, in the business world, and in other fields that use quantitative data.

There are several good reasons for the growth of interest in graphical presentations of data. As mentioned earlier, people comprehend the information provided in graphics quicker and with fewer errors than when it is presented in tables or text alone. Visual images are also more memorable than textual depictions of information (Feinstein 2006). Several types of graphics, such as dot plots and line graphs, are better suited than tables for making comparisons. Since most research is designed to compare things—such as the number of people who vote from county to county or the number of companies that merge each year—graphical displays are a preferred medium of communication in the research world. Studies have also shown that comprehension is higher when graphics are combined with text than when tables are combined with text (Gelman et al. 2002).

Since there is such a large array of options, it is impossible to give more than a flavor of graphical presentations in this chapter. Thus, it focuses on some principles of graphics and a few examples of how to use them to present research findings. The principles discussed later, if followed, will lead to the construction of graphics with high clarity and efficiency. Furthermore, even though some argue that tables are better at providing precision, there are ways to include precise information in graphics without sacrificing clarity or efficiency.

How We Judge Visual Comparisons

Some of the arguments for using graphics to present data are persuasive. Making a clear point and allowing the audience to quickly determine patterns and comparisons is vital to the successful research project. But what are some specific aspects of how people judge the elements in graphics that can help us design better data presentations? In general, creating good graphics to compare things involves balancing *distance* and *detection*. Distance concerns the sense that as objects are closer together, it is easier to compare them. Problems occur when objects are too far apart. Detection implies that in order for viewers to compare successfully they must be able to recognize differences. However, this is impeded if there is insufficient distance, such as if the symbols designed to represent the data overlap or are hidden by other aspects of the image (Robbins 2013).

In addition, statistician and graphics expert William Cleveland (1993) points out that viewers are best able to make comparisons and judge distinctions when data are positioned along a common scale. Acuity decreases from there, with the following from highest to lowest:

1. Positions on identical but nonaligned scales
2. Length
3. Angle or slope
4. Area
5. Volume and color saturation, and
6. Hue, such as shades of color

These have been used for many years to guide graphical representations of data. However, there are some exceptions to the ordering of this list. Some studies have shown that the audience's background affects the accuracy of judgment. For example, pilots are trained to use angles in maps, whereas social scientists are typically not (Kosslyn 2006). This reinforces the notion that knowing one's audience is necessary for successful graphical data presentations.

Figure 10.3 provides a visual illustration of Cleveland's list. This list is helpful in choosing the most effective ways to present research results. Examples of specific types of graphics based on several of these are presented later in the chapter.

Principles of Graphical Data Presentations

In addition to these points about how people judge distinctions in visual representations, recall some of the key principles discussed in chapter 8 that apply to graphics. It is probably

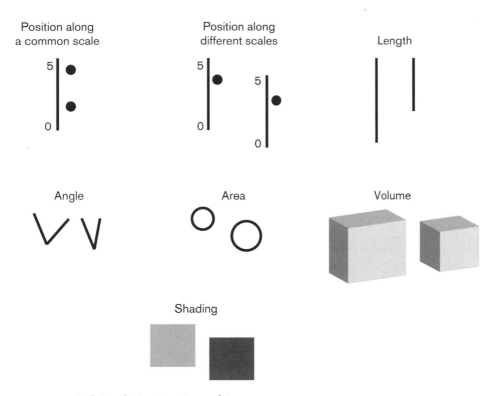

FIGURE 10.3 Judging distinctions in graphics.
SOURCE: Adapted from Cleveland and McGill (1984, 532).

a good idea for you to review these principles before proceeding. Building on these principles, here are some additional guidelines specific to graphical presentations of data:

- It is a good idea to sketch a graphic first, such as on paper, whiteboard, or touch screen, before creating it with software. This allows the researcher to consider different ways of viewing and presenting the research results so that the principles of clarity and efficiency are satisfied.

- If there is a lot of information in a graphic, consider splitting it into two or more adjacent graphics (Gelman 2014).

- Keep the formatting of graphics consistent (Wainer 2008). If lines are used to show trends in car purchases in one graph, don't use bars to show trends in bicycle purchases in the next graph. Moreover, do not change the axes in a graph or across two comparable graphs (Wainer 1984). This can be misleading. In fact, perhaps the most egregious examples of graphs involve those that use different axes (Wainer 1984; for a recent example, see Qui 2015).

- Each axis should be labeled using vertical (*y*-axis) or horizontal (*x*-axis) text. Label symbols directly rather than relying on a legend in another part of the

FIGURE 10.4 Illustration of the rule of thirds.

graphic (Bertin 1983; Gelman et al. 2002). For instance, in a line graph, label each line; in a bar chart, label each bar. Including descriptions of the bars or lines only in legends forces the reader to scan back and forth from the legend to the data; this fails the efficiency principle. If the lines are long and overlapping, label them at the beginning and the end. Make sure the labels use clear words or phrases and are large enough to be legible (Wainer 2008).

· If working in black and white and grayscale, be mindful of how different shades appear on screen or in print. Using different shades of gray to distinguish bars or lines can be effective, but may also lead to problems if the differences are not stark enough. Some graphics use different line or bar patterns (see figure 10.2).

· Use light horizontal gridlines in line graphs if precision is important; avoid dark shades or patterns that may draw the audience's attention too much. If the software allows it, use inner tick marks and place them at regular intervals. But don't use too many gridlines or tick marks because they can be distracting (Wilkinson 2001).

· Learn the rule of thirds. This is one of the first things taught to photographers and graphic designers. It can be an effective tool for drawing the audience's attention to key parts of the graphic. Imagine a frame that is divided by two horizontal lines and two vertical lines (see figure 10.4). Viewer's eyes tend to be

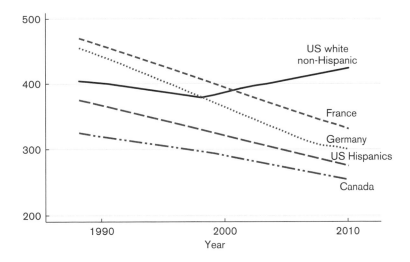

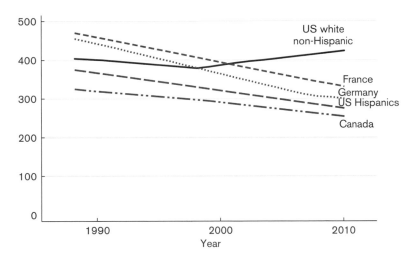

FIGURE 10.5 All-cause mortality, ages 45–54, deaths per 100,000 population.
SOURCE: Adapted from Case and Deaton (2015).

drawn to images at the intersection of these lines, such as at two-thirds across and two-thirds down the frame. Notice that this is where the child's face appears in figure 10.4. He is also facing into the frame; this can also be an effective tool when trying to draw attention to a specific area of the visual image.

- As mentioned earlier when discussing distance and detection, be aware of overlapping data. In many graphics, points and bars overlap and this can be confusing to viewers (Robbins 2013). There are some effective ways to avoid data overlap, including jittering and using hollow symbols rather than solid symbols to represent data points (Cleveland 1993). Examples of these practices are provided later.

- Unless your supervisor or instructor demands it and is inflexible, do not use three-dimensional (3D) graphics for data presentation (Kosslyn 2006). They almost always reduce the clarity and efficiency of the visual image. Size is distorted when 3D is presented on a 2D surface. There are some tools for dynamic visualization that use 3D effectively, but here we assume that the data presentations are 2D.

- If the graphic includes positive and negative numbers, such as in a horizontal bar chart or dot plot (examples of these are provided later), include a vertical line at zero and use it to contrast the geometric shapes (Kosslyn 2006).

- Some experts argue that axes—in particular, the y-axis—should always begin at zero. However, when differences are small, yet the size of the numbers is relatively large, this can make detection difficult. On the other hand, viewers can be misled by manipulating the axes to magnify differences. One guideline is to always use a zero bottom point when judging absolute magnitudes (Kosslyn 2006). This is often the case in bar charts. However, consider the two graphics displayed in figure 10.5. The first simply replicates the graphic shown in figure 10.2. The second changes the scale of the y-axis so that it includes zero. Which do you prefer? There is a lot of white space in the second graph and some experts recommend that this be avoided (Tufte 2001).

- Consider using error bars or some similar method for showing the uncertainty in statistical estimates. This may be especially important to certain types of audiences, such as those consisting of academic researchers. However, it is important that you fully understand what an error bar is based on and how it should be interpreted. If used in a bar chart, have the error bar extend above the particular bars, but there is no need to show it within the bars.

EXAMPLES OF GRAPHICS

Given the many types of graphics available, it is not practical to provide examples of each. Instead, this section discusses and displays what are perhaps the most common types of graphics used in data presentations: pie charts, bar charts, dot plots, line graphs, and scatter plots. Although there are many other types, including some intriguing options that have emerged in recent years, it is unlikely that those discussed here will fall out of favor anytime soon.

Pie Charts

Pie charts are a graphic that divides a circle into slices or wedges designed to represent parts of a whole. Florence Nightingale's coxcomb shown in figure 8.1 is an example of a pie chart, albeit more complex than the typical one found in data presentations. Even though her graphic has earned a lot of well-deserved attention, pie charts, in general, have a bad reputation. This is partly because they are often designed poorly, and also because making comparisons using angles and area is not efficient (see figure 10.3). Viewers have a relatively difficult time determining whether one pie "slice" is larger than another unless it is substantially bigger. Some experts argue that pie charts should *never* be used (Cleveland 1993; Tufte 2001). Nevertheless, since they are so common, it is helpful to understand some characteristics that increase their efficiency. The following list provides some guidelines:

- Pie charts should only be used for categorical data that represent parts of a greater whole. For example, a pie chart could be used to show the percentage or proportion of a sample belonging to different religious groups, if each member of the sample can be placed into a group. However, it would not be appropriate to use a pie chart for other purposes. For instance, suppose a pie chart on a network news program had slices representing the percentage of support for three Presidential candidates: 25%, 20%, and 17%. The problem is that these fail to add up to 100%.
- Do not use pie charts if viewers need to be aware of precise percentages. There are better options.
- Include no more than four or five slices.
- Order the slices by size, with the largest beginning at 12:00 (Wong 2010).
- Consider "exploding" a slice if it needs emphasis. This means that the slice is pulled away from the pie.
- Place the labels within the slices.
- If using multiple pies for comparison purposes, use the same order of categories in each pie (Kosslyn 2006).

Figure 10.6 provides an example of a pie chart that may be created in Stata, SPSS, or SAS. It is based on the education variable from the GSS dataset used in chapter 5. The variable is first coded into four categories and each is labeled. The pie chart is then requested. It may take a bit of trial and error to construct a pie chart that meets the guidelines listed earlier. For example, the default of all three programs is to provide the chart in color, so a grayscale scheme must be requested.

Examining the pie chart, what message does it impart? It is simply a descriptive device here, but it should still indicate something about the variable that is useful. The size of the slices suggests that the two largest groups in the sample are those who graduated from college and those who graduated from high school but did not attend college. Compared to the next two graphical tools, however, the pie chart is rather inefficient.

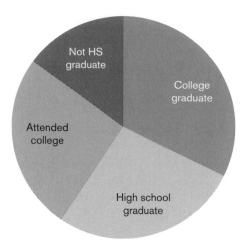

FIGURE 10.6 Pie chart example: education categories.

Code to create the pie chart in figure 10.6

```
* Stata

/* First, create and label the categorical education variable */
recode education (0/11=1)(12=2)(13/15=3)(16/20=4), gen(educCat)
label variable educCat "Education categorized"
label define educCatlab 1 "Not HS graduate" 2 "High school graduate" ///
   3 "Attended college" 4 "College graduate"
label values educCat educCatlab

/* Second, construct the pie chart of education categories */
graph pie, over(educCat) sort descending angle(90)              ///
  plabel(_all name) intensity(inten70)            ///
  title(Figure 10.6. Pie chart example: Education categories) ///
  legend(off) scheme(s1mono)

*/ Explanation of code:
   sort = sorts the slices by size;
   descending: from largest to smallest group size;
   angle = sets the angle of the first slice;
   plabel = inserts labels in the slices;
   intensity (inten70) = lightens the grayscale;
   title = creates the title;
   legend = turns the legend off;
   scheme = requests grayscale
*/
```

```
* SPSS

/* Note that the SPSS defaults for graphics may be changed from color to black .
/* and white before the pie chart is created. This can be done in the drop-down .
/* menu under Edit-Options-Charts .
```

```
/* There are also ways to set other default styles that are beyond the scope .
/* of this presentation                                                      .

/* Also note that in SPSS it is often simpler to first create the basic graphic .
/* using GGRAPH and GPL (Graphic Production Language) and then click on the   .
/* resulting graphic and use the options feature to change characteristics of .
/* the graphic; For instance, the code below simply creates a basic pie chart .
/* and then one may use options to place labels within the slices and so forth .

/* First, create and label the categorical education variable .
recode education (12=2) (0 thru 11=1) (13 thru 15=3) (16 thru 20=4) into educCat.
variable labels educCat 'Education categorized' .
value labels educCat 1 'Not HS graduate' 2 'High school graduate' 3 'Attended
    college' 4 'College graduate' .
execute .

/* Second, construct the pie chart of the education categories .
GGRAPH
    /GRAPHDATASET NAME="graphdataset" VARIABLES=educCat COUNT()[name="COUNT"]
        MISSING=LISTWISE REPORTMISSING=NO
    /GRAPHSPEC SOURCE=INLINE
    TEMPLATE=[
      "C:\Program Files\IBM\SPSS\Statistics\23\Looks\GrayScale.sgt"
      "C:\Program Files\IBM\SPSS\Statistics\23\Looks\APA_Styles.sgt"].
BEGIN GPL
    SOURCE: s=userSource(id("graphdataset"))
    DATA:   educCat=col(source(s), name("educCat"), unit.category())
    DATA:   COUNT=col(source(s), name("COUNT"))
    COORD:  polar.theta(startAngle(0))
    GUIDE:  axis(dim(1), null())
    GUIDE:  legend(aesthetic(aesthetic.texture.pattern.interior), null())
    GUIDE:  text.title(label("Figure 10.6. Pie chart example: Education
            categories"))
    SCALE:  linear(dim(1), dataMinimum(), dataMaximum())
    SCALE:  cat(aesthetic(aesthetic.texture.pattern.interior), include("4.00",
            "2.00", "3.00", "1.00"), sort.values("4.00", "2.00", "3.00",
            "1.00"))
    ELEMENT:interval.stack(position(summary.percent(COUNT))), texture.pattern.
            interior(educCat))
END GPL.

/* Explanation of code:            .
/* GGRAPH = identifies data and variables to use, sets missing data, and uses .
/* standard templates to request grayscale      .
/* SOURCE: = identifies source file from GGRAPH     .
/* DATA: identifies variables and how the chart will use them   .
/* COORD: = begin first slice at 12:00        .
/* GUIDE: = identifies the axis, turns off the legend, and provides a title .
/* SCALE: = identifies patterns, including the order of the slices        .
/* ELEMENT: = identifies the type of graph to use and the pattern of its   .
/* interior (IBM 2010)              .
```

* SAS

/* Note that in SAS there are several ways to change the color scheme to grayscale before the graphics are created. A simple way is to request the journal
style output using the ods (output delivery system) option

```
       This is the approach used to generate versions of all of the following
       graphics
*/

/* Request journal style html output - grayscale
   Note that you need permission to write to a directory for this to work
*/
ods graphics on / reset=index;
ods listing close ;
ods html style=Journal;

/* First, create and label the categorical education variable */
data gss2014data;
  set gss2014data;
educCat = .;
  if (education >= 0)  and (education < 12) then educCat=1;
  if (education = 12)  then educCat=2;
  if (education > 12)  and (education < 16) then educCat=3;
  if (education > 15)  and (education < 21) then educCat=4;
label educCat = "Education categorized"
run;

/* create value labels for education categories */
proc format;
  value edCat   1 = "Not HS graduate"
                2 = "High school graduate"
                3 = "Attended college"
                4 = "College graduate"
run;

/* Second, construct the pie chart of education categories */
Title 'Figure 10.6. Pie chart example: Education categories';
proc gchart data=gss2014data;
  format educCat edCat.;
  pie educCat / discrete value=inside clockwise descending;
run;

/* Explanation of code:
   Title = creates a title before the graphic is requested
   proc gchart = this is one of many procedures in SAS for creating graphics
   some others are proc sgplot, proc gplot, and proc g3d.
   In addition, the Graph Template Language (GTL) offers numerous tools
   for producing high-quality graphs (see Matange and Heath 2011)
   format = uses the value labels for the education categories
   pie = requests a pie chart with values inside the slices and the slices
   from largest to smallest group beginning at 12:00
*/
```

Bar Charts

This is a type of graphic that uses rectangles to represent the percentage or proportion of each category of a categorical variable, frequencies of phenomena, or summary statistics for a set of similar variables. The length or height of the rectangles indicates the magnitude of each category's or variable's value. Bar charts are preferred to pie charts since it is easier to compare lengths than it is to compare angles or volume (see figure 10.3). Bar charts may be built vertically or horizontally. In addition, a particular type of this graphic is called a *stacked bar chart*. It is similar to a pie chart but divides a bar rather than a circle into sections proportional to the size of the categories. Most experts find stacked bar charts no better than pie charts (Wilkinson 2001), although research suggests they are simpler for the average person to comprehend (Siirtola 2014). In any event, some guidelines for preparing bar charts include the following:

- Use zero as the baseline of the axis of origin.
- As mentioned in chapter 8, order the data, and thus the bars, from highest to lowest value; this makes it easier for viewers to comprehend the patterns and make comparisons (Evergreen 2014). If using shading to distinguish the bars, go from darker to lighter as the bars range from left to right or top to bottom. Be aware, though, that people tend to see darker bars as larger in magnitude (Wong 2010).
- Use horizontal bars if the labels are long and do not fit well under vertical bars. Horizontal bar charts are also useful if the variable is naturally seen as moving from left to right, such as distance traveled by car, bicycle, and motorcycle.
- Often, bar charts include groups of bars. For example, one group might represent the percent in three age groups of females next to another group of bars that represent the same age groups of males. This is known as a *clustered bar chart*. When using bar clusters, include some space between them (Kosslyn 2006).

Figure 10.7 provides examples of three types of bar charts: a clustered bar chart that represents female and male average incomes in three education categories, a horizontal bar chart that shows the number of votes received by the three leading candidates in the 2012 Presidential election, and a stacked bar chart that reconfigures the information in the pie chart shown earlier (figure 10.6). Are there problems with the clarity and the efficiency of these graphs? It seems obvious why stacked bar charts are limited. Even though this one can be improved by changing the aspect ratio, the first three categories are so similar in area that it is difficult to distinguish them. This may or may not be a helpful thing depending on the message the researcher wishes to communicate. Nonetheless, clustered and horizontal bar charts are simpler to understand since they capitalize on our ability to judge and compare length better than area.

The following presents code to construct a horizontal bar chart in Stata, SPSS, and SAS. Although there are many options available in each program, the code provides only a few that are important so that the graphs follow some of the guidelines and principles discussed earlier.

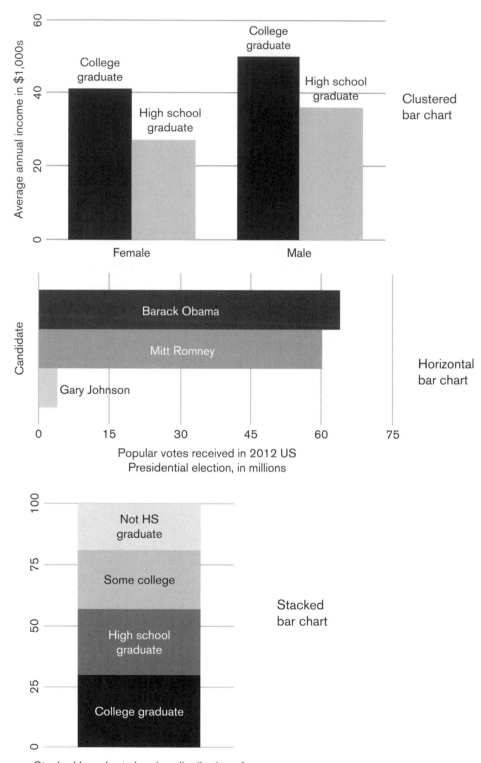

FIGURE 10.7 Three examples of bar charts.

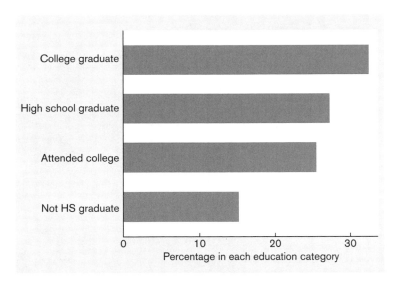

FIGURE 10.8 Horizontal bar chart of education categories.

Code to create a horizontal bar chart

```
* Stata

graph hbar, over(varname, sort(1) descending                  ///
  label(labcolor(black))) ytitle("Percent in each category")  ///
  ylabel(, nogrid tposition(inside))                          ///
  title("Horizontal bar chart of variable name", size(medlarge)  ///
  scheme(s2mono)

*/ Explanation of some aspects of code: hbar = horizontal graph; over(varname) =
   identifies the categorical variable that defines the bars; sort(1)
   descending = sorts the categories and plots them from largest to smallest;
   labcolor = color of labels; ytitle = title of y-axis;
   ylabel(, nogrid tposition) = requests not gridlines and that the tick
   marks face in; title = provides a title for the graph; scheme(s2mono) =
   request grayscale color scheme
*/
```

```
* SPSS

GGRAPH
  /GRAPHDATASET NAME="graphdataset" VARIABLES=[varname] COUNT()[name="COUNT"]
    MISSING=LISTWISE REPORTMISSING=NO
  /GRAPHSPEC SOURCE=INLINE
    TEMPLATE=[
    "C:\Program Files\IBM\SPSS\Statistics\23\Looks\GrayScale.sgt"
    "C:\Program Files\IBM\SPSS\Statistics\23\Looks\APA_Styles.sgt"].
BEGIN GPL
  SOURCE:  s = userSource(id("graphdataset"))
  DATA:    varname=col(source(s), name("[varname]"), unit.category())
  DATA:    COUNT=col(source(s), name("Count"))
  GUIDE:   axis(dim(1), label("[varname]"))
```

```
GUIDE:    axis(dim(2), label("Count"))
GUIDE:    text.title(label("Horizontal bar chart of [variable name]))
SCALE:    cat(aesthetic(aesthetic.texture.pattern.interior), include([indicate
          each category code]), sort.values([sort from largest to smallest value
          by code]))
SCALE:    linear(dim(2), min(0.0))
COORD:    transpose()
ELEMENT: interval(position(varname*COUNT), shape.interior(shape.square))

/* Explanation of some aspects of code: COORD: transpose() = creates a      .
/* horizontal rather than vertical bar chart; SCALE: linear(dim(2),         .
/* min(0.0)) = sets minimum value of bar axis at zero                       .
```

```
* SAS
Title 'Figure 10.8. Horizontal bar chart of variable name';
axis2 label=('Percent in each variable category');
proc gchart data=dataset;
  format varname varlabels.;
  hbar varname / discrete descending type=pct raxis=axis2 outside=pct;
run;

/* Explanation of code: hbar = requests a horizontal bar chart of percentages in
each category and orders from largest to smallest group
*/
```

Figure 10.8 provides a horizontal bar chart version of the pie chart in figure 10.6 (try to use the example code provided to replicate this chart). Which graphic do you prefer? The bar chart appears to do a better job of showing the relative percentages in each category. But is either one clear enough that you would be comfortable presenting it before an audience of your peers?

Dot Plots

As the name implies, these are plots made up of symbols and dots that display similar information as in a bar chart. They may be represented vertically or horizontally, although the latter is preferred in most situations. Many experts argue that dot plots are a good choice because they allow the audience to decode the data by judging position along a common scale (Cleveland 1993; Robbins 2013). As shown in figure 10.3, people are most accurate at judging differences in this manner. Dot plots are therefore preferred to bar charts, which rely on length for comparisons. Moreover, they use less ink and thus are less cluttered than bar charts (Cox 2008). Yet, these two types of graphics share many of the same principles, such as ordering by size and using zero as the baseline. However, when differences are small and thus detection is difficult, dot plots are better than bar charts because there is less visual distortion (Robbins 2013).

An important guideline is to make sure that the symbol used in a dot plot is legible. Solid and hollow circles are the most common symbol, but others are also used (triangles are more legible than squares or diamonds; Kosslyn 2006). Perhaps their main drawback is that they are not used as often as bar charts, so many viewers may not be comfortable with them.

Figure 10.9 provides a dot plot comparable to the horizontal bar chart in figure 10.8. Notice that it is a cleaner visual image than the bar chart. Even though most experts agree

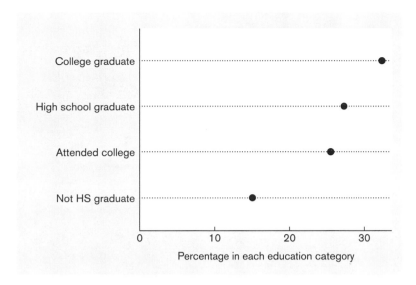

FIGURE 10.9 Dot plot of education categories.

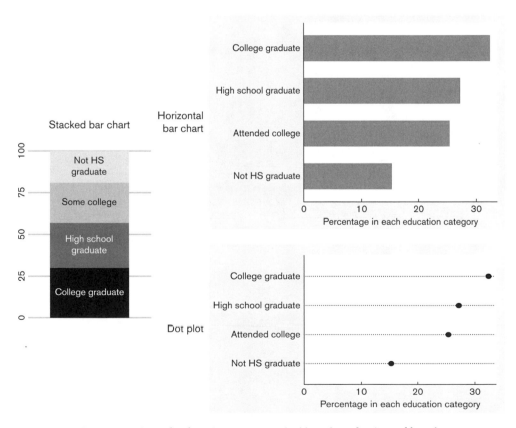

FIGURE 10.10 Percentage in each education group: stacked bar chart, horizontal bar chart, and dot plot.

Code to create a dot plot of each category of a variable

```
* Stata

/* The data are summarized by the categorical variable first, thus,    */
/* use the preserve and restore options to keep the original data in    */
/* memory                                                               */
preserve
collapse (count) idvar, by(categorical variable)
generate number = (idvar/N)*100
graph dot number, over(categorical variable, sort(1) descending)      ///
  ytitle("Percent in each category") title("Dot plot of variable name") ///
  ylabel(, nogrid tposition(inside)) aspectratio(0.75)                ///
  marker(1, msymbol(O) mcolor(black) mlwidth(medthick)                ///
  msize(medlarge)) scheme(s2mono)
restore


/* Explanation of some aspects of code: preserve = keeps data in memory;
   collapse = create summaries of categorical variables in a new dataset;
   generate = create a percent variable for each category, N is the total
   sample size; graph dot = requests dot plot; over = asks for separate dot
   line for each category; ytitle = labels the y axis; title = title of
   graphic = aspect ratio: makes it less oblong; marker = requests solid black
   circles; scheme = requests grayscale; restore = brings original data back
   into memory
*/


* SPSS

GGRAPH
    /GRAPHDATASET NAME="graphdataset" VARIABLES=[categorical variable] VALIDN([ID
        variable])[name="VALIDN_[ID variable]"]
      MISSING=LISTWISE REPORTMISSING=NO
    /GRAPHSPEC SOURCE=INLINE
    TEMPLATE=[
    "C:\Program Files\IBM\SPSS\Statistics\23\Looks\GrayScale.sgt"
    "C:\Program Files\IBM\SPSS\Statistics\23\Looks\APA_Styles.sgt"].
BEGIN GPL
    SOURCE:  s=userSource(id("graphdataset"))
    DATA:    [varname=col(source(s), name("varname"), unit.category())
    DATA:    VALIDN_[ID variable]=col(source(s), name("VALIDN_[ID variable]"))
    COORD:   rect(dim(1,2), transpose())
    GUIDE:   axis(dim(1), gridlines())
    GUIDE:   axis(dim(2), label("Number in each category"))
    GUIDE:   text.title(label("Figure 10.9. Dot plot of categorical
             variable"))
    SCALE:   cat(dim(1), include("1.00", "3.00", "2.00", "4.00"), sort.
             values("1.00", "3.00", "2.00", "4.00"))
    SCALE:   linear(dim(2), include(0))
    ELEMENT: point(position(varname*VALIDN_[ID variable]), size(size.small))
END GPL.
```

```
/* Explanation of some aspects of code: DATA: VALIDN_[ID variable] = uses  .
/* the id variable to count the number in each category; GUIDE:            .
/* axis(dim(2), gridlines())) = adds gridlines to the y-axis; SCALE:       .
/* cat(dim(1) = tells which categories to include and how to order them    .
```

```
* SAS

Title 'Figure 10.9. Dot plot of categorical variable';
proc sgplot data=dataset;
  format varname varlabels.;
  dot varname / categoryorder=respdesc stat=pct markerattrs=(symbol=circlefilled);
  xaxis label="Percent in each varname category" min=0 ;
  yaxis label=" ";
run;

/* Explanation of some aspects of code: dot = requests dot plot of
   the variables categories, from largest to smallest category, percentages,
   and filled circles as markers
   min = requests the x-axis begins at zero
*/
```

that dot plots provide better representations of this sort of information, it likely depends on the audience and what its members are used to seeing. To determine this for yourself, consider figure 10.10. It provides the stacked bar chart, the horizontal bar chart, and the dot plot adjacent to one another. Which do you think has the greatest clarity and efficiency? Assume that we are less concerned with precision and are mainly interested in general comparisons.

Bar charts and dot plots may also be used to examine the association between two or more variables. Recall that tables 9.9 and 9.10 were utilized to examine the association between education and attitudes toward gun control, as well as whether this presumed association differs by sex (see figure 9.1 for the conceptual diagram). How might these tables—especially table 9.10—be translated into a graphic? Focusing on a dot plot, think about what the distance from the origin to the symbol represents. One idea is to consider the distance from the origin as representing the percent of respondents who favor gun permits. For example, the distance for those who graduated from college is 77.2 units if measured as a percentage or 0.772 units if measured as a proportion (recall that a percent is simply a proportion multiplied by 100). Figure 10.11 provides a dot plot representation that includes all four education groups, each represented by a line of dots and a solid circle. The code to create this graph is also provided.

What do you conclude about the association between education and attitudes toward gun permits? Although there is higher favorability among those with more education, it appears to be a modest difference relative to the other three groups. Is there additional information

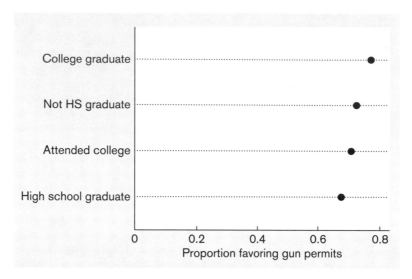

FIGURE 10.11 Proportion in favor of gun permits by level of education.

Code to create figure 10.11

```
* Stata

graph dot GunPermit, over(educCat, sort(1) descending)        ///
  ytitle("Proportion favoring gun permits")                   ///
  title("Figure 10.11. Proportion in favor of gun permits")   ///
  subtitle("by level of education") aspectratio(0.75)          ///
  ylabel(, nogrid tposition(inside))                           ///
  marker(1, msymbol(O) mcolor(black) mlwidth(medthick)         ///
  msize(medlarge)) scheme(s2mono)
```
```
* SPSS

GGRAPH
   /GRAPHDATASET NAME="graphdataset" VARIABLES=educCat MEAN(GunPermit)
     [name="MEAN_GunPermit"]
   MISSING=LISTWISE REPORTMISSING=NO
   /GRAPHSPEC SOURCE=INLINE
   TEMPLATE=[
   "C:\Program Files\IBM\SPSS\Statistics\23\Looks\GrayScale.sgt"
   "C:\Program Files\IBM\SPSS\Statistics\23\Looks\APA_Styles.sgt"].
BEGIN GPL
   SOURCE:  s=userSource(id("graphdataset"))
   DATA:    educCat=col(source(s), name("educCat"), unit.category())
   DATA:    MEAN_GunPermit=col(source(s), name("MEAN_GunPermit"))
   COORD:   rect(dim(1,2), transpose())
   GUIDE:   axis(dim(1), label(""), gridlines())
   GUIDE:   axis(dim(2), label("Proportion favoring gun permits"), delta(0.2))
   GUIDE:   text.title(label("Figure 10.11. Proportion in favor of gun
            permits"))
```

```
      GUIDE:   text.subsubtitle(label("by level of education"))
      SCALE:   cat(dim(1), include("1.00", "2.00", "3.00", "4.00"), sort.
               values("2.00", "3.00", "1.00", "4.00"))
      SCALE:   linear(dim(2), include(0, 0.2, 0.4, 0.6, 0.8))
      ELEMENT: point(position(educCat*MEAN_GunPermit))
 END GPL.


 * SAS

 Title 'Figure 10.11. Proportion in favor of gun permits, by education';
 proc sgplot data=gss2014data;
   format educCat edCat.;
   dot educCat / categoryorder=respdesc stat=mean response=GunPermit
     markerattrs=(symbol=circlefilled) ;
   xaxis label="Proportion favoring gun permits" min=0;
   yaxis label=" ";
 run;
```

you would like to have? For example, perhaps including error bars that represent 95% confidence intervals or credible intervals is appropriate. Furthermore, when considering how to represent this sort of an association, do not forget to consider the audience. Will the audience understand proportions? Or would it be better to present the association in terms of percentages or even frequencies: "about 8 out of 10 college graduates favor gun permits, whereas about 7 of 10 high school graduates favor gun permits." As mentioned in chapter 9, lay audiences tend to prefer frequencies; probabilities and proportions can be confusing (Gigerenzer 2002). Of course, these approaches to interpretation assume that precise information is important, whereas the data presentation may have as its goal general patterns. Once again, the presentation should be geared toward the particular audience the researcher wishes to address.

Should dot plots or bar charts be used to test the full conceptual model? Or will clarity and efficiency be compromised? There are no clear answers to these questions since they depend on the audience and its experience with these types of graphics. Nonetheless, figure 10.12 provides two ways that a dot plot might be used to test the model. Note that the first one simply divides the data shown in figure 10.11 into male and female panels. The second dot plot places the proportions for females and males next to each other. Recall from chapter 8 that one way to envision graphics is as layers (see figure 8.6; Wickham 2010). In the second dot plot, imagine that there is a layer for males and a layer for females. One is then placed on top of the other to form a single image. This is a useful exercise when thinking about how to design a graphic that shows associations among three variables. In any event, ponder each dot plot in figure 10.12 to determine which one you prefer. Consider the principles discussed earlier—as well as the issues of detection and distance—and decide if one or the other meets them to your satisfaction.

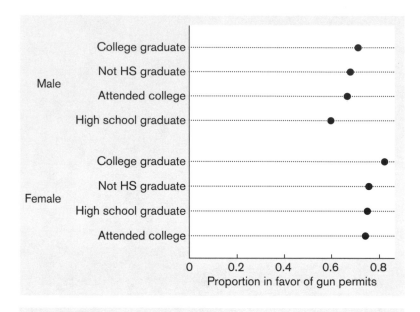

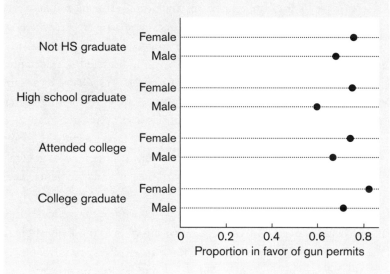

FIGURE 10.12 Dot plots of proportion in favor of gun permits by level of education and sex.

SOURCE: General Social Survey, 2014 (http://www3.norc.org/GSS+Website).

Furthermore, is this the most efficient way to represent a test of the conceptual model? When moderator effects are proposed, it is usually better to use line graphs to represent them (Kosslyn 2006). Thus, we turn next to this type of graphic.

Line Graphs

Also known as *line charts* or *line plots*, this type of graphic displays a series of data points using line segments. Some principles that apply specifically to line graphs include the following.

- Do not include too many lines, especially if they are difficult to distinguish. For example, suppose we wish to extend the conceptual model of gun control support to distinguish liberals and conservatives by their sex. This would necessitate four comparisons rather than just two. In this situation, it may be better for the sake of clarity to present two line graphs, such that one shows liberals and another shows conservatives.

- As discussed earlier, it is best to label the lines directly rather than use a legend. Most statistical software defaults to a legend.

- It is not a good idea to use line graphs with unordered categorical (nominal) data (Klass 2012). These graphs are simpler to understand when the data are ordered in some way.

- Visual acuity is enhanced when the lines do not touch the x- or y-axis (Wainer 2008).

- There is no need, except under exceptional circumstances, to include a marker to show at what point the line matches a specific value of the x- and y-axes. Line graphs are designed to display patterns and trends rather than data points.

An example of a line graph is shown in figure 10.2 (see also figure 10.5), which displays the death rates for different groups of people aged 45–54. Line graphs provide an alternative to many types of bar charts and dot plots. For example, figure 10.13 provides an another way of depicting the information displayed in figure 10.12. However, rather than comparing the relative distance between the markers in the dot plot, we may now compare differences in the vertical distance between two lines. Figure 10.13 indicates more clearly that the biggest difference between females and males occurs for those who are high school graduates only, with college graduates manifesting a slightly smaller difference. Partly for this reason, some experts prefer line graphs for demonstrating conditional associations such as the one displayed here (Gelman 2014). Nevertheless, it is important to note that one of the reasons figure 10.13 enhances our ability to see female-male differences is because the scale has changed. In figure 10.12, the proportion scale was 0–0.9, whereas in figure 10.13 it is 0.5–0.9.

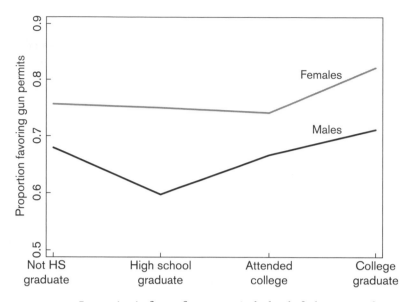

FIGURE 10.13 Proportion in favor of gun permits by level of education and sex.

An alternative way to depict the conceptual model is to treat education as continuous rather than categorical (recall this is the way education is originally measured in the dataset). The association outlined in figure 5.1 proposes that as education increases, so too does support for gun control. However, we have now seen that it is not so simple. If education is treated as continuous, then the assumption—unless some variation is proposed—is that there is a linear, or straight line, association between education and support for gun control. Recall also that this association is presumed to be different for females and males (see figure 9.1). How might this be illustrated with a line graph? One approach is to examine separate linear fit lines for females and males. You may recall that linear fit lines are usually based on linear regression models, which are designed to predict the mean value of a variable (attitudes toward gun permits) at distinct values of another variable (education). Strictly speaking, since the gun permit measure is not continuous, a linear regression model is not appropriate. Models that are designed for categorical variables are beyond the scope of this presentation. Yet, one way to vary the assumption that there is a linear fit is to use what is known as a *lowess* line. Lowess is short for *locally weighted regression*. It is a method of dividing up the data by the *x*-variable (*education*) and estimating a fit line for each portion (the local part). It then connects these lines to form a depiction of where the estimated averages for the *y*-variable (*GunPermit*) fall in narrow ranges of the *x*-variable (*education*). Lowess is also known as a *smoother* since it displays associations rather closely. Figure 10.14 provides linear fit lines and lowess fit lines for males and females that show the association between education and favorable attitudes toward gun permits.

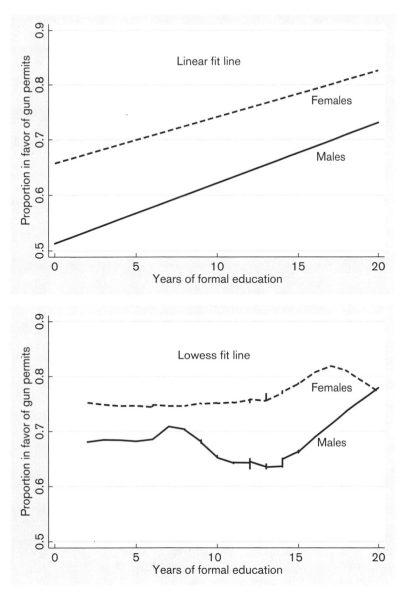

FIGURE 10.14 Linear and lowess fit lines of the association between favoring gun permits and education (in years), by sex.

Code to create figure 10.14

```
* Stata
/* Line graph of favoring gun permits by continuous education */
    twoway lfit GunPermit education if female==0,              ///
            ytitle("Proportion in favor of gun permits")       ///
            xlabel(, tposition(inside)) lwidth(medthick)       ///
            text(.68 17 "Males", place(c))                     ///
            yscale(range(.5 .9)) ylabel(#4,tposition(inside))  ///
            || lfit GunPermit education if female==1,          ///
            lwidth(medthick) text(.78 17 "Females", place(c))  ///
            legend(off) scheme(s2mono)

/* Lowess smoother depiction of favoring gun permits by education       */
    twoway lowess GunPermit education if female==0 & education>0,  ///
            ytitle("Proportion in favor of gun permits")       ///
            xlabel(, tposition(inside)) lwidth(medthick)       ///
            text(.68 17 "Males", place(c)) yscale(range(.5 .9))  ///
            ylabel(#4,tposition(inside)) ||                    ///
            lowess GunPermit education if female==1 & education>0,  ///
            lwidth(medthick) text(.78 17 "Females", place(c))  ///
            legend(off) scheme(s2mono)

/* explanation of some aspects of code: lfit = requests a linear fit line;
   lowess = requests a lowess fit line; text(# # "label", place(c)) = places
   text in the plot to identify the group the line represents; education>0 =
   the few observations for education at zero make the lowess plot difficult
   to read, so they are omitted using the if command
*/
```

```
* SPSS

/* Line graph of favoring gun permits by continuous education .
GGRAPH
    /GRAPHDATASET NAME="graphdataset" VARIABLES=education GunPermit female
MISSING=LISTWISE
      REPORTMISSING=NO
    /GRAPHSPEC SOURCE=INLINE
  TEMPLATE=[
    "C:\Program Files\IBM\SPSS\Statistics\23\Looks\GrayScale.sgt"
    "C:\Program Files\IBM\SPSS\Statistics\23\Looks\APA_Styles.sgt"].
BEGIN GPL
    SOURCE:  s=userSource(id("graphdataset"))
    DATA:    education=col(source(s), name("education"), unit.category())
    DATA:    GunPermit=col(source(s), name("GunPermit"))
    DATA:    female=col(source(s), name("female"), unit.category())
    GUIDE:   axis(dim(1), label("Years of formal education"))
    GUIDE:   axis(dim(2), label("Proportion in favor of gun permits"))
    GUIDE:   legend(aesthetic(aesthetic.texture.pattern.interior), null())
    GUIDE:   text.title(label("Figure 10.14. Linear fit line sof association
             between favoring"))
    GUIDE:   text.subtitle(label("gun permits and education (in years), by
             sex"))
    SCALE:   linear(dim(2), min(0.5))
    ELEMENT: line(position(smooth.linear(education*GunPermit))), split(female),
             label(female))
```

```
END GPL.

/* Lowess smoother depiction of favoring gun permits by education .
GGRAPH
    /GRAPHDATASET NAME="graphdataset" VARIABLES=education GunPermit female
       MISSING=LISTWISE REPORTMISSING=NO
    /GRAPHSPEC SOURCE=INLINE
  TEMPLATE=[
    "C:\Program Files\IBM\SPSS\Statistics\23\Looks\GrayScale.sgt"
    "C:\Program Files\IBM\SPSS\Statistics\23\Looks\APA_Styles.sgt"].
BEGIN GPL
    SOURCE:  s=userSource(id("graphdataset"))
    DATA:    education=col(source(s), name("education"), unit.category())
    DATA:    GunPermit=col(source(s), name("GunPermit"))
    DATA:    female=col(source(s), name("female"), unit.category())
    GUIDE:   axis(dim(1), label("Years of formal education"))
    GUIDE:   axis(dim(2), label("Proportion in favor of gun permits"))
    GUIDE:   legend(aesthetic(aesthetic.texture.pattern.interior), null())
    GUIDE:   text.title(label("Figure 10.14. Lowess fit lines of association
             between favoring"))
    GUIDE:   text.subtitle(label("gun permits and education (in years), by sex"))
    SCALE:   linear(dim(2), min(0.5))
    ELEMENT: line(position(smooth.loess(education*GunPermit))), split(female),
             label(female))
END GPL.

/* Explanation of some aspects of code: ELEMENT: line = provides linear fit  .
/* line with smooth.linear or a lowess fit line with smooth.loess           .
/* SCALE = requests that the minimum value of the y-axis be set at 0.5        .
```

```
* SAS

/* Line graph of favor gun permits by continuous education */
Title 'Figure 10.14. Linear fit of association between favoring gun permits and
    education, by sex';
proc sgplot data=gss2014data noautolegend;
  format female fem.;
  reg x=education y=GunPermit / group=female;
  xaxis label="Years of education"
  yaxis label="Proportion favoring gun permits" min=0.5 max=0.9;
run;

/* Lowess smoother depiction of favoring gun permits by education */
Title 'Figure 10.14. Lowess fit of association between favoring gun permits and
    education, by sex';
proc sgplot data=gss2014data noautolegend;
  format female fem.;
  loess x=education y=GunPermit / group=female;
  xaxis label="Years of education"
  yaxis label="Proportion favoring gun permits" min=0.5 max=0.9;
run;

/* Explanation of some aspects of code: noautolegend = omits the legend
    reg = requests linear fit lines grouped by the female variable
    loess = requests lowess fit lines
    min and max = scales the y-axis so that it spans 0.5 to 0.9
*/
```

```
/* Note that SAS does not provide a straightforward way to insert text to
   label the lines when groups are requested. One approach is to use
   annotation macros, but this is beyond the scope of this presentation
   For more information, see Liu (2015)
*/
```

Compare figure 10.14 to figure 10.13. How are they similar or different? The straight-line fit suggests a uniform increase in support for gun permits with years of education. For instance, the first graph in figure 10.14 suggests that about 62% of males and 74% of females with 10 years of education favor gun permits, whereas about 72% of males and 81% of females with 20 years of education favor gun permits. But the categorical depiction in figure 10.13 and the smoothed depiction in figure 10.14 suggest that assuming a linear pattern is a bit too simplistic. Notice, for example, that differences by education emerge mainly as people attend college. Moreover, as mentioned earlier, the largest difference between females and males occurs among high school graduates. This illustrates some important points about how graphic representations of relations among variables, if done carefully, can reveal interesting associations that many common statistical models do not. Recall the quote related in chapter 8: "The greatest value of a graph is when it forces us to notice what we never expected to see" (John Tukey; cited in Wainer 2005, 123). A word of caution is in order, though: it can be an interesting exercise to search for various patterns in the data, but doing so increases the risk of finding an association that is not valid or occurs mainly because of the particular dataset that one happens to use. After all, most datasets represent only one sample among many conceivable samples. So we need to be careful of overdoing it. It is best to strictly examine the research question and avoid fishing expeditions.

As noted earlier, line graphs are usually the best choice for examining and visually testing trends over time. Figure 10.15 is based on violent crime data that were collected as part of the US Federal Bureau of Investigation's (FBI) Uniform Crime Reports (UCR). The state-level data are for the years 1990–2012 and are part of a dataset called *ViolentCrimeTrends.csv*. This dataset was built from violent crime data available through the website http://www .ucrdatatool.gov/Search/ Crime/State/StatebyState.cfm. After importing the data into statistical software, what type of line graph would be useful? It is not a good idea to try to include a separate line for each state; a graphic with 50 lines is far too cluttered. One might consider multiple line graphs, one for each state, but this would quickly overwhelm any audience. One feasible option is to select a small number of states to compare. Figure 10.15, for example, compares three states that represent different population sizes (their population ranks are in parentheses): California (1), Kentucky (26), and Wyoming (50). Suppose the comparison is based on a research question concerning whether larger states tend to have higher violent crime rates than smaller states, but presumes that this has changed over the last couple of decades. The graphic that (weakly) examines this question is followed by the code that produces it.

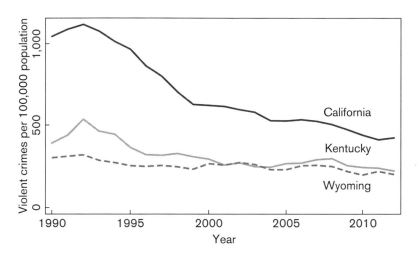

FIGURE 10.15 Violent crime rates, 1990–2012, California, Kentucky, and Wyoming.

SOURCE: FBI, Uniform Crime Reports, 1990–2012. (http://www.ucrdatatool.gov /Search/Crime/State/StatebyState.cfm)

Code to create figure 10.15

```
* Stata
/* Import the data */
import delimited [pathname]\ViolentCrimeTrends.csv

/* Create the line graph */
graph  twoway line ViolentCrimeRate Year if fipscode==6,        ///
       ylabel(#4,tposition(inside)) lwidth(medthick)            ///
       ytitle("Violent crimes per 100,000 population")          ///
       text(550 2009 "California", place(c)) ||                 ///
       line ViolentCrimeRate Year if fipscode==21,              ///
       lwidth(medthick) text(330 2009 "Kentucky", place(c))     ///
       || line ViolentCrimeRate Year if fipscode==56,           ///
       lwidth(medthick) lpattern(dash)                          ///
       text(165 2009 "Wyoming", place(c)) legend(off)           ///
       xlabel(,tposition(inside)) scheme(s1mono)                ///
       title("Figure 10.15. Violent crime rates, 1990-2012,")   ///
       subtitle("California, Kentucky, and Wyoming")            ///
       note("Source: FBI, Uniform Crime Reports, 1990-2012.")

/* Explanation of some aspects of code: twoway line = requests line plots
   of violent crime rates over the time period; if fipscode =
   requests lines for each state
   Note that three plots are overlaid, one for each state
*/

* SPSS

/* import the data .
get data / type=txt / file="[pathname]\ViolentCrimeTrends.csv"
   / delimiters=","
```

```
     /  qualifier=';"';
     /  firstcase=2
     /  variables = State A11 StateAbbrev A2 fipscode F2.0 Year F4.0
                    ViolentCrimeRate F6.1 .
execute .

/* Create a temporary dataset with just the three states .
temp.
select if (fipscode=6|fipscode=21|fipscode=56).

/* Create the line graph .
GGRAPH
    /GRAPHDATASET NAME="graphdataset" VARIABLES=Year ViolentCrimeRate StateAbbrev
      MISSING=LISTWISE
      REPORTMISSING=NO
    /GRAPHSPEC SOURCE=INLINE
  TEMPLATE=[
    "C:\Program Files\IBM\SPSS\Statistics\23\Looks\GrayScale.sgt"
    "C:\Program Files\IBM\SPSS\Statistics\23\Looks\APA_Styles.sgt"].
BEGIN GPL
    SOURCE:  s=userSource(id("graphdataset"))
    DATA:    Year=col(source(s), name("Year"))
    DATA:    ViolentCrimeRate=col(source(s), name("ViolentCrimeRate"))
    DATA:    StateAbbrev=col(source(s), name("StateAbbrev"), unit.category())
    GUIDE:   axis(dim(1), label("Year"))
    GUIDE:   axis(dim(2), label("Violent crimes per 100,000"))
    GUIDE:   legend(aesthetic(aesthetic.shape.interior), null())
    GUIDE:   text.title(label("Figure 10.15. Violent crime rates, 1990-2012"))
    GUIDE:   text.subtitle(label("California, Kentucky, and Wyoming"))
    SCALE:   linear(dim(1), min(1990), max(2012))
    ELEMENT: line(position(Year*ViolentCrimeRate), shape.interior(StateAbbrev),
             label(StateAbbrev), missing.wings())
END GPL.

/* Explanation of some aspects of code: Element = requests a line plot .
/* of violent crime rates over the time period      .
```

```
* SAS
/* Import and name the violent crime trend dataset */
proc import datafile=[ViolentCrimeTrends.csv]"
  out=violentcrimetrends replace delimiter=';,';;
  getnames=yes;
run;

data violentcrimetrends;
  set john.ViolentCrimeTrends;  /* recall that the data are part of */
run;                            /* a SAS library, here called john */

/* Create the line graph */
Title 'Figure 10.15. Violent crime rates, 1990-2014';;
proc sgplot data=violentcrimetrends noautolegend;
  where (fipscode=6 or fipscode=21 or fipscode=56);
  vline Year / response=ViolentCrimeRate group=fipscode;
  xaxis label="Year"
  xaxis values=(1990 to 2012 by 5);
```

```
   yaxis label="Violent crimes per 100,000 population"
run;

/* Explanation of some aspects of code: where = uses only the three
   states to build the line graph
   vline = requests a vertical line plot for each state that represents
   the rates of violent crimes over the time period
/*
```

Once again, the lines are labeled directly rather than with a legend. For example, in Stata the word "Wyoming" is placed in the line graph at $y = 165$ and $x = 2009$. Notice also that the positioning of the labels is consistent with the rule of thirds discussed earlier; thus, they draw the eye of the viewer much better than a legend placed in the outer region of the frame. Furthermore, since the lines for Kentucky and Wyoming are so close together, the subcommand lpattern(dash) in Stata requests a different line pattern for Wyoming. This makes it easier to distinguish the lines.

Are there any interesting patterns in figure 10.15? The most apparent trend is the relatively large decrease in California's rate of violent crimes during the 1990s. This coincided with a crime drop in other large states such as New York, Florida, and Illinois (check the trends in the dataset to verify this claim). Research has suggested various reasons for the decline, such as increases in the number of police, the end of the so-called crack epidemic, and demographic shifts in the population (Blumstein and Wallman 2006).

Imagine how one might use a table, a bar chart, or a dot plot to depict these trends. A table would include a lot of data that would be difficult to interpret (see exercise 3 at the end of chapter 8), whereas a bar chart or dot plot would likely be too cluttered. Thus, it should be clear why a line graph is useful when researchers wish to study trends.

Scatter Plots

Although there are many other useful graphics, the last one discussed in this chapter is called a scatter plot. These graphics are designed primarily for two continuous variables. They use symbols to represent where in the frame the data elements of the two variables intersect. Perhaps you recall plotting points in a coordinate system in an elementary algebra class. Scatter plots are simply another name for the results of this type of exercise. One of the problems with scatter plots occurs when researchers use relatively large samples or datasets. The symbols representing the data points often overlap to such a degree that the plot looks like a messy cloud (see figure 10.1). But, if there is a pattern in the cloud or separate clouds of data points, then scatter plots can be useful even with lots of data.

Some important principles that apply to scatter plots include the following:

- Use a marker that is easily recognizable, such as a circle or triangle. But it is simpler to distinguish different markers when they are in distinct parts of the scatter plot (Kosslyn 2006); when many are in the same area, they can overlap and make detection difficult.

- Use an open marker style, such as a hollow circle, when there are many data points.

- If using color to indicate different sets of points, make sure they are well distinguishable (red vs. blue, but recall that red appears "closer" than blue). Different colored circles can be especially effective at discriminating groups (Lewandowsky and Spence 1989). However, be cognizant of color blind viewers and black and white reproduction. Darker shades on a white background seem to work best.

- Use *jittering* to distinguish overlapping points. This is a technique that moves the points a bit so that those that overlap are separated by some space. It makes it easier to detect patterns when there is a lot of overlap in the data. Stata (*jitter*), SPSS (*point.jitter*), SAS (*jitter* macro), and R (*jitter*) all feature options to jitter points.

- Including a fit line of some sort can help to clarify the association (see figures 10.13–10.15). Make sure it is discernible, though, and provide labels directly in the plot, especially if there is more than one line. Recall the messy graphic in figure 10.1. Try to avoid this type of clutter.

- If visual acuity can be maintained, consider using labels rather than markers to identify data points (Robbins 2013). For example, if the scatter plot shows two variables and the unit of observation is countries, use the country names (or well-known abbreviations) to label their respective data points.

- Do not use an inner grid (Kosslyn 2006). If you recall plotting points in algebra class, you may have used graph paper. This type of paper shows a grid. But we do not want scatter plots to appear this way.

The following scatter plot examples are based on nation-level data on rates of endangered animal species (*EndangeredSpecies.csv*). The 74 nations that make up the dataset are mostly from the developing world. There is some research that suggests that higher levels of carbon dioxide emissions and greater energy use are associated with higher rates of endangered species (Hoffmann 2004). Figure 10.16 depicts one of these proposed associations. Since all three of these variables are measured continuously, examining their relationships with scatter plots should be useful.

Figure 10.17 provides a basic scatter plot of the association between CO_2 emissions and the rate of endangered species among the 74 nations. What does the scatter plot show? Is there a discernible association? Be careful of looking at the plot for too long. Recall the *Ganzwelt effect* (see chapter 8). It tends to occur when someone stares at a graph, such as a

FIGURE 10.16 Carbon dioxide emissions and rates of endangered species at the nation level.

scatter plot, too long. As the mind seeks to make sense of the pattern, something tangible emerges even if the pattern is simply random (Wainer 2005, 26). In any event, there is not a strong pattern in figure 10.17. A generous statement is that there is a slight positive association as one scans from left to right.

Nonetheless, notice some of the principles used to create this scatter plot: hollow circles make overlapping points easier to recognize, inner tick marks are used, and there are no gridlines. Nevertheless, are there other principles that should be considered? Is the title clear enough or is more information needed? For example, since the data are comprised mostly of developing nations, does this need to be pointed out? Will audience members understand the term "rate" or is some clarification needed, such as "number of endangered species per 1,000 indigenous species of animals"? Is there too much clutter in the graphic and this makes any patterns that may exist difficult to recognize (a clarity and efficiency issue)? What about the markers? Will audience members wish to understand a little more about which countries fall into which positions in the scatter plot? A problem with this is that using country names rather than the markers will create a very cluttered graphic. An alternative is to use the nation codes, which are labeled with two-letter abbreviations. Another idea is to label a few countries to provide a little more context.

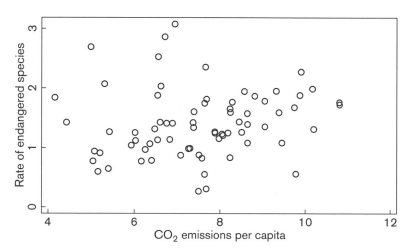

FIGURE 10.17 CO_2 emissions and endangered species, by country.

SOURCE: World Bank (http://data.worldbank.org/indicator/EN.ATM.CO2E.PC) and IUCN Red List (Vié et al. 2009).

Code to create figure 10.17

```
* Stata

/* import the Endangered Species data */
import delimited [pathname]\EndangeredSpecies.csv

twoway scatter EndangerRate CO2Emissions, msymbol(Oh) mcolor(black)   ///
      msize(medlarge) xlabel(,tposition(inside))                      ///
      ylabel(,nogrid tposition(inside))                               ///
      title("Figure 10.17. CO2 Emissions & Endangered Species,")     ///
      subtitle("by Country", size(large)) scheme(s1mono)             ///
      note("Source: World Bank & IUCN Red List, 2006.")

/* Explanation of some aspects of code: twoway scatter = requests a
   scatterplot, with EndangerRate on the y-axis and CO2Emissions in the x-axis
   msymbol(Oh) = requests hollow circles for the markers, followed by options
   to make them black and a little larger than the default size
*/
```

```
* SPSS

/* import the endangered species data .
get data / type=txt / file="[pathname]\EndangeredSpecies.csv"
  / delimiters=","
  / qualifier='"'
  / firstcase=2
  / variables = Nation A19 NationNumber F2.0 Population F9.0
                EnergyConsumption F16.14 CO2Emissions F16.14
                EndangerRate F17.15 IncomeLevel F1.0 GDP F16.14 .

formats EndangerRate CO2Emissions (f 2.0).
GGRAPH
    /GRAPHDATASET NAME="graphdataset" VARIABLES=CO2Emissions EndangerRate
      MISSING=LISTWISE
      REPORTMISSING=NO
    /GRAPHSPEC SOURCE=INLINE
  TEMPLATE=[
    "C:\Program Files\IBM\SPSS\Statistics\23\Looks\GrayScale.sgt"
    "C:\Program Files\IBM\SPSS\Statistics\23\Looks\APA_Styles.sgt"].
BEGIN GPL
    SOURCE: s=userSource(id("graphdataset"))
    DATA:   CO2Emissions=col(source(s), name("CO2Emissions"))
    DATA:   EndangerRate=col(source(s), name("EndangerRate"))
    GUIDE:  axis(dim(1), delta(2), label("CO2 emissions per capita"))
    GUIDE:  axis(dim(2), delta(1), label("Rate of endangered species"))
    GUIDE:  text.title(label("Figure 10.17. CO2 Emissions & Endangered
            Species,"))
    GUIDE:  text.subtitle(label("by Country"))
    GUIDE:  text.footnote(label("Source: World Bank & IUCN Red List, 2006."))
    SCALE:  linear(dim(1), min(4), max(12))
    SCALE:  linear(dim(2), min(0), max(3))
    ELEMENT: point(position(CO2Emissions*EndangerRate))
END GPL.

/* Explanation of some aspects of code: ELEMENT: point = requests a      .
/* scatterplot; another ELEMENT command can be used to request fit lines   .
```

```
/* as in Figure 10.14 or Figure 10.19 These are needed to construct      .
/* Figure 10.18                                                          .

* SAS
/* Import endangered species data */
proc import datafile="[pathname]\EndangeredSpecies.csv"
  out=endangeredspecies replace ;
  delimiter=',';
  getnames=yes;
run;

Title 'Figure 10.17. CO2 Emissions and Endangered Species, by Country';
footnote j=l "Source: World Bank & IUCN Red List, 2006.";
proc sgplot data=endangeredspecies noautolegend;
  format NationNumber nationabbrev.;
  scatter x=CO2Emissions y=EndangerRate;
  xaxis label="CO2 emissions per capita" max=12;
  yaxis label="Rate of endangered species"
run;

/* Explanation of some aspects of code: scatter = specifies a scatterplot with
   the x and y axes defined and labeled, with a maximum value for the x-axis of 12
   Note that the format option assumes that characters have been assigned to the
   NationNumber variable in a previous step. These are needed to construct
   Figure 10.18
/*
```

Figure 10.18 is identical to figure 10.17 except that it uses the two-letter abbreviation rather than the hollow circles to identify each country. Two things are obvious. First, there is still quite a bit of clutter, which makes detection difficult and violates the principle of clarity. Consider the points in the middle of the scatter plot. There is too much overlap to distinguish the country abbreviations. Second, even ignoring the clutter, the abbreviations may not be helpful to many viewers. It is common in the United States and Canada for North American audiences to understand abbreviations for states or provinces, but country abbreviations are less well known. Thus, if country-specific information is desired rather than simply the pattern of the association, then labeling a few of the countries, such as Madagascar (MG), Botswana (BT), and Trinidad and Tobago (TT), may be better since these are examples of countries that don't fit the presumed pattern as well as some of the others. For example, Madagascar is relatively high on the rate of endangered species, but in the middle of the distribution of CO_2 emissions.

Some experts argue that the value of a scatter plot lies in its ability to display patterns and trends rather than specific information. Thus, they prefer figures 10.17 and 10.18. However, some also prefer some sort of line to show the pattern of association better. This necessitates layering a line graph onto a scatter plot. But this risks clutter (see figure 10.1). There are also some who prefer a line graph without a scatter plot. This diminishes clutter and,

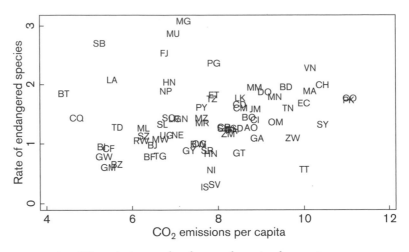

FIGURE 10.18 CO$_2$ emissions and endangered species, by country.
SOURCE: World Bank and IUCN Red List, 2006.

presumably, enhances clarity and efficiency. A problem with this approach is that the line chosen is too often a straight (linear) line. As illustrated by figure 10.14, this can miss some interesting patterns in the data, such as nonlinear (curved) associations. Nuances of the pattern, such as extreme observations, may also go undetected.

Consider figure 10.19. It provides a line graph superimposed on a scatter plot. The linear fit line is almost horizontal, thus suggesting a modest linear association between CO$_2$ emissions and endangered species among these nations. The correlation between these two variables is about 0.14. Some researchers place correlations directly in the graph to provide a bit more context for viewers (as an exercise, see if you can determine how to do this). In addition, one should ask whether a linear fit line is the most appropriate at capturing the association between these two variables. Try fitting a lowess fit line. What does it show about the association? Would it be better to use this type of line rather than a linear fit line?

As a final example of a scatter plot, suppose that a researcher wishes to observe an association between two continuous variables, and also determine whether the association differs for some groups? In other words, how would someone create a three-way scatter plot? If there are only two groups, identifying their patterns with different markers or with different fit lines is feasible. If there are more than two groups, unless they are clearly distinguishable in the graphic, then multiple adjacent scatter plots are useful.

Figure 10.20 displays a scatter plot of CO$_2$ emissions and endangered species by the nation's income level. To simplify this presentation, income level is divided into only two categories: low and high. The main problem with the scatter plot is that there is not sufficient discrimination between the low- and high-income nations; thus, the markers are not distinguishable (Kosslyn 2006). The principle of efficiency is not met in this graph. Would

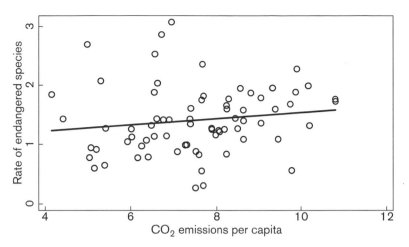

FIGURE 10.19 CO_2 emissions and endangered species, by country.

SOURCE: World Bank and IUCN Red List, 2006.

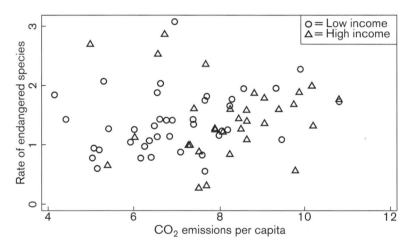

FIGURE 10.20 CO_2 emissions and endangered species, by country's income level.

SOURCE: World Bank and IUCN Red List, 2006.

the use of color help? As mentioned earlier, including different colored circles to distinguish groups can be quite effective (Lewandowsky and Spence 1989). In any event, the most apparent pattern is that high-income nations tend to produce more CO_2 emissions, but whether this is associated with endangered species rates is not clear.

Perhaps including fit lines for the two groups would be beneficial. Figure 10.21, though cluttered, includes two fit lines, one for low-income nations and one for high-income nations.

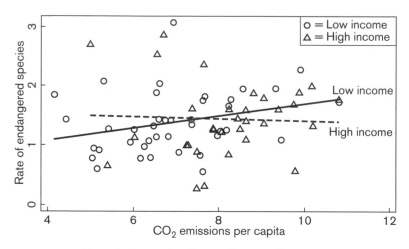

FIGURE 10.21 CO_2 emissions and endangered species, by country's income level.

SOURCE: World Bank and IUCN Red List, 2006.

Note that there are now, implicitly, four layers to this graphic. There is a slightly higher association between CO_2 emissions and endangered species for countries with low income levels, although the difference is not dramatic and suggests a weak association in general. As an exercise to try to get a better handle on whether there is any sort of association worth exploring, try lowess fit lines for both groups of countries. What do they suggest?

Although the types of scatter plots shown in figures 10.17–10.21 continue to be a popular way to represent associations that involve continuous variables, there are alternatives. Perhaps the most common is a *bubble plot*. This is a type of scatter plot in which the size of the marker represents something about the magnitude of a third variable. Suppose a researcher wishes to replicate the scatter plot in figure 10.17 but include data on population size. The plot could be revised so that the size of the circles is proportional to the population of the country. Although population size is frequently used in bubble plots, the choice depends on the research question. Nevertheless, recall that area is not an effective way to make comparisons (see figure 10.3), so bubble plots have limitations. See the website www.gapminder.org /data for dozens of examples of bubble plots.

An alternative to scatter plots some experts recommend is called a *density or contour plot*. As noted, scatter plots can get cluttered quickly when there are a lot of data points. A density plot divides the frame of the graphic into relatively small tiles, such as squares or hexagons. It then bases the color or shading of the tile on the number of data points within it. Tiles with more data points use warmer colors, whereas those with fewer data points use cooler colors. For this reason, this type of contour plot is also called a *heat map*. If grayscale shading is used, a darker shade can be used to represent denser tiles. One advantage of a contour plot is that it may be used to display three continuous variables on a 2D surface. However, they can be difficult to grasp and thus inefficient for many audiences.

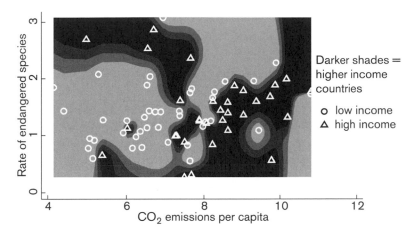

FIGURE 10.22 CO_2 emissions and endangered species by country's income level.

SOURCE: World Bank and IUCN Red List, 2006.

Figure 10.22 displays a contour plot rendition of figure 10.20 along with markers to show where in the graphic high- and low-income countries fall. Normally, the markers are not shown in a contour plot, but they are furnished here to provide a bit more intuition about how the plot works. Notice that the higher-income nations tend to fall in the darker shaded areas and the lower-income nations are in the lighter shaded areas. But does the contour plot provide any additional or unique information about the association between CO_2 emissions and endangered species? It suggests a rather odd pattern that is not easy to interpret. Thus, in this situation, a contour plot does not seem useful. Nevertheless, when there is a strong pattern, these graphics are more informative.

WHERE TO NEXT?

The fields of data visualization and statistical graphics are growing at a rapid clip. The big data movement has been the impetus for much of this growth, although it is often more concerned with using data to create a striking image that catches the viewer's attention than with specific results of a data analysis (Gelman and Unwin 2013). The social sciences have also seen increasing interest in graphical methods since, as mentioned several times, they provide a clear and efficient way to understand the results of a project (Healy and Moody 2014). Human minds appear to be designed to appreciate graphical representations of information. Researchers may use this to their advantage by developing graphical depictions of research results.

This chapter reviews just a few graphics that are commonly used to present data and the results of statistical analyses. But there are many others. For instance, we have spent little time on some popular graphics used to explore distributions, such as histograms, box plots, kernel density plots, and stem-and-leaf plots. There are also some excellent resources available for learning about other graphical tools for presenting results and how to construct them using statistical software (Aldrich and Rodriguez 2012; Cox 2014; Kleinman and Horton 2014; Matange and Heath 2011; Mitchell 2012). In addition, there are several good websites that address graphical depictions of data, including andrewgelman.com, www.datavis.ca/gallery/index.php, gapminder.org, and junkcharts.typepad.com/junk_charts. Many of the methods worth looking into are extensions of dot plots, line graphs, and scatter plots. But some others include trellis plots, network visualizations, stacked or wave graphs, decision trees, and maps with directional or density components. There is also increasing attention to dynamic and interactive graphics, such as R's Shiny apps; with SAS's ActiveX control, plotly, or GGobi; or as available on the website Gapminder (gapminder.org). Similarly, there is growing interest in methods that utilize animation to enhance visualization, or what some have termed *visuanimation* (Genton et al. 2015). This includes embedding or linking video to graphical displays of data.

As mentioned in chapter 8, the widespread availability of large amounts of data has motivated the burgeoning field of data and information visualization (*Infovis*; Gelman 2011b). The statistics and social science communities have been a relatively small part of this field; it is dominated largely by computer scientists and data science aficionados. The websites flowingdata.com, informationisbeautiful.net, and visualcomplexity.com offer an impressive visual overview of this field. Among the many intriguing methods, two graphical techniques that have emerged and seem to be showing up more and more frequently are *word clouds* and *information graphics*. Word clouds take some text, perhaps from tweets, blogs, media reports of an event, or some other source, and then represent more frequent words in bigger typeface, often both horizontally and vertically. The idea is to show that some words are used more frequently than others in, say, a presidential candidates' debate. Figure 10.23 shows an example of a word cloud based on a few early paragraphs of this chapter. Given what you now know about the research process and principles of data presentation, can you see benefits of word clouds for presenting the results of a research project? Would they be useful for an audience interested in research results or do they suffer from clarity and efficiency problems?

Another popular tool for reporting various types of data is an information graphic, which is also called an *infographic* (Gelman 2011b). Although these have been around under different names for more than 100 years, advances in computer graphics have led to their increasing use in the news media, in books, and online (see, e.g., *USA Today*'s snapshots or *The Telegraph* graphics page). Some claim that virtually any graphical presentation of data is an infographic, but examining some of the most notable examples suggests that they are designed mainly to provide a lot of information using bold colors and creative designs. They are actually more like research posters than the types of graphics discussed in this chapter. In fact, most of them include multiple graphics, but with few standard presentation styles. Their creators seem to have a preference for displaying data using clocks. A quick perusal of some infographics online shows a concern with how to get a job, the size of the legal US marijuana market, various facts about the Seattle Seahawks football team, the different ways that plastics break down in the environment, and where and when robberies occur (mostly on the street and during daylight hours). Figure 10.24 displays an example of an infographic

FIGURE 10.23 Word Cloud.

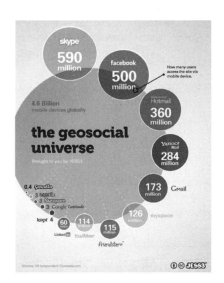

FIGURE 10.24 Infographic example.

that shows the size of various web-based services from a few years ago. This is a rather basic infographic; many provide much more detail about some phenomenon. Moreover, the original version is quite colorful (see https://commons.wikimedia.org/wiki/File:Geosocial-universal-infographic.jpg).

FINAL WORDS

It is tempting to be excited about these new developments in data presentation. Data visualizations and infographics are interesting and enjoyable to look at. They take advantage of the way human eyes are drawn to bright colors and various contrasts. However, the principles of data presentation still apply. Clarity, precision, and efficiency remain as vital goals for anyone who wishes to present data. In addition, graphical displays of data with line graphs, scatter plots, and similar graphics continue to be among the first options for social and behavioral scientists. When they are based on sound principles of data presentation, audiences benefit from clear and crisp information that helps them understand the results of the research process. It also benefits the researcher who wishes to make her work known to the wider community of scholars, policymakers, and other interested parties.

EXERCISES FOR CHAPTER 10

The following exercises use the data file *healthbehaviors.csv*. The data are based on the 2012 Health Behavior in Children Study. The codebook provides information on the variables and their codes. Once you have read the data into your preferred statistical software, complete the following exercises. Make sure you use the design principles, where applicable, that are described in this chapter.

1. Construct a horizontal bar chart and a dot plot of the variable *ethnic*.

2. Construct a dot plot of the average level of alcohol use by ethnic group (we'll ignore the fact that alcohol is a categorical variable). Identify which group reports the highest and lowest level of alcohol use.

3. Construct a similar graph as in exercise 2, but examine the average level of *fights*. Compare the dot plot in this exercise to the dot plot in exercise 2.

4. Construct two line graphs. The first has *satisfaction* on the *y*-axis and *active* on the *x*-axis, with linear fit lines representing males and females. The second has the same *y*- and *x*-axis, but uses lowess fit lines to represent males and females. What do you observe from these two line graphs? How would you explain these associations to an audience at your local community center (assume they are not experts in data analysis)?

5. Your goal in this final exercise is to use a graphical method to explore the association between *fights* and being bullied. Describe what steps you took to decide on a method, what method you used, and what it showed about this association. As the last step, do you think this association would be explored better using a table or a graphic? Explain your answer.

Introduction to Statistical Software

This appendix provides a very brief introduction to the three statistical software packages used in this book: Stata, SPSS, and SAS. It also introduces a fourth package called R that is mentioned occasionally in the chapters. Some suggested resources for learning to use these software packages are also provided.

STATA

Stata is widely used statistical software that is both powerful and relatively user friendly. Its popularity in the social and behavioral sciences has grown quite a bit over the last two decades. Some researchers consider it more flexible and powerful than SPSS, and also more user friendly than SAS or R, its major competitors. As shown in figure A1, when opened, Stata's default style consists of four windows: a command window where users may type commands, a results window that shows output, a variables window that shows the variables in a data file (assuming one is open), and a review window that keeps track of what users have entered in the command window. If a line in the review window is left-clicked, it shows up in the command window (so there is no need to retype commands). Scroll over a variable in the variable window and a small arrow appears next to it. Left-clicking this arrow places the variable in the command window, so there is no need to type variable names if one chooses not to.

When using the command window, it is always a good idea to save the Stata commands and output by opening a log file. This can be done by clicking the icon that looks like a spiral notebook in the upper left-hand side (Windows) or the upper middle portion (Mac) of Stata or by typing the following in the command window:

```
log using "regression.log"                    * the name is arbitrary
```

This saves a log file to the local drive listed at the bottom of the Stata screen. To suspend the log file, type `log off` in the command window; to close it completely, type `log close`.

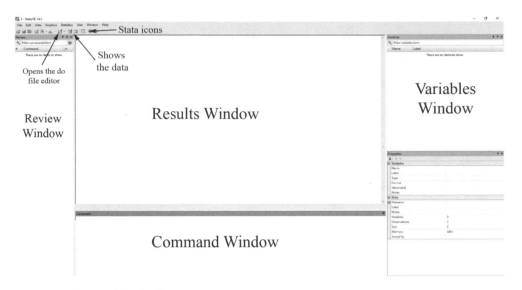

FIGURE A1 Stata statistical software.

Stata's help menu is also useful. It may be accessed using a drop-down menu or by typing `help [name of command/statistic]` in the command window. For example, to learn more about Stata's *codebook* command, type `help codebook` in the command window. Since users may write specialized commands for Stata, an alternative is to type `findit [name of procedure]` to locate specialized procedures. For instance, typing `findit codebook` in the command window opens a new window that lists not only the help menu material for this command, but other resources as well. When I took this approach, I noticed a user-written procedure called `CB2HTML` that is designed to write a codebook as an HTML file.

As emphasized through this book, it is important to learn how to write *.do* files. These are similar to SPSS syntax files, SAS program files, or R script files in that we write—and, importantly, save—commands in them and then ask Stata to execute the commands (see chapter 4 for instructions about program files in general). Stata has a do file editor that is simply a notepad screen for typing commands (see figure A2). The Stata icon that looks like a small pad of paper opens the editor. Typing `doedit` in the command window also opens the editor. But, as mentioned in chapter 4, we may also use Notepad++, TextEdit, WordPad, Vim, or any other text-editing program that allows us to save text files. I recommend that you use the file extension *.do* when saving these files, though. In the do-editor, clicking the *run* or *do* icon feeds the commands to Stata. You may also type do `"name of do file";` in the command window. However, make sure that dataset you are working on is open—or that the do file opens it—when using one of these options. Moreover, when using the command line to run a do file, Stata needs to be able to find the file in its default directory or the path to the file needs to be included in the command.

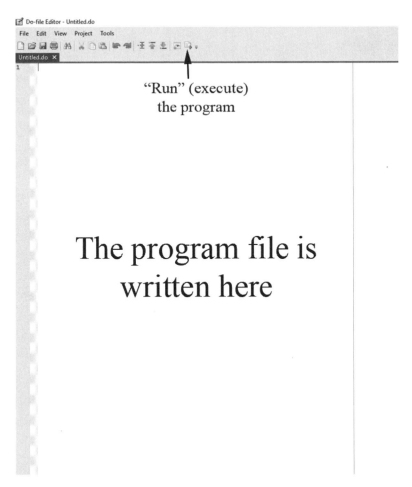

FIGURE A2 Stata's do file editor.

Additional Resources for Learning Stata

There are many exceptional introductions and tutorials that show how to use Stata. Its main website is http://www.stata.com, and you will find many resources there. The Stata blog (http://blog.stata.com) has useful entries on elementary and advanced topics. A good place to start learning how to use Stata is on its YouTube channel (https://www.youtube.com/user /statacorp), as well as on the following website: http://www.ats.ucla.edu/stat/stata. This website also includes links to web books that demonstrate how to estimate various statistical models with Stata. For more information about using Stata to conduct quantitative research, see Kohler and Kreuter (2012) and Longest (2014). If you wish to learn more about program-ming in Stata, Baum (2016) is a superb resource. Long (2009) has written an excellent book on workflow in Stata. It includes extensive information on Stata programming steps, docu-mentation, and file management that make workflow thorough and efficient.

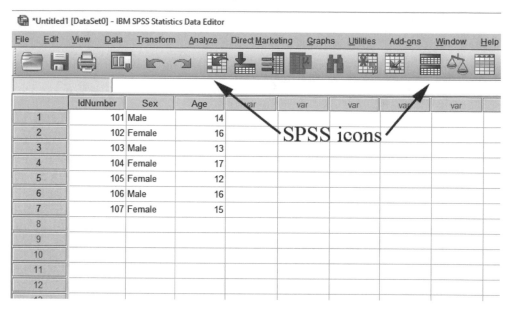

FIGURE A3 SPSS statistical software. The Data View shown here provides a data table (spreadsheet) view of the actual dataset. The observations are in rows and the variables are in columns. The tabs across the top are drop-down menus for data management and statistical analyses. You should generally avoid using the drop-down menus and rely on syntax (program) files for data needs.

SPSS

SPSS has been utilized in the social and behavioral sciences for many years, and it continues to enjoy widespread use. Its popularity is largely due to its rather relaxed learning curve. It has a relatively straightforward user interface and clearly marked options for data management and analysis. Many users rely on its drop-down menus for data management and statistical analysis tasks, although this should be avoided for most purposes (see chapter 4). Figures A3 and A4 show two ways that SPSS may be viewed.

Notice that SPSS does not use multiple windows the same way as Stata or SAS. Instead, the default option is to view SPSS in its *data view* or *variable view* window. This makes some sense since many users wish to see the data clearly first before beginning any data management or analysis steps. However, it also encourages users to use the drop-down menus rather than syntax files or a command line system.

Unlike Stata, SPSS automatically prepares an output file when commands are executed. When SPSS is closed, it asks users if they wish to save the output file. The output includes the commands entered as well as the output, so one may see the structure of the program and reproduce one's steps. Nevertheless, as emphasized throughout this book, you should rely on syntax (program) files for all stages of work with SPSS. The syntax editor is similar to the do file editor in Stata (see figure A4). It may be opened by choosing *File-New-Syntax*

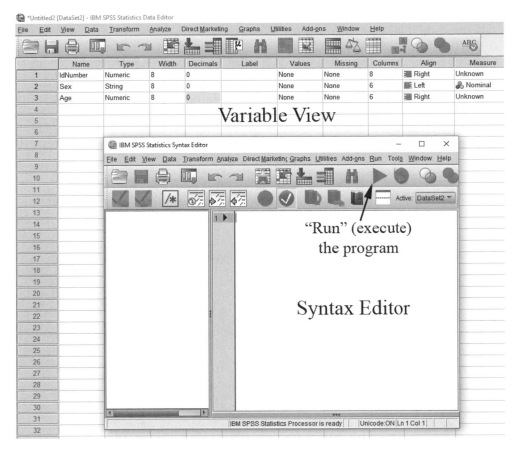

FIGURE A4 SPSS's Variable View. It shows the variable names, labels, value labels, missing values, and other information on each variable in the dataset.

from the drop-down menu. Or an existing syntax file may be opened by choosing *File-Open-Syntax*. The default extension for these files is *.sps*.

Stata's help menu offers many options to assist the user. The *Topic* option links to online resources that cover most SPSS procedures and options. There are also links to *Tutorials*, *Case Studies*, a *Command Syntax Reference*, and several others that provide complete information about SPSS and its many tools for data management and analysis.

Additional Resources for Learning SPSS

The main website for SPSS may be reached through the address http://www.spss.com. It includes many links to resources that describe how to use SPSS and for instructions about various data management and statistical procedures. Although the company that manages and distributes SPSS does not sponsor a video series, there are dozens of videos available that demonstrate numerous aspects of the software. The following websites are also useful: http://www.ats.ucla.edu/stat/spss and http://www.spss-tutorials.com. Some books that offer general overviews include Levesque (2006), Grotenhuis and Vissher (2014), and George and Mallery (2016). A book on programming that many students find useful (even though it is somewhat dated) is Boslaugh (2005).

SAS

Of the three statistical software packages emphasized in this book, SAS is the most commonly utilized outside of academia. This is because it is used widely in the private sector, by government agencies, and in medical research. The company also features several products that go beyond those available from other statistical software producers, including fraud and security intelligence software and others. In any event, it is extremely powerful and wide-ranging in its capabilities. Whereas at one time SAS was the "go-to" statistical software for many social and behavioral scientists, its popularity is no longer as high as it once was. Part of the reason is that it has a fairly steep learning curve, and many students have a difficult time when they are first introduced to it.

Figure A5 illustrates the appearance of SAS's statistical software when opened. The windows are similar to those found in Stata; however, the program file editor opens automatically. In this editor window, the user writes the data management and analysis commands. The file may then be executed by choosing the *run* icon or by highlighting specific commands, right-clicking, and choosing *Submit Selection* (*Submit All* will run all the commands in the editor). Once the commands are executed, the results are provided in an output window. The log window shows the commands that were executed and any error messages the program produces. The results window saves your output in case you run multiple program files. When you close SAS, it will ask if you wish to save the text in the editor. Make sure you save the program if you plan to use it again. Or you may write program files in a text editor. The file extension for these files is *.sas*.

SAS's help menu provides a "getting started" guide that is useful. It also has a search option in the documentation link. However, searching for a command or other procedure can be confusing to the new user. Depending on how SAS is set up on your system, it may search across several SAS products to find a search term. For example, entering *recode* in the search bar resulted in links to several procedures from SAS products such as QC, IML, STAT, and GRAPH. It can be difficult to decide which one to choose to find what you need. For most novice users, it is perhaps best to search for online descriptions written by SAS users.

Additional Resources for Learning SAS

As mentioned earlier, many new users of SAS report that it can be difficult to learn, especially for those who have used only SPSS or Stata. However, there are also some helpful instruction guides that make working with SAS easier. The main SAS support website is a good place to begin (http://support.sas.com/training/tutorial). Some other useful websites include the following: http://www.ats.ucla.edu/stat/sas, http://www.sascrunchtraining.com, and https://en.wikibooks.org/wiki/SAS. There are also many helpful videos available online

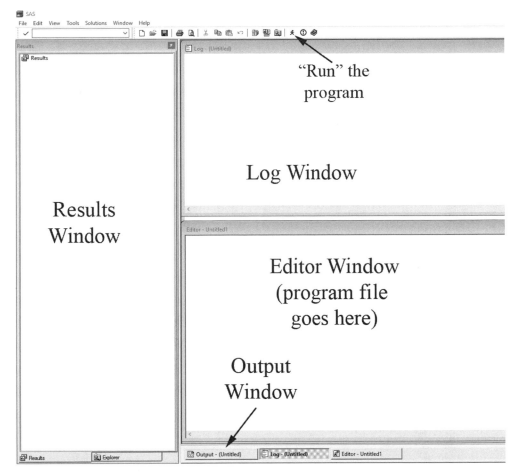

FIGURE A5 SAS statistical software.

that are worth viewing. Delwiche and Slaughter (2012) provide a relatively painless introduction to SAS. Kleinman and Horton (2014) furnish good guidance about data management and analysis using SAS. See Padgett (2011) for an introduction to statistical methods using SAS. Finally, for those who wish to learn SAS programming, a good resource is Cody (2007).

R

In the social and behavior sciences, the new kid on the block is R. However, R is perhaps the most widely used software in the statistical community and its use has grown tremendously in many scientific disciplines. Unlike Stata, SPSS, and SAS, R is open source software and freely distributed. Many of its commands and procedures are written by users and made available to others as "packages."

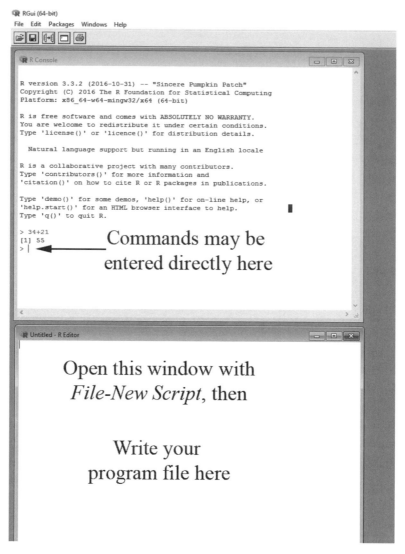

FIGURE A6 R statistical software.

Although it is free to download and use, R also has a relatively steep learning curve. It operates somewhat differently than the other statistical software that has been discussed thus far. Students with a programming/coding background have a relatively simple time learning R (it is actually a programming language), but others are not so fortunate. Nevertheless, even though R is not emphasized in this book, it is worth becoming familiar with it because its use in academic, public sector, and private sector settings is exploding. An analysis of statistical software reported in academic research articles in 2015 found that whereas SPSS is still used most often, R is now ahead of SAS as well as Stata (see http://r4stats.com

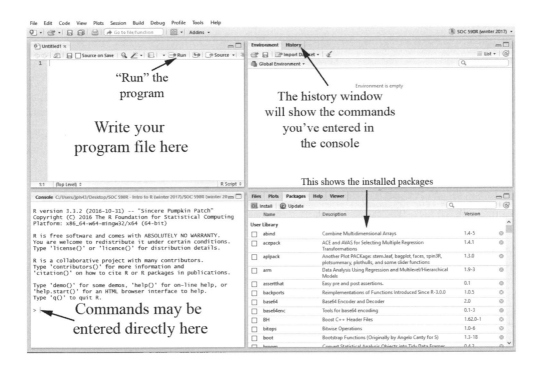

FIGURE A7 RStudio. An integrated development environment (IDE) for R statistical software. It simplifies some R tasks.

/articles/popularity). Moreover, new statistical procedures tend to be released in R much more quickly than in other software because it is supported mainly by a large and sophisticated user community. In addition, R is also well integrated with other software used to present the results of research projects, such as LaTeX. There is also an R package called *knitr* that is designed for reporting analysis results. Finally, integrated development environments (IDEs), such as RStudio® (https://www.rstudio.com) and JGR (https://www.rforge.net/JGR), are freely available to automate and simplify some R capabilities. R is also becoming the "go-to" software for data visualization. It has many excellent features that may be used to produce numerous graphics.

Figures A6 and A7 show the appearance of R and RStudio when they are opened.

Some of the biggest challenges for students who are used to SPSS or Stata and are learning R include (a) the way it handles datasets; (b) the documentation and help resources, which can seem opaque; and (c) understanding the various data types and objects that R can use. For instance, the help menu contains several options, but it is often simplest to use the ?? option in the command line. Yet, even this can be perplexing for the new user (try it: type *??recode* on the command line and hit enter). There are also myriad commands that are borrowed from other programming languages that can confuse those without a programming background. Finally, R is not very easy to use for data management. Although it can do all the things shown in the earlier chapters, it tends to take greater effort to learn how to do them compared to the other software used in this book.

Additional Resources for Learning R

Fortunately, since R is largely managed by its community of users, there is a sizable number of learning resources available. It is best to take your time when learning R and to begin practicing with datasets soon after taking it up. Its main website is https://www.r-project .org. From there, it may be downloaded for free. The site also includes manuals, links to books, and other resources. For first-time users, the best place to begin is the manual "An Introduction to R."

The number of instructional videos about R can be overwhelming. The YouTube series called *Intro to R* by Google Developers is thorough and systematic. There is also a YouTube channel titled *LearnR* that includes exercises so that users can have hands-on learning experiences. Furthermore, there are many videos that focus on using R for elementary statistical analyses.

The *Quick-R* (http://www.statmethods.net/index.html) and *R-bloggers* (http://www .r-bloggers.com) websites are good places to find various learning resources and assistance with numerous aspects of R. The following websites are also helpful: http://www.ats.ucla .edu/stat/r, https://www.rstudio.com/online-learning, and http://www.inside-r.org.

It is not surprising given its growing popularity that there are now many books that demonstrate how to use R for data management and statistical purposes. For data management with R, consider Kleinman and Horton (2014). Teetor (2011) provides a good general introduction to R, Dalgaard (2008) focuses on using R for statistics, and Mare et al. (2012) take a more conceptual approach that some new users may find helpful. Finally, there are several online discussions of workflow in R, especially regarding reproducible research.

FINAL WORDS

The choice of software can be important, but each of those mentioned in this book are well regarded and provide appropriate results virtually all of the time. I've found that knowing at least a bit about each one is beneficial, even though I tend to rely on a couple far more than the others.

However, even if you become expert with one piece of software and don't wish to learn another, there are also relatively simple ways to call one type into another. For example, if SPSS does not include a command for estimating a particular model, the user may set up SPSS to call R to estimate the model, which can then be output to SPSS (see http://www .ibm.com/developerworks/library/ba-call-r-spss). There are also ways to call R from Stata (Newson 2014) and SAS (http://support.sas.com/rnd/app/studio/Rinterface2.html). This can be beneficial to more advanced users because R tends to have the latest statistical procedures before the others. Nevertheless, for purposes of learning and practicing data management and presentation skills, any of these programs is suitable.

REFERENCES

Abbasi, Ahmed, and Donald Adjeroh. 2014. "Social Media Analytics for Smart Health." *IEEE Intelligent Systems* 29(2): 60–64.

Agnew, Robert. 2006. *Pressured into Crime: An Overview of General Strain Theory.* Los Angeles: Roxbury.

Aldrich, James O., and Hilda M. Rodriguez. 2012. *Building SPSS Graphs to Understand Data.* Los Angeles, CA: Sage Publications.

Allison, Paul. 2001. *Missing Data.* Newbury Park, CA: Sage Publications.

Allison, Paul. 2012. "Handling Missing Data by Maximum Likelihood." SAS Global Forum, Paper 312-2012. Accessed July 14. http://statisticalhorizons.com/wp-content/uploads/MissingDataByML.pdf.

Allison, Paul. 2016. "Sensitivity Analysis for Not Missing at Random." Accessed July 14. http://statisticalhorizons.com/sensitivity-analysis.

Alvarez, Marino C., and D. Bob Gowin. 2010. *The Little Book: Conceptual Elements of Research.* Lanham, MD: Rowman & Littlefield Education.

Alvesson, Mats, and Jorgen Sandberg. 2013. *Constructing Research Questions: Doing Interesting Research.* Los Angeles: Sage Publications.

American Association for the Advancement of Science. 2016. "Historical Trends in Federal R&D." Accessed June 30. http://www.aaas.org/page/historical-trends-federal-rd.

Andrews, Richard. 2003. *Research Questions.* London: Continuum.

Anscombe, Francis J. 1973. "Graphs in Statistical Analysis." *The American Statistician* 27(1): 17–21.

Attewell, Paul, and David B. Monaghan. 2015. *Data Mining for the Social Sciences: An Introduction.* Berkeley, CA: University of California Press.

Baglione, Lisa A. 2016. *Writing a Research Paper in Political Science: A Practical Guide to Inquiry, Structure, and Methods.* Los Angeles, CA: Sage Publications.

Baum, Christopher F. 2016. *An Introduction to Stata Programming.* 2nd ed. College Station, TX: Stata Press.

Baumer, Ben. 2015. "A Data Science Course for Undergraduates: Thinking with Data." *The American Statistician* 69(4): 334–342.

Baunach, Dawn Michelle. 2012. "Changing Same-Sex Marriage Attitudes in America from 1988 through 2010." *Public Opinion Quarterly* 76(2): 364–378.

Becker, Howard S. 2007. *Writing for Social Scientists: How to Start and Finish Your Thesis, Book, or Article.* 2nd ed. Chicago, IL: University of Chicago Press.

Becker, Howard S. 2008. *Tricks of the Trade: How to Think about Your Research While You're Doing It*. Chicago: University of Chicago Press.

Bell, Andrew, Ron Johnston, and Kelvyn Jones. 2015. "Stylised Fact or Situated Messiness? The Diverse Effects of Increasing Debt on National Economic Growth." *Journal of Economic Geography* 15(2): 449–472.

Bertin, Jacques. 1983. *Semiology of Graphics: Diagrams, Networks, and Maps*. Madison, WI: University of Wisconsin Press.

Blumstein, Alfred, and Joel Wallman. 2006. "The Crime Drop and Beyond." *Annual Review of Law and Society* 2: 125–146.

Booth, Wayne C., Gregory G. Colomb, and Joseph M. Williams. 2008. *The Craft of Research*. 3rd ed. Chicago, IL: University of Chicago Press.

Boslaugh, Sarah. 2005. *An Intermediate Guide to SPSS Programming: Using Syntax for Data Management*. Newbury Park, CA: Sage Publications.

Bradburn, Norman, Seymour Sudman, and Brian Wansink. 2014. *Asking Questions: The Definitive Guide to Questionnaire Design*. Rev. ed. San Francisco, CA: Jossey-Bass.

Bulmer, Martin. 2001. "Social Measurement: What Stands in Its Way?" *Social Research* 68(2): 455–480.

Buonaccorsi, John P. 2010. *Measurement Error: Models, Methods, and Applications*. Boca Raton, FL: CRC Press.

Campante, Filipe R., and Davin Chor. 2012. "Why Was the Arab World Poised for Revolution? Schooling, Economic Opportunities, and the Arab Spring." *Journal of Economic Perspectives* 26(2): 167–188.

Campbell, John Paul, Richard L. Daft, and Charles L. Hulin. 1982. *What to Study: Generating and Developing Research Questions*. Beverly Hills, CA: Sage Publications.

Case, Anne, and Angus Deaton. 2015. "Rising Morbidity and Mortality in Midlife among White Non-Hispanic Americans in the 21st Century." *Proceedings of the National Academy of Science of the United States of America* 112(49): 15078–15083.

Celinska, Katarzyna. 2007. "Individualism and Collectivism in America: The Case of Gun Ownership and Attitudes toward Gun Control." *Sociological Perspectives* 50(2): 229–247.

Cleveland, William S. 1993. *Visualizing Data*. Summit, NJ: Hobart Press.

Cleveland, William S., and Robert McGill. 1984. "Graphical Perception: Theory, Experimentation, and Application to the Development of Graphical Methods." *Journal of the American Statistical Association* 79(387): 531–554.

Cleveland, William S., and Robert McGill. 1985. "Graphical Perception and Graphical Methods for Analyzing Scientific Data." *Science* 229(4716): 828–833.

Cody, Ron. 2007. *Learning SAS® by Example: A Programmer's Guide*. Cary, NC: SAS Institute.

Cohen, Lindsey L., Laurie Greco, and Sarah Martin. 2012. "Presenting Your Research." In *The Portable Mentor: Expert Guide to a Successful Career in Psychology*, edited by Mitchell J. Prinstein, 133–144. New York: Springer.

Cox, Nicholas J. 2008. "Speaking Stata: between Tables and Graphs." *Stata Journal* 8(2): 269–289.

Cox, Nicholas J. 2014. *Speaking Stata Graphics*. College Station, TX: Stata Press.

Dalgaard, Peter. 2008. *Introductory Statistics with R*. 2nd ed. New York: Springer.

Delwiche, Lora D., and Susan J. Slaughter. 2012. *The Little SAS Book: A Primer*. Cary, NC: SAS Institute.

DePoy, Elizabeth, and Laura N. Gitlin. 2016. *Introduction to Research: Understanding and Applying Multiple Strategies*. St. Louis, MO: Elsevier Health Sciences.

DeVellis, Robert F. 2012. *Scale Development: Theory and Applications*. 3rd ed. Los Angeles, CA: Sage Publications.

Driver, Rosalind, Paul Newton, and Jonathan Osborne. 2000 "Establishing the Norms of Scientific Argumentation in Classrooms." *Science Education* 84(3): 287–312.

Duffy, Deborah L., Yuying Hsu, and James A. Serpell. 2008. "Breed Differences in Canine Aggression." *Applied Animal Behaviour Science* 114(3): 441–460.

Engels, Jean Mundahl, and Paula Diehr. 2003. "Imputation of Missing Longitudinal Data: A Comparison of Methods." *Journal of Clinical Epidemiology* 56(10): 968–976.

Evergreen, Stephanie D. H. 2014. *Presenting Data Effectively: Communicating Your Findings for Maximum Impact.* Los Angeles, CA: Sage Publications.

FDA (US Food and Drug Administration). 2016. "FAERS Reporting by Patient Outcomes by Year." July 14. http://www.fda.gov/Drugs/GuidanceComplianceRegulatoryInformation/Surveillance/AdverseDrugEffects/ucm070461.htm.

Feinstein, Sheryl, ed. 2006. *The Praeger Handbook of Learning and the Brain.* Vol. 2. Westport, CT: Praeger.

Finzer, William. 2013. "The Data Science Education Dilemma." *Technology Innovations in Statistics Education* 7(2): 1–9.

Firebaugh, Glenn. 2008. *Seven Rules for Social Research.* Princeton, NJ: Princeton University Press.

Flam, Faye D. 2014. "The Odds, Continually Updated." *New York Times*, September 29.

Foss, Sonja K., and William Waters. 2007. *Dissertation Destination: A Traveler's Guide to a Done Dissertation.* Lanham, MD: Rowman & Littlefield.

Freese, Jeremy. 2009. "Secondary Analysis of Large Survey Data." In *Research Confidential: Solutions to Problems Most Social Scientists Pretend They Never Have*, edited by Eszter Hargittai, 238–261. Ann Arbor: University of Michigan Press.

Gandrud, Christopher. 2015. *Reproducible Research with R and R Studio.* 2nd ed. Boca Raton, FL: CRC Press.

Gelman, Andrew. 2011a. "Why Tables Are Really Much Better Than Graphs." *Journal of Computational and Graphical Statistics* 20(1): 3–7.

Gelman, Andrew. 2011b. "Infovis, Infographics, and Data Visualization: Where I'm Coming from, and Where I'd Like to Go." August 29. Accessed July 14, 2016. http://andrewgelman.com/2011/08/29/infovis-infographics-and-data-visualization-where-im-coming-from-and-where-id-like-to-go.

Gelman, Andrew. 2014. "A Statistical Graphics Course and Statistical Graphics Advice." March 25. Accessed July 14, 2016. http://andrewgelman.com/2014/03/25/statistical-graphics-course-statistical-graphics-advice.

Gelman, Andrew. 2015. "Correcting Statistical Biases in 'Rising Morbidity and Mortality in Midlife among White Non-Hispanic Americans in the 21st Century': We Need to Adjust for the Increase in Average Age of People in the 45-54 Category." November 6. Accessed July 14, 2016. http://andrewgelman.com/2015/11/06/correcting-rising-morbidity-and-mortality-in-midlife-among-white-non-hispanic-americans-in-the-21st-century-to-account-for-bias-in.

Gelman, Andrew, and Eric Loken. 2014. "The Statistical Crisis in Science." *American Scientist* 102(6): 460–465.

Gelman, Andrew, Cristian Pasarica, and Rahul Dodhia. 2002. "Let's Practice What We Preach: Turning Tables into Graphs." *The American Statistician* 56(2): 121–130.

Gelman, Andrew, and Antony Unwin. 2013. "Infovis and Statistical Graphics: Different Goals, Different Looks." *Journal of Computational and Graphical Statistics* 22(1): 2–28.

Genton, Mark G., Stefano Castruccioa, Paola Crippaa, Subhajit Duttaa, Raphaël Husera, Ying Suna, and Sabrina Vettoria. 2015. "Visuanimation in Statistics." *Stat* 4(1): 81–96.

Gentzkow, Matthew, and Jesse M. Shapiro. 2014. *Code and Data for the Social Sciences: A Practitioner's Guide.* Chicago, IL: University of Chicago. March 10. Accessed July 14, 2016. http://web.stanford.edu/~gentzkow/research/CodeAndData.xhtml.

George, Darren, and Paul Mallery. 2016. *IBM SPSS Statistics 23 Step by Step: A Simple Guide and Reference.* New York: Routledge.

Gerstein, Dean, John Hoffmann, Cindy Larison, Rachel Volberg, Sally Murphy, Marianna Toce, Robert Johnson et al. 1999. *Gambling Impact and Behavior Study.* Accessed July 14, 2016. http://www.norc.org/PDFs/publications/GIBSFinalReportApril1999.pdf.

Gigerenzer, Gerd. 2002. *Calculated Risks: How to Know When Numbers Deceive You.* New York: Simon & Schuster.

Gobeil, Renée, Kelley Blanchette, and Lynn Stewart. 2016. "A Meta-analytic Review of Correctional Interventions for Women Offenders: Gender-Neutral versus Gender-Informed Approaches." *Criminal Justice and Behavior* 43(3): 301–322.

Gould, Stephen Jay. 2010. *Triumph and Tragedy in Mudville: A Lifelong Passion for Baseball.* New York: Norton.

Graham, John W. 2009. "Missing Data Analysis: Making It Work in the Real World." *Annual Review of Psychology* 60: 549–576.

Greenhoot, Andrea Follmer, and Chantelle J. Dowsett. 2012. "Secondary Data Analysis: An Important Tool for Addressing Developmental Questions." *Journal of Cognition and Development* 13(1): 2–18.

Grotenhuis, Manfred te, and Chris Visscher. 2014. *How to Use SPSS Syntax: An Overview of Common Commands.* Los Angeles, CA: Sage Publications.

Groves, Robert M., Floyd J. Fowler, Mick P. Couper, James M. Lepkowski, Eleanor Singer, and Roger Tourangeau. 2009. *Survey Methodology.* 2nd ed. New York: Wiley.

Han, Jiawei, Micheline Kamber, and Jian Pei. 2012. *Data Mining: Concepts and Techniques.* 2nd ed. Waltham, MA: Elsevier.

Hanauer, David A., Naren Ramakrishnan, and Lisa S. Seyfried. 2013. "Describing the Relationship between Cat Bites and Human Depression Using Data from an Electronic Health Record." *PloS One* 8(8): e70585.

Hand, David. 2014. *Measurement Theory and Practice: The World through Quantification.* New York: Wiley.

Harel, Ofer, Jennifer Pellowski, and Seth Kalichman. 2012. "Are We Missing the Importance of Missing Values in HIV Prevention Randomized Clinical Trials? Review and Recommendations." *AIDS and Behavior* 16(6): 1382–1393.

Harris, Peter. 2008. *Designing and Reporting Experiments in Psychology.* 3rd ed. Berkshire, UK: Open University Press.

Healy, Kieran, and James Moody. 2014. "Data Visualization in Sociology." *Annual Review of Sociology* 40: 105-–128.

Hempel, Sandra. 2007. *The Strange Case of the Broad Street Pump: John Snow and the Mystery of Cholera.* Berkeley, CA: University of California Press.

Henrich, Joseph, Steven J. Heine, and Ara Norenzayan. 2010. "Most People Are Not WEIRD." *Nature* 466(7302): 29.

Herzog, David. 2016. *Data Literacy: A User's Guide.* Los Angeles, CA: Sage Publications.

Herzog, Thomas N., Fritz J. Scheuren, and William E. Winkler. 2007. *Data Quality and Record Linkage Techniques.* New York: Springer.

Hoffmann, John P. 2014. "Social and Environmental Influences on Endangered Species: A Cross-National Study." *Sociological Perspectives* 47(1): 79–107.

Hoffmann, Roald. 2003. "Why Buy That Theory?" *American Scientist* 91(1): 9–11.

Hox, Joop J., and Hennie R. Boeije. 2009. "Data Collection, Primary vs. Secondary." In *Encyclopedia of Social Measurement*, edited by Kimberly Kempf-Leonard, 593–599. New York: Elsevier.

Hundepool, Anco, Josep Domingo-Ferrer, Luisa Franconi, Sarah Giessing, Eric Schulte Nordholt, Keith Spicer, and Peter-Paul De Wolf. 2012. *Statistical Disclosure Control*. New York: Wiley.

IBM. 2010. *GPL Reference Guide for IBM SPSS Statistics*. Chicago, IL: SPSS.

ICPSR (Inter-university Consortium for Political and Social Research). 2011. *Guide to Codebooks*. Ann Arbor, MI: ICPSR.

ICPSR. 2012. *Guide to Social Science Data Preparation and Archiving*. 5th ed. Ann Arbor, MI: ICPSR.

Johnson, David R., and Rebekah Young. 2011. "Toward Best Practices in Analyzing Datasets with Missing Data: Comparisons and Recommendations." *Journal of Marriage and Family* 73(5): 926–945.

Johnson, Timothy, and Michael Fendrich. 2005. "Modeling Sources of Self-report Bias in a Survey of Drug Use Epidemiology." *Annals of Epidemiology* 15(5): 381–389.

Jutte, Douglas P., Leslie L. Roos, and Marni D. Brownell. 2011. "Administrative Record Linkage as a Tool for Public Health Research." *Annual Review of Public Health* 32: 91–108.

Kahneman, Daniel. 2011. *Thinking, Fast and Slow*. New York: Farrar, Straus, and Giroux.

Kandel, Sean, Jeffrey Heer, Catherine Plaisant, Jessie Kennedy, Frank van Ham, Nathalie Henry Riche, Chris Weaver, Bongshin Lee, Dominique Brodbeck, and Paolo Buono. 2011. "Research Directions in Data Wrangling: Visualizations and Transformations for Usable and Credible Data." *Information Visualization* 10(4): 271–288.

Kass, Robert E., Brian S. Caffo, Marie Davidian, Xiao-Li Meng, Bin Yu, and Nancy Reid. 2016. "Ten Simple Rules for Effective Statistical Practice." *PLOS Computational Biology* 12(6): e1004961.

Keith, Bruce E., David B. Magleby, Candice J. Nelson, Elizabeth Orr, and Mark C. Westlye. 1992. *The Myth of the Independent Voter*. Berkeley: University of California Press.

Kelsey, Britta. 2005. "The Mystery of the PROC SORT Options NODUPRECS and NODUPKEY Revealed." Accessed July 8, 2016. http://www2.sas.com/proceedings/sugi30/037-30.pdf.

Khine, Myint Swe, ed. 2012. *Perspectives on Scientific Argumentation: Theory, Practice and Research*. New York: Springer.

Kim, David A., Alison R. Hwong, Derek Stafford, D. Alex Hughes, A. James O'Malley, James H. Fowler, and Nicholas A. Christakis. 2015. "Social Network Targeting to Maximise Population Behaviour Change: A Cluster Randomised Controlled Trial." *The Lancet* 386(9989): 145–153.

Kirchkamp, Oliver. 2013. *Workflow of Statistical Data Analysis*. Jena, DE: Friedrich-Schiller-Universität. Accessed July 8, 2016. http://www.kirchkamp.de/oekonometrie/pdf/wf-screen2.pdf.

Klass, Gary M. 2012. *Just Plain Data Analysis: Finding, Presenting, and Interpreting Social Science Data*. Lanham, MD: Rowman & Littlefield.

Kleck, Gary. 1996. "Crime, Culture Conflict and the Sources of Support for Gun Control." *American Behavioral Scientist* 39(4): 387–404.

Kleinman, Ken, and Nicholas J. Horton. 2014. *SAS and R: Data Management, Statistical Analysis, and Graphics*. 2nd ed. Boca Raton, FL: CRC Press.

Kline, Theresa J. B. 2005. *Psychological Testing: A Practical Approach to Design and Evaluation*. Thousand Oaks, CA: Sage Publications.

Kohler, Ulrich, and Frauke Kreuter. 2012. *Data Analysis Using Stata*. 3rd ed. College Station, TX: Stata Press.

Koschat, Martin A. 2005. "A Case for Simple Tables." *The American Statistician* 59(1): 31–40.

Kosslyn, Stephen M. 2006. *Graph Design for the Eye and Mind*. New York: Oxford University Press.

Kraemer, Helena Chmura, and Christine Blasey. 2016. *How Many Subjects? Statistical Power Analysis in Research.* Los Angeles, CA: Sage Publications.

Leek, Jeffery T., and Roger D. Peng. 2015. "What Is the Question?" *Science* 347(6228): 1314–1315.

Levesque, Raynald. 2006. *SPSS Programming and Data Management: A Guide for SPSS and SAS Users.* Chicago, IL: SPSS.

Lewandowsky, Stephan, and Ian Spence. 1989. "The Perception of Statistical Graphs." *Sociological Methods & Research* 18(2–3): 200–242.

Little, Roderick J. A., and Donald B. Rubin. 2014. *Statistical Analysis with Missing Data.* 2nd ed. New York: Wiley.

Liu, Charlie Chunhua. 2015. *Producing High-Quality Figures Using SAS/GRAPH® and ODS Graphics Procedures.* Boca Raton, FL: CRC Press.

Long, J. Scott. 2009. *The Workflow of Data Analysis using Stata.* College Station, TX: Stata Press.

Longest, Kyle C. 2014. *Using Stata for Quantitative Analysis.* 2nd ed. Los Angeles, CA: Sage Publications.

Loveless, Tom. 2015. "CNN's Misleading Story on Homework." *The Brown Center Chalkboard,* August 20. Accessed July 14, 2016. http://www.brookings.edu/blogs/brown-center-chalkboard/posts/2015/08/20-misleading-cnn-homework-story-loveless.

Mare, William B., John M. Ferron, and Barbara M. Miller. 2012. *Introductory Statistics: A Conceptual Approach Using R.* New York: Routledge.

Matange, Sanjay, and Dan Heath. 2011. *Statistical Graphics Procedures by Example: Effective Graphs Using SAS.* Cary, NC: SAS Institute.

McClelland, Christine V. 2016. *The Nature of Science and the Scientific Method.* Accessed July 14. http://www.geosociety.org/educate/NatureScience.pdf.

McCrea, Rod, Zoe Leviston, and Iain A. Walker. 2016. "Climate Change Skepticism and Voting Behavior: What Causes What?" *Environment and Behavior* 48(10): 1309–1334.

McDowell, Ian. 2006. *Measuring Health: A Guide to Rating Scales and Questionnaires.* New York: Oxford University Press.

McNabb, David E. 2010. *Research Methods for Political Science.* 2nd ed. New York: M.E. Sharpe.

Merton, Robert K. 1968. *Social Theory and Social Structure.* Rev. ed. New York: Simon and Schuster.

Milgram, Stanley. 1967. "The Small World Problem." *Psychology Today* 2(1): 60–67.

Milgram, Stanley. 1970. "The Experience of Living in Cities." *Science* 167(3924): 1461–1468.

Miller, Delbert C., and Neil J. Salkind. 2002. *Handbook of Research Design and Social Measurement.* 6th ed. Thousand Oaks, CA: Sage Publications.

Miller, Jane E. 2004. *The Chicago Guide to Writing about Numbers.* Chicago, IL: University of Chicago Press.

Miller, Jane E. 2007a. "Organizing Data in Tables and Charts: Different Criteria for Different Tasks." *Teaching Statistics* 29(3): 98–101.

Miller, Jane E. 2007b. "Preparing and Presenting Effective Research Posters." *Health Services Research* 42(1): 311–328.

Mitchell, Michael N. 2010. *Data Management Using Stata: A Practical Handbook.* College Station, TX: Stata Press.

Mitchell, Michael N. 2012. *A Visual Guide to Stata Graphics.* 3rd ed. College Station, TX: Stata Press.

Morgan, Susan E., Tom Reichert, and Tyler R. Harrison. 2002. *From Numbers to Words: Reporting Statistical Results for the Social Sciences.* Boston, MA: Pearson.

Mumford, Stephen, and Rani Lill Anjum. 2013. *Causation: A Very Short Introduction.* Oxford: Oxford University Press.

Myers, Teresa A. 2011. "Goodbye, Listwise Deletion: Presenting Hot Deck Imputation as an Easy and Effective Tool for Handling Missing Data." *Communication Methods and Measures* 5(4): 297–310.

Nagler, Jonathan. 1995. "Coding Style and Good Computing Practices." *PS: Political Science & Politics* 28(3): 488–492.

Newson, Roger. 2014. "RSOURCE: Stata Module to Run R from Inside Stata Using an R Source File." Accessed July 14, 2016. https://ideas.repec.org/c/boc/bocode/s456847.html.

Nichols-Barrer, Ira, Philip Gleason, Brian Gill, and Christina Clark Tuttle. 2016. "Student Selection, Attrition, and Replacement in KIPP Middle Schools." *Educational Evaluation and Policy Analysis* 38(1): 5–20.

Niemi, Jarad, and Andrew Gelman. 2011. "Statistical Graphics: Making Information Clear—and Beautiful." *Significance* 8(3): 135–137.

Nyhan, Brendan, and Jason Reifler. 2010. "When Corrections Fail: The Persistence of Political Misperceptions." *Political Behavior* 32(2): 303–330.

O'Leary, Zina. 2014. *The Essential Guide to Doing your Research Project*. 2nd ed. Los Angeles, CA: Sage Publications.

Osborne, Jason W. 2013. *Best Practices in Data Cleaning*. Los Angeles, CA: Sage Publications.

Oxford English Dictionary. 2016. "Research." July 8. http://www.oxforddictionaries.com/us/definition/american_english/research.

Padgett, Lakshmi. 2011. *Practical Statistical Methods: A SAS Programming Approach*. Boca Raton, FL: CRC Press.

Pager, Devah. 2008. *Marked: Race, Crime, and Finding Work in an Era of Mass Incarceration*. Chicago, IL: University of Chicago Press.

Paxton, Pamela. 1999. "Is Social Capital Declining in the United States? A Multiple Indicator Assessment." *American Journal of Sociology* 105(1): 88–127.

Pearlin, Leonard I., and Carmi Schooler. 1978. "The Structure of Coping." *Journal of Health and Social Behavior* 19(1): 2–21.

Peng, He, and Jon Pierce. 2015. "Job- and Organization-Based Psychological Ownership: Relationship and Outcomes." *Journal of Managerial Psychology* 30(2): 151–168.

Peng, Roger D., Francesca Dominici, and Scott L. Zeger. 2006. "Reproducible Epidemiologic Research." *American Journal of Epidemiology* 163(9): 783–789.

Pohlabeln, Hermann, Achim Reineke, and Walter Schill. 2014. "Data Management in Epidemiology." In *Handbook of Epidemiology*. 2nd ed. Edited by Wolfgang Ahrens and Iris Pigeot, 979–1022. New York: Springer.

Pulvers, Kim, and George M. Diekhoff. 1999. "The Relationship between Academic Dishonesty and College Classroom Environment." *Research in Higher Education* 40(4): 487–498.

Putnam, Robert D. 1995 "Bowling Alone: America's Declining Social Capital." *Journal of Democracy* 6(1): 65–78.

Putnam, Robert D. 2000. *Bowling Alone: The Collapse and Revival of American Community*. New York: Simon and Schuster.

Qui, Linda. 2015. "Chart Shown at Planned Parenthood Hearing Is Misleading and 'Ethically Wrong.'" *Politifact*, October 1. Accessed July 7, 2016. http://www.politifact.com/truth-o-meter/statements/2015/oct/01/jason-chaffetz/chart-shown-planned-parenthood-hearing-misleading.

Ragin, Charles C., and Lisa M. Amoroso. 2011. *Constructing Social Research: The Unity and Diversity of Method*. 2nd ed. Los Angeles, CA: Sage Publications.

Reaves, Shiela, Jacqueline Bush Hitchon, Sung-Yeon Park, and Gi Woong Yun. 2004. "If Looks Could Kill: Digital Manipulation of Fashion Models." *Journal of Mass Media Ethics* 19(1): 56–71.

Rehmeyer, Julie. 2008. "Florence Nightingale: The Passionate Statistician." *Science News*, November 26. Accessed July 14, 2016. https://www.sciencenews.org/article/florence-nightingale-passionate-statistician.

Remler, Dahlia K., and Gregg G. Van Ryzin. 2015. *Research Methods in Practice: Strategies for Description and Causation.* 2nd ed. Los Angeles, CA: Sage Publications.

Retractionwatch.com. 2015. "'To Our Horror': Widely Reported Study Suggesting Divorce Is More Likely When Wives Fall Ill Gets Axed." July 21. Accessed July 14, 2016. http:// retractionwatch.com/2015/07/21/to-our-horror-widely-reported-study-suggesting-divorce-is-more-likely-when-wives-fall-ill-gets-axed.

Robbins, Naomi B. 2013. *Creating More Effective Graphs.* Wayne, NJ: Chart House.

Rosoff, Stephen, and Henry Pontell. 2010. *Social Deviance: Readings in Theory and Research.* New York: McGraw-Hill.

Rugh, Jacob S., and Douglas S. Massey. 2010. "Racial Segregation and the American Foreclosure Crisis." *American Sociological Review* 75(5): 629–651.

Rumsey, Deborah J. 2006. *Probability for Dummies.* New York: Wiley.

Sabo, Roy, and Edward Boone. 2013. *Statistics Research Methods: A Guide for Non-Statisticians.* New York: Springer.

Sak, Ugur. 2011. "Selective Problem Solving (sps): A Model for Teaching Creative Problem-Solving." *Gifted Education International* 27(3): 349–357.

Sampson, Robert J., and Stephen W. Raudenbush. 2004. "Seeing Disorder: Neighborhood Stigma and the Social Construction of 'Broken Windows.'" *Social Psychology Quarterly* 67(4): 319–342.

Sana, Mariano, and Alexander A. Weinreb. 2008. "Insiders, Outsiders, and the Editing of Inconsistent Survey Data." *Sociological Methods & Research* 36(4): 515–541.

Sawyer, Keith. 2013. *Zig Zag: The Surprising Path to Greater Creativity.* San Francisco, CA: Jossey-Bass.

Schaumberg, Katherine, Christine Vinci, Joseph S. Raiker, Natalie Mota, Michelle Jackson, Diana Whalen, Julie A. Schumacher, and Scott F. Coffey. 2015. "PTSD-Related Alcohol Expectancies and Impulsivity Interact to Predict Alcohol Use Severity in a Substance Dependent Sample with PTSD." *Addictive Behaviors* 41: 41–45.

Schildkraut, Jaclyn, and Tiffany Cox Hernandez. 2014. "Laws That Bit the Bullet: A Review of Legislative Responses to School Shootings." *American Journal of Criminal Justice* 39(2): 358–374.

Schwartz, Martin A. 2008. "The Importance of Stupidity in Scientific Research." *Journal of Cell Science* 121(11): 1771.

Sedgwick, Philip. 2014. "Unit of Observation versus Unit of Analysis." *British Medical Journal* 348(3840): 1–2.

Shadish, William R., Margaret H. Clark, and Peter M. Steiner. 2008. "Can Nonrandomized Experiments Yield Accurate Answers? A Randomized Experiment Comparing Random and Nonrandom Assignments." *Journal of the American Statistical Association* 103(484): 1334–1344.

Shepard, Roger N. 1990. *Mind Sights: Original Visual Illusions.* New York: Freeman.

Shore, Zachary. 2008. *Blunder: Why Smart People Make Bad Decisions.* New York: Bloomsbury.

Shore, Zachary. 2016. *Grad School Essentials: A Crash Course in Scholarly Skills.* Berkeley: University of California Press.

Siirtola, Harri. 2014. "Bars, Pies, Doughnuts & Tables: Visualization of Proportions." *Proceedings of the 28th International BCS Human Computer Interaction Conference on HCI*, Southport, UK.

Silva, Samuel, Beatriz Sousa Santos, and Joaquim Madeira. 2011. "Using Color in Visualization: A Survey." *Computers & Graphics* 35(2): 320–333.

Smyth, Jolene D. 2017. "Designing Questions and Questionnaires." In *The Sage Handbook of Survey Methodology*, edited by Christof Wolf, Dominique Joye, Tom W. Smith, and Yang-Chih Fu, 218–235. Thousand Oaks, CA: Sage Publications.

Stake, Robert E. 2012. *Qualitative Research: Studying How Things Work*. New York: Guilford.

Stigler, Stephen M. 2016. *The Seven Pillars of Statistical Wisdom*. Cambridge, MA: Harvard University Press.

Sullivan, Daniel, and Till von Wachter. 2009. "Job Displacement and Mortality: An Analysis Using Administrative Data." *Quarterly Journal of Economics* 124(3): 1265–1306.

Swires-Hennessy, Ed. 2014. *Presenting Data: How to Communicate Your Message Effectively*. Chichester, UK: Wiley.

Teetor, Paul. 2011. *The R Cookbook*. Sebastopol, CA: O'Reilly Media.

Thomas, Gary. 2011. *How to Do Your Case Study: A Guide for Students and Researchers*. Los Angeles, CA: Sage Publications.

Tinkler, Penny. 2013. *Using Photographs in Social and Historical Research*. Los Angeles, CA: Sage Publications.

Toch, Hans, and Kathleen Maguire. 2014. "Public Opinion Regarding Crime, Criminal Justice, and Related Topics: A Retrospect." *Journal of Research in Crime and Delinquency* 51(4): 424–444.

Torpy, Janet M., Cassio Lynm, and Richard M. Glass. 2003. "Men and Women Are Different." *JAMA* 289(4): 510.

Torra, Vicenç, and Guillermo Navarro-Arribas. 2014. "Data Privacy." *Wiley Interdisciplinary Reviews: Data Mining and Knowledge Discovery* 4(4): 269–280.

Toulmin, Stephen E. 1958. *The Uses of Argument*. Cambridge: Cambridge University Press.

Tourangeau, Roger, Lance J. Rips, and Kenneth Rasinski. 2000. *The Psychology of Survey Response*. New York: Cambridge University Press.

Tourangeau, Roger, and Ting Yan. 2007. "Sensitive Questions in Surveys." *Psychological Bulletin* 133(5): 859–883.

Tufte, Edward R. 2001. *The Visual Display of Quantitative Information*. 2nd ed. Cheshire, CT: Graphics Press.

Turner, Jonathan H. 2013. *Theoretical Sociology: 1830 to the Present*. Los Angeles, CA: Sage Publications.

Uggen, Christopher. 1999. "Ex-offenders and the Conformist Alternative: A Job Quality Model of Work and Crime." *Social Problems* 46(1): 127–151.

Van den Broeck, Jan, Solveig Argeseanu Cunningham, Roger Eeckels, and Kobus Herbst. 2005. "Data Cleaning: Detecting, Diagnosing, and Editing Data Abnormalities." *PLoS Medicine* 2(10): 966.

Vartanian, Thomas P. 2010. *Secondary Data Analysis*. New York: Oxford University Press.

Vié, Jean-Christophe, Craig Hilton-Taylor, and Simon N. Stuart, eds. 2009. *Wildlife in a Changing World: An Analysis of the 2008 IUCN Red List of Threatened Species*. Gland, Switzerland: International Union for the Conservation of Nature.

Virnig, Beth A., and Marshall McBean. 2001. "Administrative Data for Public Health Surveillance and Planning." *Annual Review of Public Health* 22(1): 213–230.

Wainer, Howard. 1984. "How to Display Data Badly." *The American Statistician* 38(2): 137–147.

Wainer, Howard. 1997. "Improving Tabular Displays, with NAEP Tables as Examples and Inspirations." *Journal of Educational and Behavioral Statistics* 22(1): 1–30.

Wainer, Howard. 2005. *Graphic Discovery*. Princeton, NJ: Princeton University Press.

Wainer, Howard. 2008. "Improving Graphic Displays by Controlling Creativity." *Chance* 21(2): 46–52.

Wainer, Howard. 2009. *Picturing the Uncertain World: How to Understand, Communicate, and Control Uncertainty through Graphical Display*. Princeton, NJ: Princeton University Press.

Ware, Colin. 2013. *Information Visualization: Perception for Design*. 3rd ed. New York: Elsevier.

Watts, Duncan J. 2004. *Six Degrees: The Science of a Connected Age*. New York: Norton.

Weitzer, Ronald John. 2002. *Deviance and Social Control: A Reader*. New York: McGraw-Hill.

Whetten, David A. 2002. "Modelling-as-Theorizing: A Systematic Methodology for Theory Construction." In *Essential Skills for Management Research*, edited by David Partington, 45–71. Thousand Oaks, CA: Sage Publications.

White, Lynn. 2005. "Writes of Passage: Writing an Empirical Journal Article." *Journal of Marriage and Family* 67(4): 791–798.

White, Patrick. 2009. *Developing Research Questions: A Guide for Social Scientists*. New York: Palgrave Macmillan.

Wickham, Hadley. 2010. "A Layered Grammar of Graphics." *Journal of Computational and Graphical Statistics* 19(1): 3–28.

Wickham, Hadley. 2014. "Tidy Data." *Journal of Statistical Software* 59 (10): 1–23.

Widaman, Keith F. 2006. "Missing Data: What to Do with or without Them." *Monographs of the Society for Research in Child Development* 71(3): 42–64.

Wilkinson, Leland. 2001. "Presentation Graphics." In *International Encyclopedia of the Social & Behavioral Sciences*, edited by Neil J. Smelser and Paul B. Baltes, 6368–6379. New York: Pergamon.

Winerip, Michael. 2003. "What Some Much-Noted Data Really Showed about Vouchers." *New York Times*, May 7, p.12.

Wong, Dona M. 2010. *The Wall Street Journal Guide to Information Graphics*. New York: W.W. Norton.

Zhu, Yeyi, Ladia M. Hernandez, Peter Mueller, Yongquan Dong, and Michele R. Forman. 2013. "Data Acquisition and Preprocessing in Studies on Humans: What Is Not Taught in Statistics Classes?" *The American Statistician* 67(4): 235–241.

INDEX

Note: Page number followed by (f) and (t) indicates figure and table, respectively.